PENGUIN BOOKS

ICE TIME

SCOTT RUSSELL has been a host on *Hockey Night in Canada* since 1989. An award-winning broadcast journalist, he is the co-author with Chris Cuthbert of *The Rink: Stories from Hockey's Home Towns*. He and his family live in Toronto.

ICE TIME

*The Unsung Heroes
of Canadian Hockey*

SCOTT RUSSELL

Penguin Books

PENGUIN BOOKS

Published by the Penguin Group

Penguin Books Canada Ltd, 10 Alcorn Avenue, Toronto, Ontario, Canada M4V 3B2

Penguin Books Ltd, 27 Wrights Lane, London W8 5TZ, England

Penguin Putnam Inc., 375 Hudson Street, New York, New York 10014, U.S.A.

Penguin Books Australia Ltd, Ringwood, Victoria, Australia

Penguin Books (NZ) Ltd, cnr Rosedale and Airborne Roads, Albany, Auckland 1310, New Zealand

Penguin Books Ltd, Registered Offices: Harmondsworth, Middlesex, England

First published in Viking by Penguin Books Canada Limited, 2000
Published in Penguin Books, 2001

10 9 8 7 6 5 4 3 2

Manufactured in Canada
Text design and typesetting by Laura Brady

CANADIAN CATALOGUING IN PUBLICATION DATA

Russell, Scott, 1958–
    Ice time: the unsung heroes of Canadian hockey

ISBN 0-14-028167-3

1. Hockey—Canada. 2.Hockey—Canada—History I. Title

GV848.4.C3R87 2001   796.962'0971   C2001-900641-1

Visit Penguin Canada's website at **www.penguin.ca**

To my family, the unsung heroes of my life

Contents

Acknowledgements ix

Introduction: *The Passion Players* 1

Where have you gone, *Ron Ellis?* 13

The Team: *Glace Bay Miners* 27

The Scout: *Lorne Davis* 61

The Natural: *Andy Sullivan* 101

The Pioneer: *Angela James* 137

The Coach: *Brian Kilrea* 169

The Voice: *Bob Ridley* 207

The Family: *The Crawfords* 243

The Town: *Kamloops, British Columbia* 279

The Hero: *Ron Ellis* 321

ACKNOWLEDGEMENTS

✧ THIS TRIP TOOK A LONG TIME, but I had many willing companions along the way. I relied on their instincts to help guide me to all the right places, those often out-of-the-way spots where the soul of hockey still dwells in this country. For that simple gift, I am eternally grateful.

Cynthia Good of Penguin Books has demonstrated great faith in this project, and Barbara Berson had the vision to bring it to completion—her gentle hand has been a blessing. My editor, Meg Taylor, kept in constant touch throughout the long haul of the Stanley Cup playoffs and magically made the right words appear in their proper spots.

The production team at Penguin gave the stories the look that I had imagined all along; special thanks are due to Cathy MacLean for a super cover and to Shannon Proulx. Craig Pyette is my cousin and *Ice Time*'s publicist. During the course of my research I encountered his mother and father at the Oshawa Civic Auditorium and reaffirmed the central place of hockey in so many families.

I would like to thank Scott Sellers, now at Random House, for his belief in the book from the beginning. He is responsible for helping me to search beyond the obvious to find what really matters. Friend and *Hockey Night in Canada* colleague Chris Cuthbert was there every step of the way; I was able to draw on his knowledge and understanding of the game throughout my journey. Hall of Fame broadcaster and author Dick Irvin is always an inspiration, as is former NHL goaltender and pal John Garrett.

The people at CBC Sports and *Hockey Night in Canada* have been supportive and understanding of this outside distraction. Nancy Lee, Alan Clark, John Shannon, Paul Graham, Tim Davis, Greg Millen and Jim Hough brought encouragement to the effort. Co-workers such as Sherali Najak, Kathy Johnson, Chris Irwin, Frank Hayward, Carol Angela Orchard and Paul McDougall patiently listened to my stories as I foisted a work-in-progress upon them. David Moir was kind and helpful while we were on the road and printed an endless amount of the manuscript.

Passage to the world of hockey's wonders is made easy because of the willingness of the people involved in the game. All of the characters in these stories were generous throughout. In particular, I would like to express gratitude to Bob Seward, Richie Warren and Davey Beresford. They made my trip underground in Cape Breton a wonder. Donna Baratto shared an abiding pride in her daughter, Angela James. Scott Higgins of TSN provided me with video proof of A.J.'s greatness. Louis Crawford put me in touch with all of his family members. In Ottawa, the people at the *Citizen* found the picture that perfectly captures "Killer" Kilrea. Roy MacGregor and Dean Brown shared their considerable insight into Brian Kilrea as well.

In Kamloops, the love of the town brimmed within Don Larsen of the Blazers as well as Doris and Kerry Rubel. Darrell Davis of the *Regina Leader Post* conjured up a brilliant image of his dad. Bob Ridley and the Medicine Hat Tigers welcomed me on the bus, and the result was a rewarding trek through Alberta. Kelly Hrudey was there too, as he was throughout this hockey season. He is a generous and trusted friend who believes in the wonder of the game.

Over the course of a misty few days in Newfoundland, Peter Hanlon and Pam Sullivan brought Sully's story to life. Craig Campbell at the Hockey Hall of Fame came through again. My hero, Ron Ellis, gave me the most important thing I could have asked for—all the time in the world.

My mother, Elizabeth, and father, Scott, have encouraged me in all my endeavours. My sister, Carrie, and her husband, Brad, have always cared about hockey and supported my fascination with it. My close friend Tim Currie stokes a fire for hockey within me and motivates me more than he could ever know. They are terrific teammates, and I count on them incredibly.

Now it's finished. The book is done and the Stanley Cup is won. I can't wait to go to the local rink with Catherine and sit in the place she's kept for me, to watch as Alex and Charlotte enjoy the ice time they so richly deserve.

Scott Russell
Dallas, Texas
June 10, 2000

INTRODUCTION

The Passion Players

Top left: Ron Ellis
(courtesy Graphic Artists/Hockey Hall of Fame)

Top right: The Kamloops Blazers
(courtesy Kamloops Blazers Hockey Club)

Bottom right: Angela James
(courtesy Donna Baratto)

❖ THE ZAMBONI MACHINE HAS always fascinated me. The way it comes out before every game and between periods to create a new surface. As I watch it chug around the arena I wonder how many layers of frozen water have built up over the course of the season, how many wafers of ice there are to each rink's story. Underneath the glistening sheet I can make out veins in the ice below, the marks of thousands and thousands of skate blades. Some, I imagine, slice their way to the front of the goal crease, maybe a few of Wayne Gretzky's are there or Mark Messier's or some other hockey great.

The players seem oblivious to it all as they make their way through the gates and onto the ice. Their first strides leave frosty white trails behind them; in the corners their churning skates spew flying chips which settle against the neatly groomed dashers. Opposing goalies rasp their long skate rails over the painted blue thresholds to their respective nets. The pristine mirror is roughed up to a twinkling silver before the opening faceoff. The Zamboni machine is not five minutes gone, its fastidious driver satisfied that what he left behind is as close to perfect and true as it can possibly be.

———

Hockey players are remarkably like elephants in the most positive sense—they never forget a thing. Every player credits something or someone along the way that has made it possible for them, all the conditions right. Although the players themselves are fascinating because of their depth of skill, the size of their hearts, their courage and fortitude, it's what they remember about their journey to the NHL and stardom that most interests me.

Hockey players are often hailed as the most likeable of the professional athletes in the modern world of million-dollar contracts and endorsement deals. I'm sure it's because they compete in a forbidding game where survival requires sacrifice and ultimately a reliance on team play. People can identify with hockey players because for the most part they are humble souls who bear their scars and bruises with pride. Maybe it's because no matter where they originate, they have travelled to their chosen vocation from strikingly similar backgrounds.

Hockey is consumed with such ferocity in this country that every move of every skater is dissected, every flaw questioned, every goal celebrated, every bodycheck savoured and every win or loss replayed until it is understood completely. The players, I have found, would rather reflect on much simpler things and find solace in the unsung heroes of their own past. They drift easily into conversations about where they hail from—the town where they first believed that they might indeed have a future in professional hockey.

Rob Brown of the Pittsburgh Penguins is a veteran performer. I encountered him in the dressing room as he answered questions about why the squad was facing elimination at the hands of the Philadelphia Flyers. Dozens of reporters swarmed him, television sun guns illuminated his sweaty forehead and he offered the standard answers: "We know we have to be better in Game 6. We know there is no tomorrow."

Later, when all the cameras were gone, Brown was happy to reminisce about the place he had refined his craft. He played his junior hockey in Kamloops, British Columbia, the same city where his father, Bob, had managed the team. The younger Brown became one of the first stars of the community-owned club, which had been rescued from a migration to Saskatchewan and transformed into the model franchise of the development system. "It's absolutely the ideal Canadian junior hockey town," Brown declared. He offered as proof, not the money the team was willing to spend or the size of the arena but the people of the municipality who felt such pride in a player like him. He claimed he kept in constant contact with the billet lady—the local woman who organized the houses where the young players would sleep, be fed and cared for while living far away from home. "Doris Rubel is the best," Brown said. "She means so much to everyone who ever played there." I instantly knew this woman was as important to Brown's career as any superstar linemate he had taken a pass from over the course of his thirteen years as a professional.

Claude Lemieux is a ferocious adversary at playoff time. Winner of the Stanley Cup four times with three different teams—Montreal, New Jersey twice and Colorado—Lemieux captured the Conn Smythe Trophy in 1995 and has scored a total of 80 post-season goals, which puts him in an elite category. He is also feared and loathed by opponents because of his "no holds barred" approach when the Cup is on the line. Lemieux is the son of a truck driver from Buckingham, Quebec, and has come by his living honestly, through hard work and a competitive spirit.

Articulate in both of Canada's official languages, the thirty-four-year-old Lemieux expressed relief deep into the Eastern Conference Final of the 1999–2000 season as New Jersey battled with the Philadelphia Flyers. Since coming over to the Devils from the Avalanche in a mid-season trade, the strong-willed forward had struggled with his skates. "I have a very difficult rocker on my blade," Lemieux explained, describing the curve of the metal and the exact portion that should come into contact with the ice. "If I don't get it just right, then my balance is off and, as you know, the skates are the most important part of any player's equipment."

Lemieux knew that his former equipment manager with the Avalanche, Rob McLean of Westchester County, Nova Scotia, had been let go by Colorado at the outset of the season. It was McLean who had fine-tuned Claude's precious blades over the course of four solid years with the western franchise and was reputed to have a surgeon's skill when it came to getting the right edge for the right player. Out of need but also out of loyalty, Lemieux went to the New Jersey management and wondered if there might be a place for McLean on the Devils' staff. Five games before the end of the regular season, Lemieux was reunited with his skate sharpener and had played markedly better hockey because of it.

"I don't like to make a big deal out of it because we also have very good people here," Lemieux said, referring to the Devils' training staff. "The thing is, you have to trust the person who sharpens your skates completely. I'm just very thankful that Rob's back with me here. It makes everything a lot more fun."

Here was a player who had more than once been described as vicious, expressing gratitude towards the man who ground the steel of his skate blades for a living. Lemieux knew that McLean was essential to his continued good fortune and would never consider taking him for granted.

"It's very flattering," said McLean. "To know that such a great player would need and want me is very special." With that he turned the black boot of Claude Lemieux's skate towards the whizzing stone wheel and pressed down on the blade, creating sparks and a fine red dust. I sensed a passion shared by two craftsmen of the game.

———

The best ice in the National Hockey League is found under the protective cover of Skyreach Centre in Edmonton. Most players will tell you that the game is faster and better when played on this hard surface.

The Oilers' dressing room is a special place where each edition of the team is given recognition in framed portraits on the walls of the foyer. Silver Stanley Cup decals are placed on a blue door to the video room for each playoff game won by the franchise in its twenty-one-year history. A young man with Down's syndrome named Joe Moss is the locker-room attendant, as he was in the days of Gretzky and Messier. He vacuums the carpet and sees that the laundry is taken care of just so. The night Gretzky's number 99 was retired in Edmonton he asked for Joey Moss to be brought to centre ice, making sure that this behind-the-scenes soldier would be officially recognized.

Glen Sather is one of the most respected men in hockey. For twenty seasons he managed the Edmonton Oilers with style and turned them into a Stanley Cup winner five times. His teams have been a testament to exciting hockey, never built on the principle of jealous defence but instead on the wild abandon that accompanies skill and speed. Sather selected the players who would play for his club and he also dictated the strategy they would employ long after he handed over the coaching reins to someone else.

At the announcement of his resignation in the spring of 2000 Sather singled out a tiny handful of people by name, crediting them with his success in Edmonton. He began with the dressing room staff. "I want to say thank you to Barry Stafford [equipment manager], 'Sparky' Kulchisky [assistant equipment manager]," the Hall of Famer noted. "And thank you to Joey Moss. You guys have been great."

I have never encountered as many scouts as I have in Edmonton over the years. For the most part they are former players, and I suppose they frequent this rink because each contest here promises such a high level of play and a true test of talent. Like wise owls they peer down over half-rimmed glasses from the press level and make notes on the backs of programs. They talk hockey and share their experiences and encyclopedic knowledge of the game with anyone who will listen. The scouts, I notice, are rarely by themselves. They tend to travel in pairs or in small groups to avoid the inevitable loneliness associated with their jobs. It's not always possible when one is in the business of being a bird dog.

Tommy McVie is such a character. A native of Trail, British Columbia, he scouts for the Boston Bruins and has seen a lot of hockey in his day. "I've been fired more times than the space shuttle!" he told me in his booming voice. "I reckon I've had to move my family forty times because of hockey. My wife is always one or two moves behind me!" Once when he was coaching in the professional ranks, McVie lived in the same hotel room for four years, unwilling to buy a home for fear that he would be fired the next day. He is a shrewd judge of talent, a full-time scout relied upon by managers in the high-stakes gamble that hockey has become.

———

It is comforting to discover that certain basic elements of the game survive in the hot American south where the growth of NHL hockey will most certainly take place in the coming years. In cities like Tampa Bay, Phoenix, San Jose and Nashville the soul of hockey lives on in the modern players, whether they are Canadian, European or born in the United States. While it is true that money talks in terms of where most teams now base their operations, a less tangible code defines the ethics of the sport and the conduct of those who make it their calling.

In Dallas, the Stars delivered the last Stanley Cup of the twentieth century to the people of Texas. They employed the huge talents of an American superstar, Mike Modano, to get the job done. Modano was born in Livonia, Michigan, but had attracted the attention of NHL scouts while playing in the small western Canadian centre of Prince Albert, Saskatchewan. In concert with his father, Mike had made the decision to move to the Prairies and compete for the Raiders, a team that had won the Canadian junior championship in 1985, two years before his arrival. It was a distinguished hockey club, one whose tradition of winning Modano wanted to be part of.

The supporting cast is extremely important to the players in leading roles. Constant references are made by the young stars to their families, with special thanks to fathers and mothers who footed the bills and froze in the bleachers of community rinks. At Reunion Arena in Dallas, I ran into Dick and Lucille Morrow of Carlyle, Saskatchewan, who had driven twenty-three hours straight to see their son Brenden skate in his first playoff match against the Edmonton Oilers. They operated a small sporting goods store in their hometown, and Lucille had sharpened her boy's skates throughout his minor hockey days.

In Pittsburgh, Keith Primeau, the hulking front-line centre of the Philadelphia Flyers, made a point of telling the *Hockey Night in Canada* crew that his brother Wayne was in the crowd that night to see him play. Wayne Primeau is also a promising young NHLer with the Tampa Bay Lightning and he lent his support as Keith tried to revive the Flyers' Stanley Cup chances. "I had my opportunity at the big one last year with Buffalo and we came close," Wayne said, his eyes glued to the action. "Now I hope Keith gets a shot because he just missed winning those two years [1997–98] with the Red Wings."

Most players acknowledge a tremendous debt to their coaches, not only because of the skills they have been taught but also because of the mentoring in other areas over the years. When Jason Arnott of the New Jersey Devils heard that Tim Dickey, his junior C coach, had sent greetings he beamed with pleasure. "Tell him hello for me and that I'll be back as soon as we get this thing won," he said. "He taught me a ton. One of the best coaches I ever had."

Down the hall from Arnott, Eric Lindros was struggling to get back with the Flyers. The former Hart Trophy winner as the NHL's most valuable player was being kept out of the playoffs because of a concussion, the fourth serious head injury in his career. Instead of discussing his own misfortune, he marvelled at the recovery of his coach, Roger Neilson, from cancer surgery. Neilson and Lindros had been close over the past couple of seasons, with Roger acting as Eric's confidant as well as his instructor.

Neilson had been behind the bench with seven different NHL

teams in sixteen big league seasons and had still not won the coveted Stanley Cup. His team in Philadelphia was among the strongest in the league and seemed headed for the playoffs, but the sixty-five-year-old coach was forced to step aside because of his health. A legendary innovator, Roger Neilson's immense following stems from his junior days with the OHL Peterborough Petes and his continuing association with the craft of coaching through his various instructional schools and camps.

Lindros was just happy that Neilson had returned from surgery able to guide the team again, albeit in a more limited capacity. "He's an amazing person," Lindros said. "Now he's running every day and riding his bike!"

———

Hockey heroes, in most cases, grow up in families that value the game because it's part of their history and the folklore of the town they live in. Young players hear the game from voices on radios in dairy barns, at the gas station or on the drive home from practice. It comes across like theatre.

Some are naturals with undeniable talent. Others are coached well, taught the nuances of fitting in and go on to play for good teams until they are discovered by some scout who sends them on to the next level. Along the way a thousand characters enter into each player's story and the endearing thing is this—very few are forgotten.

It is safe to conclude that a hockey player's trip to fame is a journey of discovery, one that requires a pioneering spirit. The people and places along the way differ from player to player and over time. Each locale, each personality is important. The people profiled in this book are representative of the riches to be found across the land. Each is a symbol of something or someone that a player feels loyalty towards. They are not just a part of the process that guarantees the emergence of talent, they are the very cornerstones of the game itself. The roots of hockey are found deep in Canadian soil, and while harvesting takes place at the NHL level, the cultivation has occurred much closer to home. All the great ones are in agreement: the game unfolds beyond the surface and so much transpires because of unsung heroes—those who provide the foundations and make the precious ice time possible in the first place.

WHERE HAVE YOU GONE,

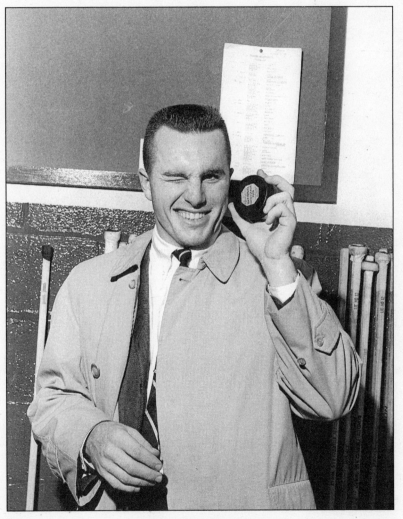

Ron Ellis?

The Wink: His first NHL *goal*
(courtesy Graphic Artists/Hockey Hall of Fame)

✧ IT'S NOT EASY TO KEEP TRACK of your favourite things about hockey—the heroic figures, the thrill of a breakaway, the rattle of the glass, maybe even the entire texture of a game you knew so well when you were young. Sometimes it all gets lost in the commercial break—one of seven per period, twenty-one per game—as we bear silent witness to hockey's penetration of the American Sunbelt. The teams become confused with markets, the players are disguised as so many free agents and the action, it seems, has drifted off course—endlessly mired in the dreaded wasteland of the neutral zone at the National Car Rental Centre in Sunrise, Florida.

Holdouts, lockouts, Group 2 compensation and video replay conspire to put a lid on so much simmering greatness out there. Take it all away and perhaps what's left behind is more than enough. A sheet of ice with circles and dots, red and blue lines over which the fastest team athletes in the world traverse—to dash and crash, load and fire, navigating by thin rudders of steel. They sail the seven seas on every shift and the best of them, I distinctly recall, are so fast that as they reach for the other end, their sweaters flutter like the jib on a schooner. Ron Ellis was like that. I miss him but I know he's lingering somewhere—waiting to burst over the boards and swoop into the limelight.

———

Those special Saturdays came only once or twice a year. To see the Toronto Maple Leafs live and in person at the Gardens was like heaven. It was as if I had been granted admission to a magic place that was reserved for only the fortunate few. My father would leave the tickets at the end of my bed long before I woke and make his way in the middle of the night to the hospital. He was on call, as usual, but had managed to get another doctor to cover him for three or four hours come game time. We would soon gather at a rink we all considered almost holy. On any given night it could include the Leafs, the Hawks (members of the original six), Dave Keon, Bobby Hull, and a ten-year-old who worshipped Toronto's fast right winger called Ronny.

Inevitably the passes had been given to my dad by a grateful patient, a kind gift considering season's tickets at Maple Leaf Gardens were precious and rare, even in those days. They were willed from generation to generation. My spot was generally in the end blues, I could tell by the stripe across the top of the ducats. More importantly, it was right beside my father, a man I spent too little time with.

Outside the Gardens, the streetcars clicked along Carlton Street and a man roasted chestnuts in the bitter cold. There was a little whistle on his cart with steam rising into the December air and my dad would always stop to give the man a quarter for a translucent paper bag full of butter-soaked popcorn. We shared the treat while walking east on Carlton and making a sharp turn north onto Church. Behind us the marquee shouted in blazing white: "HOCKEY TONIGHT—LEAFS VS. BLACKHAWKS."

Scalpers skulked in the shadows. These were the men who peddled the most-sought-after currency in the country. "Who needs tickets?" they asked of no-one in particular. The scalpers wore parkas, mostly with hoods, and seemed to shuffle constantly, never looking a soul in the eye. They had no customers to speak of, at least I never saw a transaction actually take place, and the inquiries were never shouted in those days—they floated out there, more like a sinister whisper.

Our pace quickened and I felt my father's arm around my shoulders as we approached the splashed light of the northernmost gate. "Not me," I thought to myself. "I don't need your tickets. Mine are tucked safely into the pocket of dad's overcoat." They were, to a little boy, the best seats in the house. While they were not coloured gold or situated along the rail close to the ice, they were in the end blues. From there, I could hang, almost dangle, directly over the net that the Leafs would shoot on for two of the game's three periods, the perfect position to witness the majority of goals on every occasion I sat there. I would see Ron Ellis drive down his wing, wind up and fire, and then throw up my arms as he made the net bulge right in front of me.

Once inside and through the turnstile, we hurried to the gallery of black-and-white pictures hung on the walls so high that I would have to crane my neck to look at them. I always made sure that we arrived just as the warm-up began so that I could see the players dance like water bugs and marvel at goalies Johnny Bower and Bruce Gamble as they faced thousands of slapshots without wearing a mask. The noise of the pucks, sticks and dinging metal posts drew me into the spectacular and brightly lit big top.

There was one picture in particular that captured my imagination and I dragged my dad to it every time we went to Maple Leaf Gardens. Alongside the magnificent photographs of Ted Kennedy, the famous Leafs captain, holding the Stanley Cup and meeting Her Majesty, Queen Elizabeth, there was a simple shot of a young man. He had a brush cut—a "flat top" they used to call it in those days. Ron Ellis was wearing a trench coat and was winking towards the camera. In his hand he held the puck from the first goal he had scored in the National Hockey League at the Gardens in the second game of the 1964–65 season. Ellis was a rookie, his time to shine was just beginning and as I studied the portrait, I thought how great it would be to have his life—to be a Maple Leaf and to play in this hockey rink.

Favourite hockey players enjoy unparalleled status in the eyes of young fans. They can do no wrong and regardless of their ability to score or contribute to a winning team in a particular game, they are

held in high esteem. Such was the lofty position Ron Ellis occupied in my world. He was a solidly built right winger about five
feet nine inches tall who could skate like the wind and deliver
whistling shots at the opposing team's net. From the mid-1960s to
the close of the 1970s, Ellis patrolled his position for the beloved
Leafs and inspired my belief that everything was good about the
game of hockey. He always did his job: number 6 scored more than
twenty goals a season, killed penalties and seemed to be someone
you could count on. Ellis was not a great player but he was very
good. Not a superstar, but worthy, I thought, of a great deal of
admiration. Every game he played in the National Hockey League,
he wore the blue and white of the Maple Leafs; Ron Ellis, I was
convinced, couldn't bear to pull any other team's sweater over his
closely shaved head.

That's not to say my favourite didn't have his detractors. I can
remember being invited to games with my best friend, Ian Davey.
His father had just been named to the Canadian Senate and for a
brief time was Commissioner of the Canadian Football League.
Senator Keith Davey drove us to the hockey temple on those rare
Saturday evenings and we would lounge in the plush seats of a
giant black Oldsmobile, talking about the Leafs the whole time. We
would play a game, the Senator included, predicting the score of
the impending contest and naming who we thought would come
up with the winning goal. It was a battle of our favourites and so
every time the same forecasts were made.

"I'll take the Leafs 3–1 with Davey Keon to score the winner
late in the third," Ian would inevitably declare. "You're crazy!" his
dad would pipe up. "It'll be the Leafs all right but Bob Baun will
get the big goal." Bob Baun, I should mention, was a wonderful
defenceman but he was a stay-at-home type of player who during
the course of his seventeen seasons in the NHL accumulated the
grand total of 37 goals. It's not to say Baun hadn't scored the big
one because he once put the puck in the net while playing on a

broken leg and the Leafs won the Stanley Cup. It's just that number 21 averaged only 2 goals a year and it meant that the Senator was rarely right in our little game; he was however, committed to Baun, his favourite player.

I, too, would never stray from Ellis, and I always made my pick last because I knew my friend and sometimes rival, Ian, would challenge it. "I guess I'll take the Leafs 5–3 over the Red Wings tonight," I always started tentatively because, after all, I was the guest in this situation. "And I have to say that Ronny Ellis will be the big star. He'll not only score the winner but he'll get two tonight. That's the way I see it!"

The reaction was swift and sure, a knowing nod from the front seat where the Senator reserved judgment like the politician he was. Ian, on the other hand, would slap his knee and begin to laugh. "Russell, you say the same thing every time we play this game! Ron Ellis this . . . Ron Ellis that. You've got Ron Ellis on the brain! Besides, he never does anything but go up and down his wing and if he does get a chance he goes right by the net and shoots on the bad angle. Ron Ellis is *not* going to score the winner tonight!"

It was an argument I could never win. My friend Ian was too tied up in his favourite player, Dave Keon, the slick centre and Toronto's captain at the time, to have an objective opinion. But I always thought he had opted for the obvious choice and in succeeding years, after Keon had left the Leafs for the World Hockey Association, Ian's favour fell on another superstar captain, Darryl Sittler. I was firmly planted in Ellis's camp throughout, and over time I was proven correct on many of those cold Saturdays in the Toronto winter. Ron Ellis scored 332 times in the more than one thousand games he played with that one team. I may not have predicted every one of them and they weren't all decisive goals. Still, I savoured every one and my loyalty, of which Ellis was totally unaware, was richly rewarded.

His number had changed over the years. When Ron Ellis first broke into the league after having been a key member of the Memorial Cup–winning Toronto Marlboros in 1964, he had two white ones tattooed on the back of his brilliant blue sweater. It was because his coach with the Leafs, "Punch" Imlach, liked the number eleven and it had at one time belonged to a pretty good former right winger with the Toronto team named Bob Nevin. As an aging player, Nevin had been traded to the New York Rangers and Imlach wanted a good year out of Ellis so he gave him his favourite hockey number. Ellis responded by scoring 23 goals in his first full season in Toronto and finished as the runner-up to Roger Crozier, the sterling Detroit goaltender, in the voting for the Calder Trophy as the NHL's best rookie.

Alas, his number didn't last because Imlach was known to change his mind and play the winds of fortune when it came to his hockey team. Another prospect, Brit Selby, graduated from the junior Marlboros in time for the 1965–66 campaign and was touted as a potential rookie of the year. Imlach was superstitious enough to believe the number on his back might have something to do with his success and asked Ron Ellis to hand over his sweater. Ellis agreed and reverted to number eight, which he had worn that Memorial Cup year with the Marlies.

Sure enough, Brit Selby was named the Calder winner in 1966, outdistancing Kamloops, B.C., native Bert Marshall of the Red Wings and Ellis's production dropped to 19 goals, four less than he had scored in his brilliant inaugural year. There was no fuss or complaining and Ellis stuck with the new number through the Stanley Cup playoffs of 1966–67, helping the Leafs to the championship by scoring the first goal in Game 6, which eventually eliminated the favoured Montreal Canadiens. I'll never forget as "Red" Kelly delayed at the blue line and fired the puck at

"Gump" Worsley in the Montreal net. Ronny Ellis was like a jet as he got to the front of the crease and pounced on the loose puck, burying it to give the Leafs a lead at the Gardens. It was superb to see the young player's elation at having performed perfectly in such a critical situation.

So he won the Stanley Cup as number 8, but I remember Ron Ellis most vividly as number 6. The Leaf penalty timekeeper in the late 1960s and on into the '70s was a man named "Ace" Bailey, a Hall of Famer who had starred for Toronto in the 1920s and '30s. He loved the way Ellis played the game—speed being the first priority and of course an obvious commitment to covering his opposite number on the wing.

Bailey's number 6 had been retired by the Leafs, one of only two at that time, the other being number 5, which was worn by the late Bill Barilko. Barilko had scored the Stanley Cup–winning goal in 1951, and then been killed in a plane crash days later. Bailey stopped Ellis in the corridor of Maple Leaf Gardens after the Cup was won in 1967, and asked Ellis if he would do him the honour of wearing the old number 6 should Bailey be able to convince owner Harold Ballard to bring it out of retirement. Ellis was understandably delighted at the compliment to his playing ability and gladly donned the rejuvenated jersey. While wearing it, he scored over 20 goals in nine consecutive seasons, a Leafs record, which still stands. Beyond that Ellis made Bailey proud every time he whizzed by the penalty box at the Gardens.

There could be no other number from that moment on for a devoted follower of Ron Ellis. Leafs fans in those days wore the same number as their favourite player—which led to great arguments at curbsides when we played road hockey because there was generally more than one disciple of a certain player or players among us. "I get to be Mahovlich tonight," one kid would whine. "If I don't get to be number 27 then I'm taking my net and going home," countered another determined fellow.

Frank Mahovlich, Dave Keon and Tim Horton drew the most
competition as we fashioned rudimentary Leafs jerseys from old
pillowcases and donned them over winter jackets on Kellythorne
Drive in suburban Toronto. The disputes were eventually solved
through barter and, believe it or not, compromise. Everyone was
eventually satisfied, nobody more so than me. I always got to wear
number 6 because Ellis was the favourite of very few others. He
was not flashy and that suited me just fine. He was dependable and
that's how I always saw myself.

———

I played in a house league called the Parkwoods Civitan for a team
sponsored by the local shoe salesman. They had named me the assistant captain of "Harold Barnes Fine Footwear," and I proudly had my
mother sew the "A" on my brown-and-white sweater just where Ron
Ellis had placed his with the Leafs. I had asked for and received the
number 6 at the outset of the season, and all was well with the world.
It was a given that I would patrol the right wing, just as Ellis did, and
I quietly went about my business. While it's true that I was not the
most prolific scorer in the atom league, I was the offensive leader of
my team and they could count on me to deliver the occasional decisive goal on those very early mornings at the Fenside Arena.

I had become Ron Ellis, only younger, and did everything I
could in order to perform the way he would have wanted me to. I
was even shy like he was. The year before, he had come to our closing banquet with Brian McFarlane, the hockey broadcaster, and
played the guitar while we all wolfed down hot dogs and soda pop.
"King of the Road" was the song Ellis sang as he strummed along
on his six-string guitar. He didn't give a speech, deferring to
McFarlane, the accomplished orator from *Hockey Night in Canada*.
Ellis stayed to sign autographs at the end of the festivities but
looked a little uncomfortable, as I recall. It's not that he was

unfriendly; I think he just wasn't sure what all the fuss was about. In any case, I didn't want to impose on him and left the banquet just thankful that my idol had been there.

Everything was going fine until one Friday night I came down with a horrible case of the flu. My throat was so swollen that I could barely speak and I lay awake through the dark hours sweating nervously and hoping that things would clear because I had never missed a game. Ellis was the same way. He rarely was injured and never dogged it because of some little ailment. Number 6 of the Leafs personified the player who always showed up for duty, and I had come to believe that was a must for my own modest career. My father had other ideas.

"If you play and sweat really hard when you have this kind of flu then you can make yourself seriously ill," he argued. "You could get rheumatic fever and then you'll hurt your heart. Maybe you'll never play again!"

I wouldn't listen to reason and believed mistakenly that my father the doctor would be convinced of the importance of my attendance at the game that morning because of his belief in the principle of "playing hurt." Surely he could understand the nobility of it all. "Ronny Ellis would play even if he was sick," I croaked, as Dad closed the door of my bedroom and left the vaporizer hissing. My father was also an admirer of Ellis, and I believed invoking the great player's name would aid my case.

As the hour of the game approached with me still swaddled in the bedsheets, sweating and shivering, my father reappeared and took my temperature, which was fully five degrees above normal. Then he gave me devastating news.

"Look, when you're sick and can't play they have to call one of the substitute boys from the waiting list. It just so happens that Ross Wixon from across the street got the call to play for your team today," he explained. It sort of softened the blow because after all, if I couldn't play, a friend and road hockey buddy was the next best choice. "Here's the deal," my dad continued. "We have to run your sweater over to Ross so that he can use it for today's game."

That was it! He was *not* getting my sweater! Ross Wixon had forever been a Davey Keon fan and had no interest in Ron Ellis at all. To let him have my number 6 jersey would be tantamount to treason—Ellis, I was sure, would not approve of this arrangement. We argued and I cried like a child for at least half an hour. Couldn't they see the unfairness of it all? I was being told that I was not only replaceable but that someone who had no allegiance to my favourite player could benefit from the magic powers of his number. Such was the influence that Ron Ellis had over my entire hockey being.

I faded fast and was drifting off to sleep when my father taught me a lesson that has remained with me to this day. "Remember when 'Punch' Imlach asked Ronny Ellis for his number 11 and gave it to Brit Selby?" he inquired. I meekly nodded my head and knew all of a sudden what was coming next. "And remember how 'Ace' Bailey gave his number to Ellis?" Again I nodded and at the same time pulled the covers a little further over my quivering mouth so as to avoid showing my dad the gathering pout. "If you give another player your number, it's like helping him out. It's an honour. And it's exactly what Ronny Ellis would do in this situation."

He was right and I knew it. My mom went to my equipment bag in the basement and fetched that neatly folded number 6 and took it across the street to Ross Wixon's house. I fell fast asleep and woke later in the day to find out that "Harold Barnes Fine Footwear" had defeated "Warner Lambert Pharmaceuticals" by a score of 3–1. Everything had turned out all right and a few of my teammates called me up just before supper to tell me about the game and to say that they missed me in the dressing room, even on the power play. Ross Wixon himself phoned. "Thanks a lot for lending me your sweater, I really had fun," he told me. "I guess Ronny Ellis is good luck after all!"

On those wonderful Saturdays my dad took me to Maple Leaf Gardens we entered the bowl to find out that the lights were the brightest and the colours certainly the most vivid in our experience. Gold, red, blue, green and in the nosebleed section, the vast expanse of grey. There was a contraption that hung from centre ice—a triangular blue box with a white maple leaf painted on it and whirling fans on either side to make the flags flap while the national anthem played.

Over the years, what we saw there was phenomenal. The Big "M" swooping, Eddie Shack clearing the track, Harold Ballard scowling from his bunker with his faithful sidekick, "King" Clancy, alongside. "Spinner" Spencer spun and Lanny McDonald sported the biggest moustache in NHL history—it was a lock. My favourite, Ronny Ellis, darted down the wing and once or twice every game I was there, brought the crowd to its feet with a tremendous rush and a slapshot that caused the red light over the glass behind the net to beam brightly.

Ellis was chosen to play for Team Canada in the Summit Series of 1972 and along with his linemates Bobby Clarke and Paul Henderson, suited up for every critical game. Ronny never scored in those eight magical games but he was on Valery Kharlamov, the Soviet sniper, like glue. Harry Sinden, the Canadian coach, had assigned Ellis the critical checking role and must have known that such a devoted team man wouldn't consider letting him down.

I was in the end blues at the Gardens when the NHL season following the Summit Series began. The Maple Leafs staged a ceremony at centre ice to honour the Toronto players who had played so brilliantly for Canada in the dramatic victory. Defenceman Brian Glennie received polite applause and there was a standing ovation for the newly crowned national hero, Paul Henderson, as he had delivered that famous winning goal. But I had eyes only for

Ron Ellis and the way he shyly stepped forward to hear the fans shower him with praise. It was evident from the cheering that more and more fans had grown to appreciate Ellis for the great talent that he was.

More people were gathered in one place than I had ever seen before, and I looked over at my father and thought how lucky we were to be there too—high up in the end blues, crowded close to our neighbours and hanging over the hot white ice.

There was no play-by-play when you were actually in Maple Leaf Gardens and, in fact, it was something that I will admit to missing. There was no Bill Hewitt biting off his words. "Armstrong over to Ellis and that failed to click," he would say, as only he could. In his absence, I listened to the sounds of the magic place and the crowd as it groaned and then collectively held its breath when Ron Ellis steamed down the right wing. My dad nervously shushed me as I whispered, "C'mon, Ronny! . . . Go, Ronny!" We listened and paid attention to a game that stopped for nothing—much less a commercial break.

I'm convinced that I saw it all from where I sat. I saw the Leafs win and more often than not I saw them lose, because after the Stanley Cup year of 1967 they sank into a period of mediocrity. I loved the three stars that they announced when the game was over and hoped that Ellis would be awarded one whenever I was there to appreciate it firsthand. "And the third star . . . Ron Ellis!" Paul Morris, the Gardens' public address announcer, would intone. Ellis would skate full speed from the gate, stop in a shower of snow shavings, and then skate back with his stick raised to the cheering fans. Nobody was louder or prouder, I guarantee it, than I was.

THE TEAM

The Glace Bay Miners

The 1955–56 Cinderella Miners

(courtesy Bob Seward)

✧ ON A FRIDAY NIGHT LATE in March, a playoff battle rages in the west. The Edmonton Oilers are struggling to stay ahead of their arch-rivals, the Calgary Flames. One spot in the NHL's post-season is available, and the two teams desperately need the revenue that the Stanley Cup tournament could deliver to their respective franchises—franchises made fragile by a burgeoning league now dominated by wealthy American clubs. Even though the Flames and the Oilers are not playing head-to-head on this night, the old rivalry could affect the outcome of the race.

The Oilers are hosting St. Louis at the Skyreach Centre. A long-time nemesis of Edmonton's team, Al MacInnis is a stalwart on the Blues roster. A former Flame and one-time winner of the Conn Smythe Trophy as the playoffs' most valuable performer, MacInnis possesses the league's hardest shot. On familiar ice, he goes gunning for Edmonton's playoff aspirations.

In the press box, Edmonton native and former NHL goaltender Kelly Hrudey watches MacInnis like a hawk. Hrudey is in his first year of retirement and now makes his living as a *Hockey Night in Canada* analyst in the west. He is particularly concerned with how newly acquired Oilers goalie Tommy Salo will handle the heat of the playoff race. Hrudey is troubled by Salo's inactivity in the first period. "Give me something," Hrudey cries out, anticipating Salo's thoughts. "Let Al MacInnis wire one from centre and I'll be ready—get me into the game!"

MacInnis, it seems, is always on the ice. A couple of months shy of his thirty-sixth birthday, the Blues number 2 takes only fifteen to thirty seconds of breathing time before leaping over the boards to re-engage the action. Smooth strides and efficiency mark his play. Now in his eighteenth season, MacInnis is easily the league's most dangerous threat from the blue line. He leads all defencemen in scoring, with 54 points in 71 games, and seems a sure bet to claim his first Norris Trophy as the NHL's top rearguard.

There is also a nasty streak to Al MacInnis. Never one to back down, he scraps in a scoreless first period with a much larger Oilers forward named Mike Grier. Punches are thrown. Grier's glove swipes at the defenceman's face like the huge paw of an angry grizzly bear. MacInnis stands his ground and goes about his business. He is the only player on either team from east of Quebec City, a proud Maritimer—a Cape Bretoner and the son of a coal miner.

―――

"Hockey is big in Cape Breton," MacInnis has noted. "It's second only to religion or horse racing down there."

He was born in a little place called Inverness but calls the village of Port Hood his home. The rugged, windswept coast of Nova Scotia's island was alive with hockey in his youth. Until he was fifteen, MacInnis played with the squirts, peewees, bantams and midgets in the town of Port Hawkesbury, about thirty minutes down the road. There were endless tournaments in places with names like Whitney Pier, Dominion, Sydney and Glace Bay. From there, like so many before him, he left the Maritimes to seek his fortune on a wider stage.

First it was to Regina and a year in the Tier II Saskatchewan league. Then MacInnis went to the mighty Kitchener Rangers of the Ontario Hockey League. Impressions he made in central Canada were lasting ones, and he became one of the most sought after prospects in his draft year of 1981. The Calgary Flames selected him as the fifteenth choice in the first round. Their coach was another Cape Bretoner by the name of Al MacNeil. He knew of MacInnis's reputation and of the booming shot that would become a staple of the Flames' Stanley Cup foundation and a championship year in 1989.

―――

In the third period at Skyreach Centre, the Oilers have built a 2–0 lead over the Blues on the strength of two goals by Stratford, Ontario, native Rem Murray. Through the first forty minutes of play MacInnis has logged almost twenty minutes of ice time. It is the most by any player on either team. He continues to churn up the rink making pinpoint passes and creating scoring chances. MacInnis kills penalties, runs the power play and deftly retrieves the puck in his own end after avoiding a threatening and potentially crushing bodycheck. With time quickly escaping from the Blues, they pull their goalie. Grant Fuhr, the former Oiler great, dashes to his bench, and Al MacInnis leaps into action. "Watch this," says Kelly Hrudey. "This is where Al's really dangerous."

You cannot help but notice the eyes. As he cradles the puck on his stick and traces the threatening side of the Oilers blue line, MacInnis never looks at the tiny black disc. His hands shift effortlessly over the shaft of his stick, the blade of which rarely leaves the ice. The eyes peer from under his helmet, which is tight against his forehead. Back and forth they move, constantly searching for the open man or perhaps the unobstructed path to Tommy Salo's net. It would not be unfair to say that MacInnis's eyes widen in the offensive zone and especially when he gets closer to the other team's goal.

With forty seconds left, Mike Eastwood wins a faceoff and draws the puck back to MacInnis. Receiving it and darting sideways to the middle of the rink all in one motion, he reverses the play and slides a searing pass to Scott Young standing completely alone at the side of the Oilers net. Young rifles the puck past a sprawling Tommy Salo and it's a 2–1 game. Al MacInnis has his fifty-fifth point of the season but nothing more. When the siren goes, the most prominent player in the arena hangs his head just a little and swallows his team's loss to the surging Oilers.

His career is made up of more than a thousand points scored and a thousand penalty minutes. Once, in 1991, at the age of

twenty-seven, MacInnis accumulated 103 points in a single season
and he has played in ten All-Star games. There is no question that
he is the greatest NHL player produced by the principality of Cape
Breton, Nova Scotia. Still, Al MacInnis, even though he is an individual star, takes losses to the team very hard. It is quite some time
before he emerges from the training room after conferring with
younger teammates and his coach, Joel Quenneville.

"Sorry to have you wait," MacInnis offers with the friendly lilt
of a Maritimer. He has nothing on but a white towel wrapped
around his waist and a huge ice pack taped to his shoulder. Red
floods what should be the white of his left eye. There is a welt high
on his cheekbone, the result of the earlier dealings with Mike
Grier. For all the world, MacInnis looks less like a multimillionaire
and more like the coal miner's son in the sweltering sweat of the
visitors' locker room. Gaunt and exhausted, he talks about the place
he came from and the strength of his community.

"They used to work in the mines, and the tunnels would go for
miles under the ocean," he recounts. "It was a tough way to make
a living, for sure."

His mother was a schoolteacher and his dad worked in what
MacInnis calls "the Pit." It is a common expression in Cape Breton,
and refers to the dark and forbidding holes in the ground where
livings have been extracted in the form of coal for most of the last
century. Along with the mines, Cape Breton has been a location
where steel is made and where oil has been refined, always with no
long-term security. A difficult place to make a good living but
home nonetheless, and Al MacInnis talks warmly of his past.

"If you didn't have anything else then you didn't realize it was
tough at the time," he remembers. "With the people down there
anything extra went to the kids. You know, for a hockey stick or a
pair of skates or a roll of tape. Anything you needed, it was there."
Including education for those who chose it. His brothers played
hockey at St. Francis Xavier University in Antigonish. Al selected

a different route, one that led him away from home but on a path that could not fail to take him back. "At the time I didn't realize how hard my parents worked," he recalls. "It was only when I got older that I understood all the hours they put in for what I was able to have."

Remembering the hardship of his formative years even while basking in the riches of professional hockey, MacInnis describes the daily grind of his father's work in the refineries and mines and his own salvation through hockey. "He became like the rink manager in our hometown." MacInnis grins. "When the arena was built, there was him and another fella who looked after it when their work was done. What a bonus for us!"

Al MacInnis, who has made his fortune in the Canadian west, and more recently, the United States, feels the need to give something back to his community. He now owns part of the Cape Breton Screaming Eagles of the Quebec Major Junior Hockey League. They occupy the state-of-the-art Centre 2000 in Sydney, which was built for the Canada Winter Games in 1987. Until the mid-1990s the rink was the home of the American Hockey League Cape Breton Oilers, an affiliate of the NHL's Edmonton Oilers. Once the parent club moved its farm team closer to home and based it in Hamilton, Ontario, Cape Breton was left without high-level hockey. MacInnis wanted to do something about that.

"The junior team for me was a special team," he says. "In that part of the world we were rarely able to see any major junior hockey. I wanted to be part of a team where kids from around the island could go to Sydney and see players develop. Then maybe the next year they would see one or two of those players go and play in the National Hockey League."

MacInnis sprinkles his story with the word *hope*. Hope, he believes, is created by someone from the community reflecting the talent that is inherent to the place. Someone who has been as successful as he has been. "When you see it you tend to believe it more," he stresses. "You can see the progression, and that was one of the big things that influenced me in bringing the junior team to Cape Breton."

Washed and squeaky clean, more than a little bit sore, Al MacInnis looks up as coach Quenneville announces the departure of the team's bus in five minutes. A night's rest in Edmonton and then a plane to Chicago for the Blues' next game as they continue to secure their playoff position. Bruised and battered, the great defenceman offers a lasting link to his past. "You know, my father would come home for supper and my younger brother and I would sit on his knee and we'd look up at his face and it was pitch black," he says, staring straight ahead. "The memories I have of him are coming home for supper and all I could see were the whites of his eyes."

———

Davey Beresford is at the wheel of an old red Dodge, whisking us through the grizzly dawn, heading west from Glace Bay. He is a stumpy five-foot-three defenceman of the DEVCO Oldtimers' Hockey League. That's DEVCO as in Cape Breton Development Company, the Nova Scotia government agency that is struggling to keep the coal mines in operation on the island. The province uses the coal to generate electricity and ships some of the two million tons it produces each year overseas. The problem is, the mines are downsizing. Only two are left in serious operation, the Phalen Colliery and the Prince Colliery, which is where we are headed, 57 kilometres outside Glace Bay. Davey has agreed to take me on a tour underground at Prince because the closer Phalen mine had a roof cave in the other day.

"The last time DEVCO hired anyone was back in 1988, and it was only a few men at that," Davey says, after taking a long haul on his giant-sized Tim Hortons coffee. "The miners' futures are in serious trouble."

There were 4,800 men working in the mines when Davey
started underground in 1975. There are fewer than 1,700 now. In
two years' time the tradition of coal mining in Cape Breton could
be lost forever, with the last of the collieries closed. The workers
fear that their meagre existence will disappear with the loathsome
holes in the ground that have dominated their lives. "I've been in
the Pit nearly twenty-five years and I won't get a pension," Davey
says bitterly. "I'll get a severance."

As we approach the tiny community of Point Aconi, where
the Prince mine is, Davey is buzzing because of his duties at the
tenth annual Vince Ryan Memorial Oldtimers' Tournament,
which begins that evening. In addition to being a miner, Beresford has been a hockey player most of his forty-four years and will
run the show at the College of Cape Breton rink, one of eight
that houses the four-day tournament involving ninety-two teams
from across the Maritimes, the rest of Canada and the United
States. Many of the players are former miners who are returning
home to play and raise money for a worthwhile cause. The tour-
ney, which is named after a late Glace Bay Miners hockey star,
will make available eight $500 scholarships to senior students from
the community's high school. Davey beams. "I do it because I
love to go to graduation to see the scholarships handed out. It
gives you a real feeling of accomplishment—that what you do
can make a difference to somebody."

In the mine office, yellow lights buzz as the supervisors gather
in hushed tones. Men in checkered shirts open long black ledger
books and jot down notes with pencils while asking questions of
the others. "I was wondering if someone could look into that
hydrocarbon smell and take samples from the water or something,"
intones a very serious gentleman with glasses. These are the eighteen
bosses of the men who are going into the Pit this morning, a shift
of 120 who will spend from 7 a.m. until 3 p.m. underground and
draw the coal to the surface. They are the men who toil deep under

the Atlantic Ocean, 900 feet down and about three miles beyond the shore of Nova Scotia. It is a formidable consideration, especially when it hits home that I'm going with them.

"Make sure you don't lose your buddy like the last fella, Davey," jokes a black-faced miner returning from an overnight shift. In the Lamp Room, Davey Beresford and I outfit ourselves with the necessary safety gear. Around the waist of my bright orange coveralls, I clasp on a heavy battery belt. A black hose attached to the belt snakes its way to the lamp I fit snugly onto the equally bright orange construction helmet. Wearing heavy rubber boots, I begin my walk towards the train that will take me on a gradual descent to "the Wall" thousands of feet away, to the place where they cut the coal. "It's where they pay the bills," says Davey.

A cool breeze at the back of my neck, I stoop to fit into the train that will move down Number 2 slope. It is a grey, rusted metal hull, and inside the men are barely visible save for the glitter of teeth and the occasional blinking eye. An enormous man with a heaving belly is sprawled across from us. He crams chewing tobacco into his mouth and then chases it with a wad of blue bubble gum.

"I got a pal in town from Pittsburgh for the tournament who brought me some new chew," Davey offers.

"I'll be over to get me some of that," grunts Shelly Snow.

"You don't know where I live," says Davey, chuckling. "Oh yes, I do, boy!" roars Snow. "You live at the rink."

The squeamish feeling begins to build inside my gut as I read passing signs. "Self Rescuers Must Be Worn While in the Mine." The clicking of the train seems to last forever as we continue towards the face of the tunnel. The dampness is overwhelming and the lights on our helmets only partially illuminate the gloom. A 49,000-foot steel cable drags the rig on this endless route, and some miners sleep while others play a hand of cards.

A tall man with a black moustache and heavy Cape Breton

accent wants to talk about his beloved Montreal Canadiens. Angus Davidson's job is to muck the belts that move the payload and keep them free of any obstruction. "Yessir, when Dale Hunter scored in '81 to beat the Habs I threw the TV out the front door," Davidson says with barely a grin. "Yep, that was $268, two weeks' work and a TV gone 'cause of that boy. Not to mention twenty years of pain and suffering since."

When the train stops to let us off at the entrance to the tributary that leads to the Wall, Angus leans his head out and asks a parting question. "What are you doing here anyway, buddy?"

"I'm just visiting for the day," I reply.

Angus snorts. "Days can be pretty long around here." I can only begin to imagine.

Davey is built for the mine. Short and squat, he moves easily through the diminishing space. We are on our own now, on the way to the crew that is already cutting the coal. Others have remained on the train and will go farther into the hole, to explore or to reinforce the tube with new jacks and timber. "I love the life," Davey is saying as I try to avoid banging my head on the ever-lowering roof. "When you're underground everyone's your buddy." I know that if I ever let my buddy out of my sight, I'll be a goner.

Ahead of us is blackness and there is a certain amount of water underfoot. Barely squeezing between pieces of machinery is not an easy chore, and claustrophobia is becoming a concern. As we turn a corner, Davey swings open a huge door and a rush of air escapes. We move into a new and wider space that seems brighter. There, sitting on a yellow transformer of some sort, is a man with the blackest face and the whitest eyes I have ever seen.

Davey introduces Bobby Keefe as one of the supervisors at the Wall who is just coming off his shift. "How much longer you got, Bobby?" Davey asks.

"I would say just about thirty-three days," Keefe responds. He has worked underground for thirty-three years and will soon retire, perhaps one of the lucky ones who will get a pension. A little man, Keefe is a fifty-three-year-old goaltender who still plays, on occasion, in the DEVCO league. It was his idea twenty-five years ago to start the oldtimers' league for the miners. A way to get the fresh air of the hockey rink into their lungs after coming off a shift in the Pit.

"Some of our shifts would be from three in the afternoon to eleven at night," Keefe recollects. "So we'd book the ice for two in the morning. Everyone came."

He shakes his head, raises a shushing finger to his charcoal lips and asks that we not let anyone know he's been sitting on the machinery to keep himself warm. I shiver at the thought of all those years in this place and try to pry more information from Bobby Keefe about his playing days. "Not many of those left," he mumbles. "I'm like the rest of the fellas. Got no wind left."

Davey motions me on and we bid farewell to Keefe, who remains steadfast on the humming transformer. With his arms folded he leans towards the next entrance and the chamber where the coal is being harvested. A 600-foot-long sparkling black wall rises seven feet from top to bottom. It is the reason why the miners have come all this way from the surface. "You'll see the big hockey puck in there," says Keefe, a white smile gleaming from ear to ear.

The Glace Bay Miners hockey team has always been fascinating to an observer from central Canada, where the NHL and the professional game have long been entrenched. An illustrious hockey tradition seems incongruous in this weather-beaten community, so detached from a major commercial centre. Then again, the residents of Glace Bay had never been in close proximity to the acknowledged stars of the game like Richard, Howe, Orr and others. They were someone else's heroes, and the people of Glace Bay, as was the case in other Maritime centres, had to create their own. Who better to assume the role than the miners themselves?

Upon my arrival in Glace Bay, Davey Beresford had taken me to the modest clapboard home of newspaper reporter Greg Hines. The grey-haired Hines whisked me to the back room, which served as the parlour as well as his office. Without a word, he extracted a pile of yellowed scrapbooks and notepads from a roll-top desk and spread the whole collection on the coffee table. Sitting down in his rocker, he eyeballed me, twiddled his thumbs and said not a word. His wife arrived with tea and pineapple upside-down cake, placing them before me on the table. "Nice to meet you, mister," she said. "Would you like milk in your tea or do you take it clear?"

Thus began a ramble by Hines about a team close to his heart. The Miners go back to the early 1900s. Glace Bay itself was established as a community in 1901, around the time that the coal-mining industry began in Nova Scotia. "It was even said that in 1908 they paid their players," Hines said with a wry wink, a hint that imported hockey players would become a fact of life in the Maritimes because of the sheer smallness of the local talent pool.

It was in the pre–World War II years that senior hockey came into its own in the region. The blossoming coincided with the arrival of artificial ice in Sydney, which is a fifteen-minute drive from Glace Bay. The teams that formed the league of four were the Glace Bay Miners, the Sydney Millionaires, the North Sydney Monarchs (later the Victorias) and the small community of Reserve Mines had a team for one year.

With Sydney's new arena, the team from Cape Breton's largest city had a distinct advantage over the others. The men who worked in the mines in the Glace Bay area decided that playing second fiddle to the Millionaires wasn't for them. "The Forum was built with a checkoff," Hines said of the Glace Bay Miners Forum, which opened its doors in 1939. On the first night, the Miners, clad in their traditional crimson and white uniforms, handed the Sydney Millionaires a 5–4 loss in front of a whopping 4,000 fans. An import player named Mark Linklater had three goals in that game for the Glace Bay side.

The checkoff meant that each miner's paycheque had a deduction of a few dollars a month to finance the building of the arena. "They did everything, the miners did," Hines said. "They built hospitals, paid for the doctors, built churches and the Forum as well." It has always been the way in Cape Breton—the community taking care of its own needs in the absence of funding from government or outside agencies.

It was a rollicking time for hockey. The rivalries were intensified by the fact that teams would play five or six nights a week and face each other twenty times or more in a single season. The *Cape Breton Post* of 1941 called the Glace Bay Miners "the Red Warriors of the East." It was heady stuff, a time when many games ended in donnybrooks and police escorts for victorious visiting teams were required to ensure safe passage home.

The Oliver "Boots" Baird incident of 1941 is one of many that have become enriched through the passage of time in Glace Bay hockey circles. It seems that the club management sent Baird, who was the Miners goalie, on a forced vacation. They then imported "Legs" Frazier from the North Sydney team, which had been eliminated from the playoffs. Frazier was clearly Baird's superior in the nets. The Miners went on to face the powerful Sydney Millionaires in the next round of the playoffs. With "Legs" between the pipes, the Miners jumped to a 3–0 lead in the series and all seemed to be going according to plan for the Glace Bay side.

The problem was, the Millionaires management had hired private investigators to scour the island and find "Boots" Baird's whereabouts. They did so in some tavern miles away from the more populated locales of Sydney and Glace Bay, and they dragged "Boots" back to Glace Bay and forced the Miners to put him back into the goal in "Legs" Frazier's stead. Sydney ended up tying the series at three games apiece and eventually went on to win the seventh and deciding game. "Boots" Baird was immediately tagged with the blame, as the Miners had again been disgraced by the cocky Millionaires from Sydney. The Cape Breton victors later lost to the Regina Pats in the Allan Cup final.

The fallout was swift, according to Greg Hines. "Glace Bay residents boycotted the merchants from Sydney because of what they did," he recalled. "There were road blockades set up to prevent people from Sydney entering Glace Bay with any goods. They just stopped doing business with the larger centre for a period of time. The rivalry was that great."

Hines suggested that a 1940 playoff game between Glace Bay and Sydney had the largest indoor crowd in Cape Breton history. It was measured at 5,252 souls, far beyond the fire marshal's capacity guidelines. The infraction was a regular occurrence on the island, as people flocked to the warmth of arenas to see their local boys play. It was a welcome distraction from the lives of darkness they led underground.

Between 1942 and 1945, play in the Cape Breton Senior League was suspended because of World War II. But by 1946–47, action started up again, with the three teams of Glace Bay, Sydney and North Sydney resuming their old rivalries. And the import players started coming back because there was money to be made.

A junior league formed during this period consisted of the Glace Bay Miners, the Sydney Millionaires and the North Sydney Franklins. Parker MacDonald was one of the feature performers. He was a Sydney native who would go on to play fourteen seasons in the NHL with five clubs and score an impressive 323 points in 676 games from 1952 to 1969. MacDonald's greatest accomplishment was playing left wing on a line with Gordie Howe and Alex Delvecchio in Detroit.

The junior league had only three teams, but again, the intense rivalry born of familiarity was a drawing card. They would average more than 2,000 fans a night at the Forum in Glace Bay, and each team endured a marathon schedule of ninety games. Six nights a week there was junior hockey taking place on the island and the arenas were close to full. Such numbers are rarely heard of in today's brand of development hockey anywhere in Canada.

It was in 1952 that Glace Bay and Sydney, the two most successful clubs in the Cape Breton Senior League, joined the Maritime Big 4, a super loop that included the best in the region: Saint John, Moncton, Halifax and Charlottetown. It was known as the Maritime Major Hockey League and it was able to attract considerable talent. There was money to be banked, but the players would have to earn it. A gruelling schedule called for each team to play four games a week over the course of twenty-two and a half weeks. That was more games by twenty than the NHLers played, and it was hard work. "But Bud Poile said it was his biggest payday yet," Greg Hines recalled with a chuckle—a reminder that imported stars were the order of the day.

———

Norman "Bud" Poile sounded spry when he answered the phone at his Vancouver home. The one-time general manager of the Philadelphia Flyers and the Vancouver Canucks, who had been a pioneer of NHL expansion in the late 1960s and early '70s, was seventy-five now. Poile played a single season for the Glace Bay Miners in 1951–52, when they were a part of the Maritime Major Hockey League. "It was the World Hockey Association before the WHA actually existed," Poile said. "The payrolls and the salaries were astronomical, but we played ninety-six games a season!"

Poile, a native of Fort William, Ontario, had toiled for seven seasons in the NHL with New York, Boston, Detroit, Toronto and Chicago. A right winger, he had collected 229 points in his 311 big league games, as well as a Stanley Cup with the Maple Leafs in 1947 after they defeated the Montreal Canadiens in six games. After his success in Toronto, Poile was traded to Chicago as part of a four-player package heading to the Blackhawks from the Leafs. Going the other way was the stellar Max Bentley, who would eventually become a revered NHL Hall of Famer.

Poile's pro career took a turn to the minors in the 1950 season, when he went to Tulsa of the United States Hockey League. From there he packed up his family, including his three-year-old son, David—now the general manager of the Nashville Predators—and headed east to Cape Breton and the promise of a big salary in a place called Glace Bay.

"It was a crash course for anyone who was serious about getting into the hockey business," Poile emphasized. "I did everything there. I was the manager, I coached, I played and was the trainer. The only thing I didn't do was drive the bus, I don't think!"

Poile became the star of the Miners in his short stay there. Crowds loved him, and he responded with a productive season, scoring 33 goals and adding 60 assists for a total of 93 points. In recognition of his efforts, he was paid between $300 and $400 a week, and in the year he spent in Glace Bay he might have earned close to $8,000, a huge sum for a professional hockey player at the time.

"The miners had a checkoff to pay for the season tickets," Poile remembered. "The tickets were only about a dollar or a dollar and a half each, but they paid for them directly and we had a lot of people in the rink. Most nights it was 3,000 and that was a lot in the Glace Bay Miners Forum."

Poile went on to win the Lester Patrick Award for outstanding service to hockey in the United States. As a general manager with the early Philadelphia Flyers teams, he culled a loyal fan base in a new NHL city and took great satisfaction from his efforts. Still, he recalled his time in Glace Bay with particular fondness because of the innocence of the game and its motives.

"Hockey was an outlet for them," he said. "I was down in the mine and I went as far as the third level, and let me tell you that was as far as I wanted to go. The guys that worked in the mine, they were some tough cookies."

After having played in the bright lights and the big cities of North America, Bud Poile had found hockey at the grassroots at least for a little while. It was not glamorous but it somehow brought him closer to the game. "My son, David, played road hockey with a piece of coal, and we made some wonderful friends there," Poile reflected. "The thing with it was, you weren't spoiled when you played down there. You did it all. You just had to."

Poile later managed the Vancouver Canucks on the opposite coast of Canada, but thoughts of the hockey he had witnessed in Cape Breton lingered. He called it the next best thing to the NHL at the time. "The rivalries were amazing," he said. "Sydney and Glace Bay hated each other. It's probably because the people there are tremendously loyal. Loyal to their communities."

Bud Poile moved west to the Edmonton Flyers and the Western Hockey League after his brief time in Glace Bay. He had earned a good chunk of money and become a better hockey man. With a discerning eye, he had valued the level of the competition and the talent of the players in Maritime hockey. Most important, he had become aware of the game's attachment to its community, a paramount fundamental of hockey that in later years governed Poile's evaluation of talent that came from the region.

"There were some tremendous players in that league. In those days with only six teams in the NHL it was tough to make it," he concluded. "A lot of those players might have been top professionals in the expansion era. But even if you did find a prospect it was tough to get that person to leave their home. And if they did leave for a time, they would soon want to go back, so you couldn't keep them." Such was the lure of the embattled but resilient mining community of Glace Bay, Nova Scotia.

Greg Hines continued to rock in his chair and sip at his tea while spinning stories of a hockey team most Canadians have never heard of. Hines thrust a crumpled photograph towards me. "Now the 1955–56 Cinderella Miners," he crooned. "They were the biggest underdogs anybody's ever seen!"

Down the road in another house, Tim Hines—no relation to Greg—is in complete agreement. One of the Cinderella Miners, he revels in his memories of that special team. Tim Hines is sixty-three now and retired after working in the mines for twenty-nine years. Most of his days were spent "brushing," or moving the mountains of excess stone left from burrowing into the earth. The work was done by five men with shovels. It has left Hines a wiry and feisty specimen. "I made good money in the coal mine," he said. "Not a fortune but a good living."

His passion was hockey. Even now he plays twice a week in the oldtimers' league. When he was eighteen, he was a left winger with the Glace Bay junior Miners, and for a time he was the toast of the town. "I was the brains of the team," he said, only half jokingly. "I play anywhere I can now."

The junior Miners of 1955–56 were a struggling club. They played a thirty-five game schedule and they had been mightily inept. Memory fades when it comes to futility, but Tim Hines recollected that there were but two wins in the entire season. "Sydney and North Sydney had import players," he explained. "We had all local guys. And they paid their players. That was a big part of the problem."

At season's end each of the four teams in the Cape Breton Junior League qualified for the playoffs. One of the clubs was operated by Xavier College, but it dropped out because it could no longer afford to operate. That made a couple of their better players available to Glace Bay, as it desperately attempted to improve its prospects for the first-round matchup with North Sydney.

"The first game of the playoffs we were going to drop out," he recalled. "We had no money at all. We were $25 in the hole."

The crowds at the Glace Bay Miners Forum had been shrinking steadily as the fans watched their team flounder. Some say only thirty to forty fans would show up to see the team play. It was left to a group of nine men in the mining community, one of whom was Tim Hines's father, to form an executive and pay the team's bills. It was a risky investment, to be sure.

In the opening series with North Sydney, the Miners got down 3–1 in the best-of-nine playoff with the eventual winner going on to play the Millionaires. Things looked bleak for Timmy Hines, who was a member of an overmatched team. He played among a threesome called "the Peanut Line" along with "Red" Angus Mac-Neil and Fran Finlayson. "The three of us together, I think they weighed us in Sydney one night, totalled 360 pounds," Hines recalled. "We had a guy on our team right here." He pointed to a black-and-white photograph. "There's 'Porky' MacMullin. He was 250 pounds alone. Weighed near as much as our entire line!"

Somehow, the Miners started to win and the crowds returned to the Forum. Perhaps it was a certain resolve in the face of extinction that drove them on. In any case, they won two games in North Sydney and then came back home. Game 7 belonged to the Miners as well, and they were on the verge of creating a huge upset. It was about this time that the faithful began calling the Glace Bay team the "Cinderella" Miners in recognition of their unlikely drive in the playoffs. Game 8 finished off North Sydney, and the local boys were on their way to play the imports in the lineup of the much richer Sydney Millionaires.

"It was the mother of all series," Greg Hines had told me earlier. In the end, it went to the ninth and deciding game, to be played in Sydney. "I listened on the radio," the newspaper reporter lamented. "I wasn't going down there, because if Sydney won I just couldn't face it."

Amazingly, the underdog team from Glace Bay led late into the game. The crowd in Sydney's arena was ferocious and the roar deafening when the Millionaires tied the game 2–2 with twenty-five seconds remaining in regulation time. It appeared that Cinderella's time was nearly up. Surely a team that had won only a couple of games all year was no match for the league-leading Millionaires.

"We had a faceoff in our end and there was Freddy Courtney, one of the best junior players around here, taking it for our team," Tim Hines recounts. "I remember it like it was yesterday. He won the faceoff and carried the puck. I followed him, and after the two defencemen went for Freddy I picked up the puck and scored. That's exactly how it happened." It is as if Hines had won the Stanley Cup all by himself. "Everybody jumped on the ice and we were pretty nearly killed," he went on. "We had to get a police escort out from Sydney. They had all these imports, see, a pretty good team. We never expected to beat them."

The story of the "Cinderella" Miners has become legend in Glace Bay. The Miners went on to beat Halifax but eventually lost out to a team from St. Jean, Quebec, in the playoff run that year. It didn't matter. They had beaten hated Sydney, and unexpectedly so. At the end of it all, the squad that started the playoffs $25 in the hole had made a profit of $8,000 for the nine men who had financed them at the eleventh hour. In typical Maritime fashion, the players were given the money to share among themselves. "Not only that," Greg Hines remembered, "but every player was offered a job in the Pit if he wanted it."

Tim Hines toiled in the Pit but only in order to play hockey. "When you stepped out onto the ice, everything went blank. It was all hockey. You didn't think of nothing else except hockey."

His stories of time underground are of low ceilings made for the shortest of men. Weeks on end in the winter when he descended into the tunnel before dawn and returned to the surface after dusk. Endless stretches when a miner never saw the light of day. His work clothes were his own in those days, coveralls that are today supplied by the company. "Back then you could stand your clothes up in the corner and they'd stay there by themselves," he recalled. "They were that dirty."

It was a life he got used to. Hines didn't think about the danger of going underground day after day. It was just something he did. He chose to focus on his time out of the Pit, and his allies were the other miners. "I'd get day shift on the evening I was supposed to be playing," he says. "Your boss always knew where you were going that night, so he'd put you in a place where you could run away easy." "Running away" is the term used for miners who skip off at lunch time and stow away in the rigs that run to the surface at midday. It was an unspoken rule that hockey players on Glace Bay's teams had permission to run away.

The little man in the clapboard house has become one of the most famous players in Glace Bay hockey history because of a single goal in a regional game against arch-rival Sydney. It was a Miners victory on the strength of a miner's effort. The player had become symbolic of the team in every respect. "When I scored that overtime goal, that's something I'll never forget," Tim Hines said proudly. "People still talk to me about it today."

———

"OK, boys, ready to rock and roll?" John Walsh operates the shear, a 45-ton machine that cuts the coal near what seems like the centre of the earth. It looks like the giant hub of a tractor wheel with claws jutting from its circular centre. In advance of the cut, water jets from its extremities to dampen the wall and prevent sparks in an unstable gaseous environment. "That baby would be perfect to chatter up the ice on any rink before the Zamboni smoothes her out," Walsh wisecracks.

In the cramped space to the side of the belt that collects the shear's offerings, a team of miners huddles. Some are electricians, some operate the jacks that move constantly along the machine's path to support the tunnel's roof. All of them are black faced and damp, seeking warmth in their physical proximity and also from the generator that hums at the head of the path.

One cut of the Wall, a length of 600 feet and 2 feet deep, yields $37,000 worth of coal. As it churns away, the shear creates an overwhelming amount of thick black dust which fills the chamber.

"It's a team. I rely on these fellas and they rely on me," Davey Beresford is saying. The men move, as if choreographed, along the face of the wall, up and down as the machine gobbles up the puck-black coal.

"Hello, Scott Russell, CBC *Hockey Night in Canada*, this here's Ron MacAdam," a voice booms from an invisible intercom. Davey hands me a little box to talk into.

"Go ahead, Ron MacAdam," I respond to the electrician, who has called from some far reach of the mine.

"What was the score of that game in Edmonton last night?" he inquires.

"Two–nothing Canadiens over the Oilers," I say.

"Habs are going all the way, boy!" Ron cheers before signing off.

With his back to the generator and his feet against the wall of the tunnel, Peter Capstick considers his circumstances. "Are we just existing down here?" he asks of no-one in particular. "When you see the kind of salaries they get in the NHL and us about to lose our jobs with no pension at all, I just don't get it." The men who surround Peter nod their agreement, and I turn to watch the shear cutting deeper into the Wall. The team of men marches along, and Peter moves the jacks over just a touch. The chamber we are working in is constantly shifting.

I suddenly realize that the miners are like explorers, risking their lives every day to extend the boundaries of an uncharted region beneath the ocean. These are the same miners who will play hockey in the oldtimers' tournament at night so that scholarships will be awarded to bright young people from the community—students who will never have to be miners like them.

The principal of the Glace Bay High School, Angus Mac-Mullin, had told me what the cutting of the coal would be like. "It's like a moment frozen in time," he said. "Watching coal being cut means you're in a place where no-one has been before and where no-one will ever go again."

———

The Bayplex is perched on the shore of the Atlantic Ocean, a state-of-the-art community centre that incorporates a hockey rink within its pristine confines. It's a whiff of the modern beside the unsinkable spirit of the Maritimes: from the paved parking lot you can see the Glace Bay lighthouse flashing green, and under the asphalt lies the foundation of the old Forum.

Davey Beresford and I walk into the lobby and are greeted with the frantic activity of opening night at the Vince Ryan Memorial Oldtimers' Tournament. The Jiggers and the Keith Lakers are engaged in one of the opening games in the 35-and-over division. In the upstairs lounge of the $4 million government-funded arena, Keith's and Moosehead—the traditional brands of eastern Canada—flow freely. There is a fifty-fifty draw in the lobby with hockey gloves and jackets as the prizes.

A beautiful red score clock dangles from centre ice, and the crimson and white that adorned the old Glace Bay Miners uniforms predominate. Greg Hines had informed me earlier that Vince Ryan was a name I should become familiar with. "Vince Ryan was the Gordie Howe or the Guy Lafleur of Cape Breton, if you want to put it that way," he said. "The crowds came out of the wood-work to see him play."

Staring at the smooth white sheet of ice over which the old-timers chugged, I saw no markings beyond the red and blue lines standard to any rink. There was one glaring exception: a large caricature of a hockey player clad in Glace Bay colours and wearing a miner's helmet and lamp. Underneath the picture was the miner's name. Vince Ryan.

John Vincent Ryan hailed from a tiny community called Donkin just outside Glace Bay. He dominated junior and senior hockey in the area throughout the 1950s and '60s. Far from an overpowering physical talent, Ryan possessed a certain mystical quality that made him a favourite son. The *Cape Breton Post* of 1960 hastened to explain what separated him from the rest of the players. "The veteran Vince Ryan, on the husky side but still sporting a lot of ability to get going at lickety-split pace," the writer marvelled in January of that year. "Vince has always been a favourite out Glace Bay way. And that's the way it should be because nobody gave out with more honest work than the pudgy centre. A few seasons back some started giving up on Vince—'putting on too much weight,' they said. It certainly isn't showing this season in his effectiveness."

Ryan was reputed to have the hardest shot in the league and a finishing touch around the net without equal. Several times as a junior and later a senior, he led the league in scoring, always the captain of his team. Wearing his traditional number 8, Vince Ryan might have been a professional in another time. Many locals say he could have easily made a National Hockey League roster in the post-expansion era. His linemates, Naish Batten and Elmer "Porky" MacMullin, were Ryan's disciples. "He was born to skate, that guy," MacMullin said on the occasion of Ryan's death in 1989 at the age of fifty-six. "He possessed the greatest set of legs I have ever seen."

Vince Ryan was much more than a hockey player who combined uncanny skill and finesse. He was a local. A boy born just up the road from Glace Bay who went on to star with the Miners. Not one of the famous imports as Bud Poile was, but a homegrown talent and a man who spent thirty-three years working in the Pit at the same time he was striving to be better on the ice. "Vince and I worked in the mine together," Tim Hines of the "Cinderella" Miners told me. "We were the only ones on our senior team who worked in the Pit.

"You'd come out of it and play hockey. That's pretty rough. You'd go down to the Pit at seven o'clock in the morning and you'd come up at three in the afternoon. You'd go home and eat and get washed and then you're travelling to North Sydney. By the time you get home from work it's maybe a little after four. You have to be to the bus by four-thirty. You don't have much time. You play at eight o'clock in North Sydney and you don't get home here until midnight. Well, you've got to get up at five in the morning and go to the mine and go down in the Pit again. So it wasn't too easy!"

Beneath the ocean in the Prince Colliery that morning, I had seen the miners cut coal and had been allowed to handle the controls of the giant shear for a moment myself. The men had wanted to talk about hockey and their favourite teams. Angus Davidson, the devout Montreal Canadiens fan, was eating chalk and washing it down with a glass of water to cure his heartburn. He claimed it was anxiety because of the Habs' recent slide in the standings. The Pit was the size of the city of Halifax underground, and along with the rest of the team, Davey Beresford and I were headed for daylight not long after two in the afternoon.

Piling into the rig, we were greeted by Vince Serroul, a soaking-wet electrician who was shivering and on his way up to get dry. A wet miner is in serious danger if he stays in the tunnels' exceedingly damp environs for any length of time. Serroul opened his coveralls at the neck and revealed a brilliant pendant made of gold. It was the logo of his favourite NHL team, the Toronto Maple

Leafs. As Serroul flipped ajar his lunchbox and wolfed down a
salami sandwich, he talked of the hockey foremost in his mind.
"Got to run away 'cause I'm playing in the Vincey Ryan tonight."

———

Richie Warren looks tired all the time. With his old blue hockey
jacket hanging loosely over his slumping frame, the only chairman
the Vince Ryan Memorial Oldtimers' Tournament has ever known
fields a thousand questions a minute in his war room above the ice
at the Bayplex. "I remember the first year when we had twelve
teams we wondered what would we do if we made a profit and we
decided on scholarships," Warren says. "The scholarships are the
future of Cape Breton. Our young people are leaving. There is no
work for them here. Perhaps some day they'll do something good
and come back. Start something here themselves."

Warren is fifty-one and spent twenty-three years underground
as a miner. Now he's employed as a welder on the surface, but soon
his job will be threatened, like everyone else who works for
DEVCO. Since September, he reckons he's spent 2,000 hours working out the details of this tournament, which includes ninety-two
teams in fifteen divisions, men and women from as far away as
California. Thirty-three celebrities have been invited. Dozens of
volunteers assist because they are devoted to hockey and the memory of Cape Breton's greatest player, Vince Ryan. But mostly they
help out because they respect Richie and what he's trying to do.

Over the ten years of the tournament forty scholarships have
been awarded to local students, and a trust fund of $14,000 collects
interest in the bank on the main drag of Glace Bay. The yearly
budget for the tournament is $195,000, and Richie makes sure that
every penny is spent the right way. This is the most important
hockey event in Glace Bay every year. "There's people that I see

once a year and they tell me the same thing," says Warren. "They come here to see the others they have missed all year. Hockey is the way the community gathers itself again."

Bustling around the rinkside is a small white-haired man with fire in his eyes and a sparkling set of teeth that appear to be his own. Austin McCormick is in charge of decorations at the Vince Ryan tournament and he's making sure that everything is in place on this, the debut night of the tenth-anniversary edition. He worked forty-four years as a mechanic on the Wall and has escaped the mine's clutches to play hockey into his seventy-sixth year. Austin is a member of the Canadian Tire Miners, the oldtimers who are the last remnants of Glace Bay's once glorious team.

"I had ten kids to look after, so I worked six or seven days a week underground," says McCormick. "The only reason I looked forward to hockey was that I had a little enjoyment for myself."

At five foot two and weighing in at 140 pounds soaking wet, McCormick is lean and muscular in spite of his advancing years. A defenceman, he claims he still has plenty of wind and is surrounded by good players who take care of him. There is reason to believe he will play the game until he drops. "The only thing that's going to stop me is that I'll have to go to the cane," he says. "Once the cane sets in then I'll finally quit hockey."

The strange thing is, McCormick began to play the game, in an organized setting, just before he retired. The reason for his devotion to hockey is explained by his experiences in the coal mine. "I remember one Sunday we were called out to work and one of my buddies got trapped by a piece of stone." McCormick loses his easy smile. "We had to go back in and get him out. It's all part of being on a team and I loved every bit of it. I wouldn't trade that feeling for anything."

Turkey supper at Tim Hines's house is as traditional as I thought it might be. The place is jammed with senior citizens in town to enjoy hockey the old-fashioned way. In the kitchen, women in white tournament baseball caps with logo T-shirts to match are ferrying foil trays of food in and out of the living room. There are beets and mashed potatoes, stuffing and turkey. Apple pie and ice cream and hundreds of bottles of beer are being consumed, and everyone seems to be laughing. The women, led by Florence Hines, stop only to have their ball caps autographed by the men who wander through the room. The women haven't a clue who any of them are.

Around a giant card table in the main sitting parlour, the celebrities who have come to town for the Vince Ryan Memorial Oldtimers' Tournament are content. Ivan "the Terrible" Irwin, a seventy-two-year-old former defenceman with Montreal and the New York Rangers rubs his big hands over his full belly. Across the way, Pete Conacher, the son of Charlie "the Big Bomber," smiles at Irwin, his friend and long-time teammate with the original NHL Oldtimers. Conacher played 229 games in the pre-expansion National Hockey League with Chicago, New York and Toronto between 1951 and 1958. He scored 86 points and is so proud to have played in the era of the original six.

They are minor celebrities by most people's standards. Irwin and Conacher were not perennial All-Stars, nor did they win Stanley Cups. They never had endorsement deals and they earned about $7,000 a year to play a game they devoted their lives to. Perhaps that's why they love coming to Glace Bay to participate in the tournament the miners put together. Well into their golden years, both Conacher and Irwin feel like the coal miner's kin. Working people—whether they are on or off the ice.

"We are in awe of them," Conacher says of the miners who are his hosts. "It's not the other way around because we played pro hockey. This is tough down here. These guys really earned their spurs."

Irwin is a huge man with a bald head who possessed a rabid temper when he played pro hockey in the NHL and later the American League in Providence, Buffalo and Cincinnati. In his later years he has developed a philosophical side, which gives him an appreciation for the importance of hockey in smaller centres like this. "This is the grassroots of the whole thing. This is the start of it all," Irwin argues. "The people here have hearts as big as blooming footballs. You don't find that in most places today. But you do here."

Conacher folds his arms across his chest and gently nods in agreement. "When we are in the dressing room, we're not doing the talking, we're doing the listening. We're listening to how these guys live and how they think," he stresses. "It's team survival down in those mines. We're playing a game and they're playing for keeps."

The celebrities are quick to draw comparisons between themselves and the miners and in the process they clearly link hockey to life in this resource-based community. "You have to understand, we didn't earn very much money but we had an awful lot of pride, and everything depended on pride," Irwin says. "We love hockey, and there is a bond that's made amongst the group of us that is hard to break. We are very close knit."

Pete Conacher further clarifies the affinity between the old-time hockey player and the residents of Glace Bay in terms of the paramount importance of loyalty. "Guys in our era didn't think money. They thought team and team spirit," Conacher explains. "We wouldn't dream of trying to go somewhere else because of a few more dollars. We wanted to stay where we were and play with the same guys the next year. To have to go somewhere else was an embarrassment and you didn't like that." So it is with the celebrities' hosts, the miners, who cling to their place in the world against all the odds.

On the second day of the tournament and my last in Glace Bay, the sun was peeking through the rolling black clouds and rays of warmth descended on the clapboard community. At the Bayplex, a portable marquee had been set up, the parking lot was jammed, and a full television mobile was poised near the front door. It was just after seven in the morning.

Inside, two teams of high-school players were bustling over the indelible Vince Ryan's picture on the ice. They were young women, and harsh shouts exhorting linemates to "Pick it up, ladies!" were clearly audible. Everywhere, the Cape Bretoner's twang filled the air. It was like being at a community picnic where the chatter is laced with laughter and a singsong rhythm. One of the girls' teams was wearing the red and white colours so traditional to Glace Bay. "Miners" was stitched on the front of their jerseys.

Richie Warren, the tournament chairman, had just finished struggling through a live interview broadcast on *Breakfast Television* throughout the Maritime region. "I'm no good at that, buddy!" he said with a little grin. "They should have rung you up, Scott." With that he turned to make sure the Tim Hortons concession was being properly assembled. Big cardboard trays of doughnuts had arrived and a plastic keg of coffee was wheeled in.

Several folks were gathered in a common room just off the lobby. Cheerleaders from the high school were practising their routines. Others gathered around a video screen to watch old 8mm footage of the Glace Bay Miners and particularly number 8, Vince Ryan. A striking man with salt and pepper hair and a cableknit sweater was explaining a series of old photographs to some willing children and their attentive parents. Bob "Bugsy" Seward, the unofficial historian of the tournament and a former Glace Bay Miner himself, was engaging in a little folklore.

"He was like an idol to these people in a very narrow culture," Seward told me. "He was naturally the fella that was going to lead us in the big battles against Sydney. It was a small-town, big-town

thing." Seward worked in the mines as a young man alongside
Vince Ryan and was his teammate with the senior hockey team
here from 1963 to 1966. From there he attended Acadia University
on the mainland and starred for the Axemen. He later returned to
Glace Bay and now teaches mathematics and economics at the
high school.

"These guys in the mine, they embraced Vince Ryan then as
one of theirs," Seward explained. "Even today, people who are
generations removed from when he played still do not want to
let him go."

Davey Beresford sat down for a second and was all ears. His day
off from the Pit had begun early, and monumental duties for the
tournament lay ahead. It was going to be a twenty-hour day for the
little defenceman, but he was always ready to listen to tales of the
greatest hockey star Cape Breton had ever known.

"My sense is, economically and socially this place is crumbling,"
Seward continued. "We have very little to hang on to. The people
who were involved in sport when times were better, and particularly miners like Vince, remain extremely important."

The lure of the team in Glace Bay is astounding. The Miners no
longer exist in reality but they do in every person's heart. To con-
ceive of men from "the Deep" emerging to lead the charge against
rivals from other, larger communities speaks of a certain rugged
heroism. To have seen what they do beneath the earth to carve out
an existence in this unlikely setting has been sobering and startling
all at once. Hockey was the chance for the miners to express themselves on the surface, for their families and friends to understand
their lives, which had been hidden too long underground.

Bugsy Seward broke into a smile with the knowledge that I
understood what he was getting at. "The identity with Vince Ryan
and the coal industry is our legacy," he said. "A small, isolated,
declining community with an industry based on drudgery, and
we've still got this. To have anything like a hockey tournament

with one of our local heroes as the focus of it just brings us together and makes us something we always wanted to be. We wanted to become a community."

———

Days later, Al MacNeil and the Flames had just been whipped 5–1 by the Toronto Maple Leafs at the Saddledome in Calgary. Al was the assistant to coach Brian Sutter and brought wisdom and experience to a young team desperately trying to stay alive in the playoff race. MacNeil, a Cape Bretoner and native of Sydney, had been the Flames coach in the early 1980s and is now their director of hockey operations as well as helping out behind the bench.

MacNeil was one a handful who had emerged from Cape Breton over the years to make a big impression on professional hockey through eleven seasons as a defenceman with the Leafs, Canadiens, Blackhawks and Rangers. As a rookie coach, he took Montreal to the Stanley Cup in 1971 and endured a fractious relationship with Henri "the Pocket Rocket" Richard. After that success, he returned to his native Nova Scotia and was the general manager and coach of the Voyageurs in the American Hockey League. He took the Vs to three championships before returning to the NHL and the Flames organization in the late 1970s. It was with Calgary that he brought fellow Cape Bretoner Al MacInnis into the NHL in 1981.

In shirtsleeves, standing by the door of the coaches' room at the Saddledome, the sixty-four-year-old MacNeil talked about home. He acknowledged the others who had made it to the big time. Doug Sulliman, he pointed out, came from Glace Bay. Sulliman, a big right winger, had scored 328 points in 631 games with New York, Hartford, New Jersey and Philadelphia through the 1980s. He spoke of Mike McPhee, who had won a Stanley Cup with Montreal; Paul Boutilier, the one-time New York Islander; and Bobby Smith, the current general manager of the

Phoenix Coyotes, who was born in North Sydney, MacNeil was quick to say.

"There was always the Glace Bay Miners," he said wistfully. "Them and the Sydney Millionaires. I was weaned on them." He rattled off the names of players he had known in the old Cape Breton League, names that I had heard during my time in Glace Bay. There was Burt Sleep, Vincey Ryan, Fred Courtney, "Porky" Mac-Mullin, Naish Batten, Fran Finlayson and a hundred others. "I don't want to forget any of my buddies," MacNeil said. I doubted there was any danger of that.

"To these guys hockey became a driving force," he said. "It was a mining area and sport was a major factor in the community. Maybe because of the hard work these people did, the rivalries became so much more intense."

Like moss on a stone, MacNeil will always be attached to the island. He still goes back to Cape Breton every summer to see his mother, and he is constantly homesick after all these years "away." "There was something about the place," he whispered, tears welling in his eyes. "It made people who did strong things. They were a fierce, competitive type of people."

MacNeil looked around at the pictures in the Calgary Flames' inner sanctum: Canadians from the west like Theoren Fleury; Kent Nilsson, the Swedish-born star; from Hell's Kitchen in New York, former 50-goal-scorer Joey Mullen. The coach's eyes came to rest on the great defenceman Al MacInnis of Port Hood, Nova Scotia. "My family still lives there and I would say that I'm pretty tied to Cape Breton," MacNeil offered. "My mother has always followed hockey, and to this day she's mad at us for trading that coal miner's son."

THE SCOUT

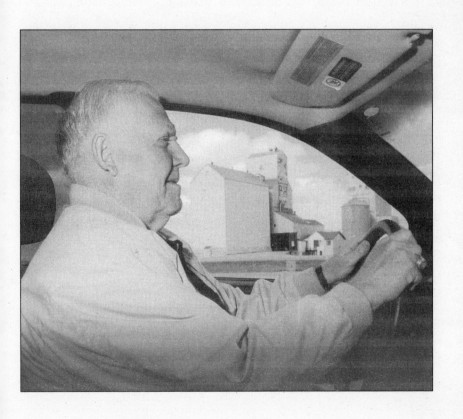

Lorne Davis

Heading Out to Lebret
(courtesy Regina Leader-Post)

✧ THE SUN HANGS LOW IN THE vast Prairie sky on this late October afternoon. Looking east from the twenty-fourth floor of the tallest building in Regina, I can easily spot the line where the city stops and the grain fields begin. Far below me snakes a freight train, the wheat symbol and CANADA stencilled large on the bulging bellies of the dark brown hopper cars, stretching in an endless chain to the horizon.

A little earlier, at the airport, I had encountered John Ferguson Jr., the assistant general manager of the St. Louis Blues, just back from the Swift. With a flight bag hanging off each shoulder, the son of the notorious Montreal Canadiens enforcer John Ferguson was clearly on an extended odyssey. He had seen the Swift Current Broncos play the Calgary Hitmen the night before and was headed one province west to scout the Lethbridge Hurricanes and the Red Deer Rebels of the major junior Western Hockey League. From there, Ferguson was bound for the Stampede City to attend a match between the Calgary Royals and their cross-town rivals, the Canucks of Alberta's Tier II loop. Friday would find him in Spokane, Washington, evaluating more hockey talent. Home to Providence, Rhode Island, for Halloween on Sunday.

"Just another scout on the road," Ferguson sighed, then hurried off to catch his plane bound for Alberta.

I was staying in this breadbasket of the land to see another hockey game. By coincidence, it involved a team that Ferguson's father had played with a long time ago. The Melville Millionaires, a historic franchise in the Saskatchewan league, were to be the visitors that evening in the town of Lebret, an hour east of Regina in the Qu'Appelle Valley where hockey raged white hot even as the frigid winds began to whip over the plains. I was going to attend the game with a scout employed by the Edmonton Oilers—to see the contest through his eyes. To freeze in the wooden bleachers alongside a "bird dog" and find out if there was anything out there worth looking at.

At 5:45 that evening, Lorne Davis marched into the lobby of the Delta Regina and grasped my hand with a bear-like grip. For thirty-three of his sixty-nine years, he has travelled hockey's roads in Canada, the United States and Europe searching for talent. Most of this time was spent in the Prairies, where so much of the National Hockey League's history begins and ends. The white-haired man led the way to his Jeep Cherokee, which he'd left warming just outside the front door knowing it wouldn't be touched. In a moment, we were wheeling towards Lebret and the Eagledome and a Tier II contest that Lorne predicted wouldn't yield much to get excited about. We were going anyway.

The stories flowed easily as we made our way east on Highway 1 towards Winnipeg. A stunning sunset brushed a salmon wash across the huge sky. "It's just so beautiful," Lorne said with a chuckle as he nestled into the leather seat, one finger on the wheel. "Kinda makes you want to get out your paints, doesn't it?"

Lorne Davis grew up on a family farm just outside the city close to a tiny place called Lumsden. But he had little interest in working the land and decided to try his luck at hockey, as a right winger. Born a decade before the outbreak of World War II, Lorne flourished in the safety of Saskatchewan's rinks and developed skills that would lead him to the upper echelons of the game. Over a twenty-year career that began just after the war, he played with the junior Regina Pats and the senior Montreal Royals. There were professional stops in minor league cities: Victoria, Vancouver, Buffalo, Edmonton, Hershey, Providence, Winnipeg and Muskegon. He made it to the NHL and played briefly with Chicago, Detroit and Boston. He was a part of Father David Bauer's Canadian national team program in the late 1960s and coached at the 1980 Olympics in Lake Placid, New York.

The greatest moment of his life, he told me, was when he won the Cup with the Montreal Canadiens in 1953. "We just got our

Stanley Cup rings two years ago," he said as he flashed the diamonds and gold around the third finger of his left hand. "They didn't give out rings in those days, you know. When they found out that 'the Rocket' and Frank and Pete Mahovlich didn't have rings, they sent them out to us. I mean, how can you knock an organization like that?"

He was a playoff call-up, a player who had toiled the entire season with the Buffalo Bisons of the American Hockey League. Montreal was desperately looking for help, as they were down three games to two in the semi-final series against the Chicago Blackhawks. Along with Davis, Calum MacKay, Eddie Mazur and Jacques Plante were inserted into the lineup. The Canadiens ended up winning a game in Chicago to tie the series but not without some trepidation on the part of a nervous Lorne Davis. "I remember my man got away from me," he recalled with a wince. "It was the second shift of the game and thank god, Jacques made a big save on Lindy MacFadden."

Lorne scored a couple of goals the rest of the way as Montreal eliminated Chicago in seven tough games and then dispatched Milt Schmidt and the longtime rival Boston Bruins in five to win the Cup. Davis was a role player on the same team as Maurice "Rocket" Richard and Jean Béliveau and was, at times, awestruck by the talent that surrounded him. He was traded to Chicago and then on to Detroit before winding up his big league career with the Boston Bruins in 1960. He had played only ninety-five games and accumulated a modest total of 20 scoring points. "I'm kind of embarrassed about my career," he said, looking out the window. "I didn't do all that much, really."

Then he sat silent for a few moments, his silhouette dark against the twilight on the other side of the glass. For Lorne Davis, hockey always had a brighter side, a glittering underbelly. "I was fortunate to play with Rocket and Gordie Howe, two of the greatest players and two marvellous guys." He nodded. "When I stop to think that there were only six teams in the big league in those days, it was special to have played."

Traded to Boston along with perhaps the greatest goaltender of all time, Terry Sawchuk, Davis was near the end of the road at the outset of the 1960s. It was back to the American League and eventually to the Regina Capitals, a Saskatchewan senior team based close to his home. By 1964 he was travelling and playing in Europe with the Winnipeg Maroons, then coaching in the Canadiens organization with the Muskegon Zephyrs of the International Hockey League. "It was a disastrous time," he admitted to me. Trying to fulfill the dual roles of player and coach was not working.

He left coaching and joined the Canadian national team under Father Bauer, the legendary Catholic priest who had become the mentor to one-time or aspiring professionals willing to play for their country at the Olympics and other international events.

"I picked Father Bauer up at the airport, assuming that he wanted to go out to Notre Dame College in Wilcox," Lorne recalled. "That's where Father Athol Murray was, and they were good friends." The Notre Dame Hounds wore the colours of a rural Saskatchewan boys' school and had garnered an almost mythical reputation for producing great hockey players as well as solid citizens blessed with admirable agrarian values. "But it turned out he wanted to go over to my house. Before I could get out of my car, Father Bauer walked through my front door, and I heard him asking my wife if it was OK that I play with the national team. My wife told him that it certainly was, and that was it. Father Bauer had it planned all along."

Two years of barnstorming through Europe with the likes of Brian Conacher and Fran Huck. Two years of competing well but, more often than not, losing to the Soviets, the Czechs and the Swedes. A stark reminder to a veteran player that the game went far beyond the borders of his native country, but the experience opened Lorne's eyes to the explosion of hockey talent outside Canada.

His on-ice career over at the age of thirty-six, Davis went home to Regina. "I tried to be an ordinary person. I worked as a salesman." He glanced at me. "I thought it was one of the phoniest jobs in the world. You were trying to sell, and that made you do things that you normally wouldn't do. I tried it for a couple of years, but I was miserable."

A brush fire glowed in a field south of the highway. Against the gathering dusk, the orange warmed the darkness like the last embers of a dying fire. Suddenly, it sent a plume of jet-black smoke into the last gasp of clear blue sky. "The harvest was taken in about three weeks ago and they're just burning off the stubble," explained Lorne. "Doesn't make much sense pollution-wise but it's kind of pretty, isn't it?"

By the late 1960s an old Montreal associate, Scotty Bowman, was coaching and in management with the expansion St. Louis Blues. He asked Davis to come aboard as the team's talent scout for western Canada, and Lorne jumped at the chance. Leaving his three children, Darrell, Liane and young Brad, at home in Regina with his wife, Shirley, he was back on the road with tickets to nearly two hundred games a year all over the country.

"I remember I made three trips into Ontario that first year I worked full time for St. Louis. One was thirty-one days, one was twenty-nine and the other was twenty-eight. My family was still pretty young, and I really wondered whether I wanted to do this while my kids were growing up. I know I neglected them sometimes—not being able to go to the rinks with them and stuff like that. But they certainly didn't grow up hating the game or hating me because of it. I think sometimes they're a little bit proud of their dad."

Shirley died in 1993 of cancer. She had been his high-school sweetheart and she shared Lorne's love of hockey, becoming a valued confidante as he struggled to understand the young players he found himself evaluating. Clearly, he missed her. "When I had doubts about players, I would ask her opinion. She had good instincts. Women see things that men don't sometimes."

Lorne's oldest son, Darrell, is the football reporter for the *Regina Leader Post.* His daughter, Liane, is a power-skating instructor who works with the Regina Pats and the Edmonton Oilers. Brad, the youngest, grew up while his father was lingering in the rinks and is now a third-year amateur scout for the Oilers. It's a sports family but one that makes its mark beyond the fields of play, travelling the roads, looking for what's out there and in some way helping to secure the continued existence of a way of life. The scout earns a five-figure salary, plus expenses, a far cry from the incomes of players he'll discover over the years.

"Some of my cousins have farms," Lorne mentioned as the sun slipped below the horizon. I reflected that in his own way Lorne is helping to gather in the Saskatchewan harvest. The hockey players have been cultivated and the scout is making his rounds to inspect the crop. Suddenly, Fort Qu'Appelle appeared through the windshield: the spire of a church and across the road the floodlight at the arena's threshold. "I've treated it as a noble thing to do," Lorne said as he pulled up to the rink. "I've always been proud of what I've done as a scout."

A certain romantic mythology is attached to scouting. It involves the lonely soul huddled near the top of the stands in the bitterly cold rink, holding a cup of steaming coffee in one hand, silently watching and taking notes. The object is to find the diamond in the rough. He goes from town to town, rink to freezing rink, hoping that some unknown kid with blistering speed will streak down the right wing, ward off his opponent with the brute force of an outstretched arm, load and then fire a booming slapshot that billows the net behind an overmatched goaltender. In an instant, the scout knows in his gut that a remarkable talent is staring him in the face.

It turns out that only part of the myth is true. The reality is forbidding rinks, gallons of coffee and thousands of miles on the road, yielding countless confirmations but almost never a startling revelation.

―――

At the sparkling new Air Canada Centre, where the Maple Leafs play in downtown Toronto, there is a skyscraper attached to the hockey rink. The address is 50 Bay Street, not far from the financial district. On the eleventh floor are the branch offices of the National Hockey League. (Marketing, television production and public relations are all housed with the commissioner of the league in Manhattan.) Here in Toronto, the National Hockey League deals in the most precious commodity it owns: its players. This is the home of the NHL's Central Scouting Bureau.

Frank Bonello's space is remarkably well organized. On his desk there's a computer, neat stacks of binders, and a telephone. For a dozen years, Bonello, a Toronto man in his mid-sixties, has been the director of the league's scouting service. A one-time coach and general manager of the Toronto Marlboros, Bonello is thought to be among the most experienced judges of hockey potential anywhere. In a starched white shirt, grey flannels and polished black brogues, Bonello shuffled around his office showing me lists.

"It's gotta be a couple thousand that we evaluate at one time," he figured. "Aw geez, it's gotta be more than that even!" He reached into a shelf above his desk and brought down a thick folder bearing the neatly printed label "National Hockey League Central Scouting Service 1999–2000 Master Schedule." As Bonello leaned over me and flipped through its pages, I noticed codes for the teams in twenty-six leagues around North America. There were hundreds and hundreds of clubs, from the National Hockey League to the Golden Horseshoe Junior Bs. The book contained a telephone

directory, a schedule of major events and tournaments and a week-
by-week calendar of every game that was taking place in every one
of the leagues listed. Thirty-three weeks of hockey were catego-
rized, graphed and plotted. Every scout who had anything to do
with the National Hockey League had one of these books in his or
her possession and used it as a bible.

"You can't be going somewhere just to see if there's anything
there," Frank was saying. Scouting, in fact, is much more scientific
than I had imagined. Ten full-time observers work for the NHL
covering North America exclusively. Add to that seven part-timers
as well as eight more in Europe under the direction of Frank's colleague Goran Stubb, who is based in Helsinki, Finland. Each of the
thirty big league teams employs a dozen or more scouts. It brings
the total to close to four hundred who watch and judge hockey
players worldwide. And that's just at the top level. A ton more catch
on as bird dogs for various junior and college teams. There are literally thousands of rink rats on the lookout for players in order to
keep the game supplied with its raw materials.

Scouts rank players according to their performance at a number
of viewings. "Wherever possible a prospect is seen a minimum of
five times, with a top prospect being seen many more times than
that," Bonello said. In each case, the scouts will rank a player
numerically according to his potential, skating ability, competitiveness, checking, puck skills, physical play and hockey sense. At the
end of the season an entry draft guide profiles the top prospects as
ranked by Central Scouting. This information, provided to each of
the member clubs, makes the huge task of talent evaluation and
selection more manageable. In addition, four separate rankings are
produced, one each for skaters in North America and goaltenders
in North America and the same two categories of players everywhere else in the world.

Frank Bonello is an easy man to talk to. He has seen it all and
won the Memorial Cup with his Marlboros in 1973 and 1975

while at the helm of one of the most productive junior hockey machines the game has ever known. Graduates from Bonello's years in Toronto include Hall of Fame left winger Steve Shutt, Stanley Cup winner John Tonelli, Mark and Marty Howe, charismatic goalkeeper Mike Palmateer and countless others. Bonello spent time scouting with the Oakland Seals and the Toronto Maple Leafs. He knows hockey inside out but scoffs at the idea that there is much method in labelling players accurately. "Anybody that gets accolades for selecting a certain player in the draft should step back and take a hard look at himself. Let's face it, there's a lot of luck to it."

Bonello is a practical man, sort of like a stockbroker who is helping his NHL clients evaluate where they should make investments and where they should not. It's a business proposition involving millions and millions of dollars in the modern scheme of sport. "The amount of money paid to top prospects means that scouts are under pressure to pick the right player, particularly with first-round selections," he noted. As with any investment, hockey players have to be properly appraised not only with regard to quantifiable statistics but also with a view to their potential performance. "In hockey, if you don't produce, it doesn't matter what your height and weight are," Bonello told me. "The only thing that matters is what you do with your talent."

This is one of the most frustrating yet enchanting aspects of a game as fluid as hockey. Speed and skill alone will not ensure an exciting and successful player. Neither does being six-foot-five guarantee that a defenceman will dominate the blue line and instill fear in those who skate against him. This is where the ability of the scout to use intuition becomes paramount and where all of the thousands of game reports prepared by Central Scouting are rendered somewhat inadequate.

"It's hard to put your finger on this intangible thing we call heart," Bonello admitted. "But it's the vital quality for a hockey player and can make up for other shortcomings. It's at the centre of our discussions when we have our final meetings to determine rankings. A player who we think is soft gets marked down, regardless of how well he skates and shoots."

The qualities of courage and heart are not easily measurable but they are readily recognized. Thousands of players have skated in front of Frank Bonello's eyes and he can recall very few who have successfully "bluffed their way to the big leagues," as he put it. Short spurts of enhanced performance in order to impress the scouts in the local arena are as transparent as the visors some players wear to shield their eyes. "Scouts are extremely wary of this 'flash' ability," Bonello reckoned. "Regardless of how flashy a player might be when he is on a streak, no scout wants to recommend a player tagged as giving good effort only part of the time."

That could mean an entire scouting staff losing their jobs because a general manager gets fired after a series of bad draft years. While it is a natural line of work for a retired player, it is a profession that calls for an almost complete understanding of the complexity of the game and its nuances. Success on the ice does not guarantee that someone will be a good scout in his retirement.

"Like everything else in life, a good scout has to be a hard-working individual," Bonello emphasized. "When you go out to scout you can't be tired. You can't be bothered and have something else on your mind. A scout has to apply himself properly and know the game of hockey inside out, but he cannot survive in the game for long without developing an ability to make correct decisions on all of the talent that is out there."

———

I recall the scouts in the upper levels of the NHL press boxes as they made their notes during the course of the season. Hunched over lineup cards, they scribbled almost constantly, more feverishly when the blast of a whistle brought a stop to the play. The professional scouts focussed on players who their employers felt could help the team make a run at the playoffs or perhaps at the Cup. Evaluations were being made on each pass, on countless hits and with every stride that the scrutinized player took.

Who are the scouts? Duane Sutter is a former NHLer and member of the famed Sutter clan from Viking, Alberta, one of six brothers who once played in the National Hockey League. Having left his assistant coaching job and the security of the Panthers bench, Sutter has taken to scouting. "It's not bad," he said. "A lot less stress but a lot more travel."

I noticed there were others who had strong connections to the game doing the scouting. In San Jose, the former Prince Albert Raiders coach and Western Hockey League luminary Terry Simpson was watching players for the Minnesota Wild, an expansion team still a season away from competition in the NHL. "It's a challenge for me to help find players," Simpson said. "I've never scouted before, and to be on the ground floor when we put a team together on draft day in June is an opportunity that excites me."

Ron Hextall, who won the Conn Smythe trophy with the Philadelphia Flyers in 1987 as a result of his goaltending heroics in the Stanley Cup final against the eventual champion Edmonton Oilers, had only recently come to scouting, after hanging up his pads. Watching a game in New Jersey with his new boss and former tough guy Paul Holmgren alongside, Hextall was extremely conscientious as he logged his notes on both the Devils' and the Leafs' lineups. "It's a tremendous eye-opener for me," he said during a break in the action. "Playing in net, you knew other players were skilled. Now you see all the talent that's out there."

For former players, who make up the majority of the scouting ranks, the motivation is rarely one as openly selfish as that of making a startling discovery. It is rare to see a modern superstar retire to a scouting life. More often than not, the foot soldiers of the game become its eyes and ears and its connection to the future talent base. "Most of the time it's someone who wants to stay in hockey," Frank Bonello explained. He gave the example of George Armstrong, the former captain and four-time winner of the Stanley Cup with the Toronto Maple Leafs. Armstrong had been scouting since he left a coaching job with the Toronto Marlboros when Bonello was the general manager. "He played all those years and didn't get into too many things other than hockey," Bonello said. "He coached junior hockey for seven years and then he tried scouting to keep his hand in the game. It's a business that he loved and it's been a huge part of his life. It continues to be that way."

The average age of the scout reflects the respect accorded to the senior statesman. Well into his sixties, Frank Bonello shows no signs of slowing down. Even though he runs the Central Scouting Bureau from his desk high atop the office tower, he still works 150 games a year. "When you consider that there are six months of hockey, or 180 days, that's only 30 days that you don't go to a game," he proudly calculated. "For instance, Friday night I was in Guelph, Saturday Barrie, Sunday afternoon I saw St. Mike's and then the same night went to a game in Brampton. Four games in three days. Not bad, you know!"

Bonello was once told by Paul Beeston, then president of the Toronto Blue Jays, that at least three members of every scouting staff should be over the age of sixty-five. Bonello was in full agreement. "An older man has seen so many different types of players come through. He can relate to certain types of guys." To further explain the amount of grey hair in his business, Bonello was quick to underscore a gentle wisdom that comes naturally with age. He smiled and waved a warning finger. "You can't be a good scout and see everything in black and white. There has to be a grey area in there. It's not right to make quick decisions on who can't play and who can't miss. There has to be some tempering of opinion and evaluation."

In the end, Bonello denied that the scouts were unsung heroes of the game. Most, he said, made a good living and were well appreciated by their organizations. He acknowledged that it was hard work and, at times, lonely. He knew all too well that there were lean years and those that produced bumper crops. Bonello lamented what he believed to be a slight drop in the quality of the product not only at home but in Europe as well. Still, he said, the gatherers had a job to do. They had to feed an appetite for talent. "Scouting is your lifeline for players," he said.

———

Lorne Davis parked the Jeep on the "50-yard line" right in front of the door to the Lebret arena. The Eagledome is short and squat—a bunker for hockey—with a huge neon sign to illuminate the parking lot as cars rolled in from around the Qu'Appelle Valley. "Isn't that a beautiful church?" Lorne said, pointing across the street.

The church stands at the crossroads of this little place. Perfectly symmetrical and made of granite flagstone, the Sacred Heart Catholic Church was established by the Qu'Appelle Mission in 1865. It seemed far too grand for the tiny community that surrounded it. "In fact, the capital was supposed to be out here at one time," Lorne said. "This is where they were going to make it and then the railroad came through where Regina was and they moved everything overnight from here."

He had run a hockey school in the Fort Qu'Appelle area for three years in the mid-1970s. It had been purchased from Bill Lesuk, the former Los Angeles King who is now one of the head scouts for the Phoenix Coyotes. "Talk about old barns," Lorne said of the school's original rink. "You could see the moon right through the roof. You'd get there in the morning praying that there was still ice. If there was, you knew you were blessed." After the old rink burned down in 1978, Lorne moved the school to the

Agridome in Regina. It ran for two weeks in the summer with sessions of about 130 kids and it became so popular that at times he
had to turn away as many as six or seven hundred aspiring players.

He employed the coaches from Notre Dame College in Wilcox
as instructors, preferring them to NHLers or major junior players
because of their intuition about hockey and their commitment to
teaching. Graduates of the program include Wendel Clark, the former captain of the Toronto Maple Leafs; one-time Boston Bruin
Gord Kluzak; and Peter Schaefer of Yellow Grass, Saskatchewan,
who is making a name for himself with the Vancouver Canucks.
There were also representatives from one of the most prominent
hockey families in the province: the late Doug Wickenheiser, Montreal's first-draft choice overall in 1980, as well as his cousin Hayley,
who has become a star with the Canadian women's team.

"She was in the top three of her class," Davis said of Wickenheiser. "I used to have a special room for her to sleep because she
was the only girl and wanted to board at the school like the rest of
the players. Once in a while I forgot to wake her up, so she'd be a
little late."

He was forthright about his evaluation of talent even at the outset of the meeting. According to Davis you were either a "player"
or you were not and likely never would be. He even had an expression for it: "N.F.G.E. No F—ing good, ever!" To him Hayley
Wickenheiser was a player regardless of her gender and he was
going to make everyone aware of it. "She had really short hair
when she was at the school and none of the other players knew she
was a girl. By the end of the week, I thought I had better let the
boys know exactly what they were up against."

As we entered the white-tiled lobby of the Eagledome, Lorne
stopped to pay our admission at a card table. Two tickets at $6.50 a
pop—light years away from the price of a ticket at most NHL games
these days. Lorne waved me off as I reached for my wallet. "I'll
sneak you through on my expenses," he said with a wink.

The Lebret Eagles of the Saskatchewan Junior Hockey League were now in their seventh year of operation, but this season they were struggling—ticket sales had dropped off and a handful of coaches had come and gone. Too bad, really, because the team had such noble goals. The franchise, which maintained an integrated lineup, had been established to give native hockey players opportunities to compete at a high level. Since its inception, aboriginal skaters from all over Canada had come to Lebret to play for the Eagles. There were currently nine native players on the roster.

"I have lots of friends who went to the old Indian school out here," Lorne was saying as he showed me the trophy cases on the wall. "They were just tremendous athletes!" The lobby was bustling now, and Lorne was clearly well known—the elders of the community slapped him on the back and shook his hand, even the children waved or yelled out a hello. I was told about the reserves in the area: the Standing Buffalo, the Muskowekan and the Kawacatoose. The Star Blanket Band owns the Eagles, and its chief, Fred Star Blanket, stopped by to greet Lorne before making his way to the play-by-play booth to call the game on radio.

There was a mandatory trip to the canteen for coffees. He bought a trayful, enough for us and for his friends, the other scouts who were busily marking up the photocopied lineup sheets they had bought for fifty cents. Peter Sullivan of Central Scouting and Bryan Raymond of the Columbus Blue Jackets welcomed me into the inner circle.

"Smysniuk's been here all along, he's an '80," Lorne commented as he passed the coffees around. "Late '81s and '82s are what we're after. Like this guy, number 5, Heshka, he's a late '81." The guys marked down the name from the Melville Millionaires' lineup as if they had just discovered the last present under the Christmas tree. Lorne extracted a bright yellow highlighter from his leather coat and with his big hand—bearing an Edmonton Oilers Stanley Cup ring—made a single stroke over the name.

Players are not referred to as, say, eighteen- or nineteen-year-olds; instead they are slotted into groups according to the year they were born. It has to do with their eligibility for the National Hockey League draft and whether they have sparked the interest of big league teams as they mature at the age of eighteen. "I don't know, maybe sometimes we're too quick with an assessment," Lorne said. "But you can pretty well be sure that if he's an '81 birthday and has gone through the draft, unless there's vast improvement over that year, he's not going anywhere. It's a tough thing to say but it's generally true."

The others nodded in agreement. Bryan Raymond peered over his half-glasses and turned an ear to Lorne, who was by now sitting back and rocking his chair as he waxed on about all the players he had seen come though this arena. Raymond, a part-time scout for an expansion NHL franchise, is also a local golf pro. He deferred to Davis's knowledge of the game. "Lorne knows everything and everybody," he said matter-of-factly. He then went right back to his roster and noted something by Bryan Heshka's name on the Millionaires side of the sheet.

Peter Sullivan wore a brightly coloured ski jacket and was the most serious of the three. One of the ten full-timers with Central Scouting that Frank Bonello had told me about, Sullivan looked young for his forty-eight years. A native of Toronto, he had produced one fine season with the Winnipeg Jets when they first entered the National Hockey League in 1979–80. A centreman who was nicknamed Silky, Sullivan managed 24 goals and 35 assists that year for the Jets. Prior to that, he had been one of the stars of Winnipeg's World Hockey Association lineup, a team that included the famed "Golden Jet" Bobby Hull as well as European stars Anders Hedberg and Ulf Nilsson. In the later years of his career, Sullivan played for the Wichita Wind of the Central Hockey League and then tried his luck overseas in the Swiss league before retiring in 1986.

"A lot of people look at Lorne and respect what he's accomplished," Sullivan said of his buddy. "He's got so many connections to the game. He played, he coached and now he's scouted. He's got a knack for hockey, and that's something that you can't teach." Davis was already embroiled in another conversation with a youthful scout he'd never met before, a fellow whose leather bomber bore the crest of Western Michigan University. Sullivan shook his head and turned to his voluminous notes. "Scouting's a gift, and Lorne's got it," he concluded.

By now Lorne had trashed his coffee cup and was eager to get into the arena. According to him, it was a sin to travel to a hockey game only to miss the opening faceoff. The four of us passed through the double doors into the rink. The cool air, complete with the lingering exhaust fumes of the Zamboni machine, were perfect reminders of where we were and what our purpose was. Unlike the plush theatres of the NHL, this was a local rink. There were three rows of bleachers and rock 'n' roll music blaring from the ancient speaker over centre ice. "I don't think we'll have trouble with seats, eh," Lorne grunted as we strolled to the right. The object was to get up high for the best view. Lorne struggled with the first bleacher step until one of his friends gave him a gentle push on the rear end. "I like this coming to games with you, Sully," Lorne laughed. "I need all the help I can get."

"Ladies and gentlemen, welcome to paradise!" the public address system boomed as the two teams burst onto the ice. "The Eagledome announces the arrival of the Melville Millionaires and your very own Lebret Eagles!" With that, the two hundred or so fans shouted their approval for the home team, clad in gaudy white sweaters with blue, yellow and copper trim, and booed the Millionaires. Melville was a well-established franchise, having competed in the Saskatchewan league in one way or another since 1910. Graduates included John Ferguson, the former Montreal Canadiens enforcer, and Hall of Famer Detroit Red Wing Sid

Abel. Silver dollar signs decorated the Millionaires' uniforms, as if to proclaim the financial status of the team compared with the last-place Eagles.

"Must be a lot of brothers on that team," Lorne deadpanned as I scrambled to look at the Melville lineup. It revealed not one repeat in family names. "The Danka boys are a pretty well known clan in Saskatchewan hockey," he said with a chuckle. I realized that every member of the Millionaires had DANKA plastered on the back of his sweater. It was the team sponsor, a company that manufactures business machines. Lorne, Sully and Raymond just smiled and shook their heads as I finally caught on.

Members of the Star Blanket Band sang a traditional native hymn, complete with drums, as the players stood at attention on their respective blue lines. Then came the national anthem. After that, the opening faceoff, and from the get go the action was fast and furious. Peter Sullivan had moved closer to centre ice, turning his back to us, enraptured by the progression of the game. At every stoppage in play he scribbled notes with a pencil. Raymond chattered on with Lorne about every player as if they had seen each compete since childhood.

"Nice pass, but the guy didn't get it," Lorne blurted out. "Man, you can set the table but if they don't want to eat, what can you do?" He folded his arms across his chest and swivelled his head to and fro as the contest went end to end at a frightening clip. It was much livelier than any NHL game I had seen in ages. The combatants were smaller but quicker, it seemed. Maybe it was our proximity to the clash itself. "There's something about sitting close to the ice like this," Lorne said, as if he had read my mind. "It makes the game that much faster."

There were quick little observations from Davis as he watched it all unfold, small comments to his colleagues or to anyone in general about the principal performers on either side. "Geez, he could put his stick in a suitcase, couldn't he?" he remarked about a Lebret player who, indeed, had a very short weapon and carried it more like a lacrosse stick. The smallest performer on the ice was number 12 of Melville, Jody Boulet. He buzzed around with alarming effectiveness, finding the cracks in the Eagles' defensive structure. Easily one of the most dangerous Millionaires, Boulet had Lorne watching for a while. "Look at number 12! I hope he's not mean." Davis smiled. "He probably causes all the trouble. Watch, he'll stick some guy sooner or later."

Melville opened the scoring with almost nine minutes elapsed in the first period of play. Number 19, Mike Markell, turned the trick with a flick of his wrist that propelled the puck past Tynan Smysniuk, the Lebret goalkeeper, in an instant. Lorne was immediate with his assessment: "He came off his wrong wing and it was a good shot too." With his lineup clutched in his hand, Davis made no effort to write down a précis of the play he had just witnessed. There was just a quick flip to open the folded sheet and a check beside Markell's name.

It seemed to me that without a record, the thousands of plays and players that a scout would see over the course of a season might become a giant blur. Not according to this veteran observer. "I find if I take notes it takes my attention away from the game," Davis claimed. "When I go home and I think of the name of the player, everything comes right across the screen in front of me. I don't think that I miss anything by not taking notes. I can visualize everything he did in that game. Everything he didn't do. What his strengths and weaknesses are. I have no problem with that. You should be able to do it after so many years in the business."

It made sense. After all, he was paid for his ability to observe and to make judgments about hockey players based on what struck him at the moment. It was unlikely that notes on some scrap of paper would do anything to change his mind given a second and distant reflection. "What about the computer?" I asked. His eyes narrowed as he suddenly understood that he had been found out for the technocrat that he had become. I knew that, as part of the Oilers staff, Lorne was required to file reports on his scouting trips into a computer program, which became a part of the team's database. From the compiled information, Edmonton would make its decisions on draft day. No detail was too small to notice and consider.

"The computer was a bit of a struggle because I had never typed in my life and I was scared of computers," he admitted. He folded his arms and returned his gaze to the ice where the Eagles had completed a successful power play, Tyler Shantz on the receiving end of a beautiful behind-the-net pass from Patrick Gosselin, to tie the game at 1–1. "Sully, did Shantz play in the Western League for a while?" Without waiting for his pal's response, he continued, "I never go on the Internet or anything like that. But I think I've got the hockey end of the computer pretty well mastered."

———

A world away, another scout was online, evaluating players he would never set eyes on. "C'mon down, I'm in the basement," a voice yelled over the banging of workmen in Jim Price's Guelph, Ontario, home. I slipped past the renovators and descended to the recreation room, which had been turned into the nervous system of player information for five National Hockey League teams: the Nashville Predators, the Tampa Bay Lightning, the Atlanta Thrashers, the Columbus Blue Jackets and the New York Rangers. A squadron of computer terminals hummed early in the morning, each assigned to a team. At the controls was Price. He looked up and quickly shook hands before returning to tapping statistics into the machines.

"With the number of players, the information required has increased incredibly," Price told me. "What the computer has allowed the scout to do is to decipher the information, to pull out what they need to know about each of the players." While we talked he was feeding the heights and weights of players currently in the Swedish league into each of the five teams' databanks.

Now in his mid-thirties, Price had been the director of information with the Canadian Hockey League for nine years before striking out on his own early in 1997 to form RinkNet Consulting Services, offering high-tech scouting and player information systems. He had a hockey background, which included scouting, as assistant general manager with the Brantford Alexanders, the Hamilton Steelhawks and the Niagara Falls Thunder of the Ontario Hockey League. Educated in computer programming at Conestoga College in the Kitchener area, Price figured there was a way to quantify the talent of a hockey player and produce an accurate chart of that player's potential. Still, he understood that the game is not an exact science. "You're never going to replace a scout seeing a player and evaluating what he sees," Price stated.

The phone rang and Price excused himself to engage in a conversation with Lucas Bergman, Nashville's amateur scout in Europe. Bergman was calling from Stockholm and trying to get his computer synchronized with the rest of the Predators staff so he could update the information in his system. With all the scouts, coaches and management online, Nashville had about twenty people on their network. What was more incredible was that the database included extensive profiles of 20,081 hockey players around the world.

"You're not seeing players come out of countries that no one has ever seen before," Price said, having further destroyed the myth of the needle in the haystack. "Finding the undiscovered player has gone by the board now. There is so much information for so many countries that it would be very tough for a player to slip through the cracks and go on to become a good NHL player."

Prominently displayed on the home page for each team's scouting systems, Price had included a litany of icons and information categories. There was a section for rosters, another for player profiles, still another for game reports. A scout can click on the query icon to search for a player who meets certain desirable specifications based on the parent club's needs. For instance, Price asked the Nashville computer for a six-foot left winger who was at least 195 pounds with blazing speed. When he pressed Enter, the screen instantly filled with a list of twenty or so young men from around the world. Beside each name was the player's age, his team and his overall numerical rating based on the Nashville scouts' evaluations, as well as the number of times he had been seen by the scouts and who these scouts were.

The Nashville system is an indication of how wide the scouting web now reaches. Price showed me that the team could create depth charts on itself and other teams. The club could also identify where its strengths and weaknesses were and zero in on a need to replenish stock at certain positions. Sources of players were created and ranked against others. In a category called Lists, Price demonstrated how prospects from American colleges, European junior leagues and everywhere else on the face of the earth were ranked and reranked every month. Players' biographical profiles were posted on the system. There was a place where each scout could file his expenses and plan his travel itinerary. It was an all-encompassing information environment in which I found it hard to place Lorne Davis and his cronies out west.

Hockey had become increasingly modernized at the NHL level. Too much money was at stake for an error to occur at the draft table. Nashville's general manager, David Poile, had been one of the leaders of the revolution that saw the old guard recognize the value of the computer for providing scouting information. A native of Toronto and a graduate of Northeastern University in Boston, Poile had begun in the NHL as an administrative assistant with the Atlanta Flames in the mid-1970s. He served his apprenticeship as an assistant general manager in Calgary, then moved on to Washington and guided the Capitals to the playoffs fourteen of the fifteen years he was vice-president and general manager. In assuming the top management position with the expansion Predators, Poile had spent an entire year setting up the organization and scouting talent before the team hit the ice.

"Scouting is the most important thing that you do as an organization," Poile told me as he watched his Predators play the Vancouver Canucks on the eve of Halloween. "When you talk about a team being built in the traditional sense, and especially an expansion team, you don't go out and sign a whole bunch of high-priced free agents. You build through the draft and count on younger players—which means that scouting is everything."

In the 1999 Entry Draft, the second year the Predators operated, Poile engineered seven of the first seventy-two picks and a league high of fifteen picks overall. It's an indication of how important selecting developing players is to this hockey executive. A survey of the Predators choices revealed that they had come from all over the world. His scouting staff is the largest in the league, and it even included a scout based in the Maritimes. "You can't be everywhere," Poile admitted. "You can't be in the Maritimes today and in Russia tomorrow and in B.C. the next day. It doesn't work like that. There's just too much hockey to cover. You can only spend so much money on scouting, but there are players coming from everywhere now so the best coverage you can get is the key."

I had run into Darrell Young, the Predators Maritimes scout, on an airplane. We were both returning from the All-Star Game in Tampa Bay, Florida. He had a pile of notes beside him and was rapidly transcribing them into his laptop computer. Young, a former coach of Dalhousie University's hockey team and the brother of one-time NHL goalie Wendell, had had a hand in evaluating the

Predators first-ever amateur draft choice, David Legwand of the
Ontario Hockey League Plymouth Whalers. "He knew how to get
to the open ice," Young had said. "He was there before the puck
got there. His on-ice vision was incredible."

Young sees about 120 games a year working part time for David
Poile and the Predators. He is determined that no stone be left
unturned, and that means the provinces of New Brunswick, Nova
Scotia, Prince Edward Island and Newfoundland, which have been
neglected by most NHL organizations in the past. He respects Poile's
intuition and defended his own place in the organization. "David is
one of the most intelligent people in the game," Young said. "He
wants you to challenge him and his thinking in order to make the
organization better. There aren't too many general managers in the
NHL who would do that."

Young went back to his computer, as if to demonstrate what he
was talking about. Clicking on icons and pointing at the stats as
they appeared, he was every bit the modern hockey scout. "You
can backtrack and find out what happened three or four years ago,"
Young explained. "Especially with younger players, you might
want to find out who has grown a lot in the last couple of seasons."

David Poile smiled when I told him of the delight that one of
his scouts took in the computer. He nodded as he leaned over the
rail at the press box in Vancouver, watching his team, which had
developed into a sternly competitive unit in only its second season.
"Some of us in hockey can't see how we were functioning successfully without them. The computer is what it is. It's a database for all
of our people to refer to on a daily basis. It's a place to get organized. The computer came along at the right time for hockey."

Another call came at Jim Price's house. Another moment to
relinquish his keyboard and help out a scout out there on the road
having trouble with a frozen system, preventing him from accessing
the online network. "This lockup thing should happen only in
a blue moon," he told Paul Castron of the Columbus Blue Jackets.

"I think you're going to have to get this looked at. Are you going to Columbus anytime soon?"

Price admitted that moving beyond the traditional way of operating hadn't always been smooth. It had taken some scouts a long time to get comfortable with the new technology. "You know, if you're sixty-nine, the initial contact with the computer can be a little daunting," he said. "But you'd be surprised at how quickly those guys are catching on. They see how critical the information is for them and, beyond that, the entire organization they work for."

Price pounded away at the keys, eager to keep his five NHL clients up to date. Soon his shift workers were scheduled to arrive—he had hired four students to help him feed all the information into the machines. It was clear that Price had exploited the game's growth to modernize an old occupation. Still, he was a hockey man and as such was realistic about the place of technology in a game of intuition. "This game will never be a robotic type of game," he stated. "It's still going to come down to what a scout thinks. A guy like Lorne Davis will have all the numbers now, but it's still what he thinks about a certain player that counts, and it's up to general managers to understand that scouts have delivered before based partly on instinct and hope that they will do it again."

———

Lorne wasn't seeing much to get overly excited about in the game between the Lebret Eagles and the Melville Millionaires. Then again, he didn't expect to, because these days it's not often any player from the Saskatchewan league will be drafted by an NHL team. Over the years, though, Lorne Davis has been a trusted pair of eyes for the Oilers. He was instrumental in helping Edmonton build its exciting teams of the 1980s with players like the superlative defenceman Paul Coffey, goaltender Grant

Fuhr and perhaps one of the most prolific playoff competitors of all time, Glenn Anderson.

He is a wise observer and sparing with his praise because of what he has seen in the past. "I'm really disappointed in our hockey in the last little while," he said, eyes fixed on a 3–1 game. "You know, I can go to some junior games and watch an entire 60 minutes and not see one good play." Just as he finished speaking, number 7 of the Millionaires, Dave Shields, unleashed a rocket to make it a three-goal gap in favour of Melville. "They've made some great shots," snorted Davis. "Thing is, I don't know if the goaltending's horseshit or if they're that good."

Desire is one of hockey's most overused adjectives. For years Canadians have believed it existed exclusively in players who were reared in this country. The lyrical and heroic image of the hard-working skater has been trumpeted by fishermen in the east, loggers in the west and Prairie farmers alike. A reflection of his country, the Canadian player may not always be the most talented or skilled, scouts have argued, but no one can match his heart. It is a theory that many an experienced scout, like Lorne Davis, has ardently subscribed to. It's why the most satisfying NHLers they have developed have not always been the most likely.

"I could say that I am proud of Grant Fuhr and Paul Coffey because I had something to do with both those players being chosen," Lorne said. "But the one guy I was exceptionally proud of was Kelly Buchberger. The way he turned out and became the captain of the team."

Kelly Buchberger is thirty-three and a native of the tiny town of Langenburg, Saskatchewan, a stone's throw from the Manitoba border. It should be noted that Buchberger could never be mistaken for an Oilers star in the mould of Mark Messier or Wayne Gretzky. Yet he has been an important captain of the team during a time of turmoil and of survival. Twice he has played on Stanley Cup teams, but he has come into his own during the lean years of the Oilers present. He has been steadfast and strong as the brightest lights have moved on to much bigger NHL cities in search of enormous contracts. Only in the last expansion was this loyal servant of the club made expendable. Left unprotected by Edmonton, he was grabbed by the fledgling Atlanta Thrashers and made the first captain of the new franchise. Even far from home, Buchberger treasures his Edmonton days and the man who made sure he came there.

"Lorne was the guy directly responsible for me making it to the NHL," Buchberger told me on the phone from his home in suburban Atlanta. "He scouted me when I was in Moose Jaw and was always there more than anybody else when I was playing."

Kelly Buchberger was an unlikely player. Horribly scarred on his legs from a farm fire in his youth, he struggled to attract the attention of the scouts first as a member of the Tier II Saskatchewan league Melville Millionaires and then with the Moose Jaw Warriors of the Western Hockey League. "You talk about somebody being raw," Lorne remembered. "It was unbelievable. The one thing he always had was that he could skate. He had great desire, even as a junior. With that you could forgive him not having the puck-handling skills that the other guys had."

It was Buchberger's "desire" that captured Lorne Davis's attention, and the young man's devotion to the game. While not a dangerous scorer, Buchberger was a tremendous competitor and was willing to fight the battles that less talented players sometimes must to succeed at any level of hockey. In the 1985 amateur draft, Davis persuaded the Oilers scouting staff to take a chance on the kid and his more than 200 penalty minutes per season as a junior. The Oilers selected him well down the list—in the ninth round, 188th overall. "Anything beyond the third round of the draft is really a crap shoot," Buchberger related. "I knew going to the Oilers in the ninth round that my battle would be uphill all the way."

A scout will tell you that once he has laid his reputation on the line and the team that employs him has shown faith in his judgment, a sense of ownership develops towards the players who are drafted on his recommendation. So it was with Lorne Davis and his "long shot," Kelly Buchberger. He was, after all, attempting to crack the lineup of what many have called the most exciting team of all time. "After we drafted him, I went back and watched him each year several times and I'd see definite improvement," Lorne recalled.

"I would always look up in the stands to see if Lorne was there," Buchberger said of the time after his selection. "I wanted to make the team so much and knew that I would have to impress him in order to do it." Things were not always smooth. His last year in Moose Jaw with the Warriors, Buchberger strayed from his concentration on hockey and had too much fun outside the arena. It was the wrong road to go down, one that could only lead to trouble and a once-in-a-lifetime chance wasted. Davis came to the rescue and took Buchberger to his hockey school as a summer instructor. There he blossomed and regained his focus for the game and his future in it. "So many kids and Lorne was always there," Buchberger said proudly. "You can't have been in Canada too long if you don't know what it's like to be at a hockey school like this. People like Lorne showed faith in me. I spoke with him and his wife a lot and they told me to believe in myself and that, through hard work, I would make it. They were right."

Indeed they were. Kelly Buchberger played a dozen years with the Oilers and scored 240 points while becoming an essential element of the Stanley Cup story in Edmonton. "It was something special to be an Oiler," said the one-time dark horse. "Especially for a kid like me who had grown up in small-town Saskatchewan. It was like one big family all the time. It didn't matter if you were a fourth liner or a front liner. You were treated the same every day."

Upon reflection, the scout who stood up for Kelly Buchberger recognized that it's all about the pride that results from the less talented pupil finding a place for himself in class. "You know, it's what you feel down here," Davis said, motioning to his ample belly. "The first time you see a guy is the best evaluation." Kelly Buchberger made good on his first impression and will never take for granted the scout who made his career possible. "He has become a very important person in my life," Buchberger said of Lorne. "Without him I would not have been able to do what I have done in hockey. I owe much of my success to Lorne. There is no question about that."

Lorne Davis's enthusiasm for the game is infectious. He chattered throughout the proceedings in Lebret that night. By the end of the second period, the Millionaires of Melville threatened to make it a runaway contest. They were up 5–2, but the resolve of the crowd was intact and so was the old scout's desire to hang in for the third period. He had talked of ducking out early but was swayed by the rink's attraction, the speed of the action and by the children who played behind the end boards with the scruffy Lebret mascot. "People sure do love their hockey in little towns," he said, full of admiration.

The players skated out for the final frame and the costumed fox, wearing the hometown Eagles sweater, high-fived everyone in sight and generally made a nuisance of himself. A man sporting a black Arctic Cat baseball cap turned to us and offered some hope. "Don't worry," he said. "In another month somebody will run him over with a snowmobile!" Lorne, Sully, Bryan and I all laughed. The referee dropped the puck and the players were away. All eyes turned to the ice and the mascot sat down to see whether the beloved locals could make their way back from a three-goal deficit.

Lorne had been on the road before coming to the game with me that night—nine games in eleven days from which he had just returned a few hours before picking me up at the hotel. There had been stops in Medicine Hat, Calgary, Lethbridge, Calgary again, Kelowna and Seattle. Then it was back to Kelowna for a couple more contests before finally boarding a plane and flying back to Regina to set up for the next trip, which would be to the east. That journey would take him to thirteen hockey games over the course of eleven days.

The west was the toughest travel by far—long distances, short hops on small planes and vast distances covered by car. In Ontario it was different, and Lorne harboured a slight smugness about the challenge of scouting the Prairies as opposed to the urban jungle of central Canada. "I keep telling our Ontario scouts, my son Brad and Ed Chadwick, that I'm going to take them to North Bay, Sudbury and Sault Ste. Marie and show them where the rinks are," he huffed. It was a thinly veiled but good-natured knock at two guys who were dear to Lorne Davis's heart. Chadwick, a former goalie with the Leafs and Bruins, was a longtime associate who had just recently retired as a full-time scout with the Oilers, but who also refused to give up the game completely. Brad Davis was relatively new to the profession and had learned everything at his dad's knee.

———

The father's son was joyous as he took my 10 a.m. call at his motel in Belleville, Ontario. He had scouted the Belleville Bulls and the Kingston Frontenacs the night before and had been able to catch the tail end of the 2–1 Edmonton victory over the Montreal Canadiens from the Skyreach Centre. "At first I couldn't find it anywhere," Brad Davis told me. "I had to go to the strip club across the street. There I am facing away from the stage trying to catch the last two periods of a hockey game in Edmonton!"

The life of a scout on the road is not a glamorous one. On average, Brad Davis, who makes his home in Kitchener, Ontario, sees fifteen to twenty hotel rooms a month. His wife, Debbie, is a nurse and had moved from the west shortly before I spoke with Brad to be closer to her husband. She has 180 games a year to look forward to as Brad scouts twelve major junior teams based within a three-hour radius of their home. With so much talent on display so close at hand, it's like shooting fish in a barrel. "This is a piece of cake compared to what Dad has to do," Brad confessed. "He always said you could work this league on a bicycle."

The younger Davis played hockey for Weyburn of the Western Hockey League for a short time but made his mark in the game as an official. He refereed in the American Hockey League, a step below the big time, and was a stalwart of the major junior WHL presiding over a couple of Memorial Cup championship series. During the NHL officials strike in the fall of 1993, he refused to break the union and work as a replacement referee. In the aftermath of the labour dispute he saw his prospects at the NHL level quickly shrink. Now into his third year as an Oilers scout, Davis is gradually feeling comfortable with a new fraternity. "The other scouts told me I had to put in three full years before I lose the handle 'three hour.' They call me that because back when I was a referee they hated going to my games—they were so long."

Scouting came naturally to Brad. The youngest of the family, he never saw his father play the game, and his home life consisted of Lorne appearing every now and again during the winter in order to change the clothes in his suitcase. He recalls his dad being gone for trips of twenty or twenty-five days and never remembering his child's age other than to say, "He's a late '66." It was a life spent in the rinks of Saskatchewan watching the best juniors develop into future stars of the NHL. "It was Swift Current or Moose Jaw or Prince Albert. I'd sit in the stands beside Dad," Brad recalled. "I always picked out players and I think I got that from him. It was always a player and not the team. The elements that made up the team, I suppose, and not the team itself."

More than anything, Brad Davis has carried on a family tradition, which allowed him to stay in the game long after his time as a player had elapsed. This is consistent among scouts—an ability to

make the game a living beyond the obvious application as a player.
He is only thirty-three, but Davis has what seems like an eternity
of hockey in front of him. The ultimate life for a boy who, even as
a man, craves the life of the rink rat. "I wouldn't ever want it to
sound like we are hangers-on because we have gotten this far on a
certain knowledge of the game," he cautioned. "We have a job to
do and we are part of it. We are not on the ice or behind the
bench. We aren't making the crucial decisions that general managers do but we are around the game at the grassroots level every
day. We're paid to go out day in and day out and find players.
That's our job."

Before hanging up the phone, Davis explained how much he
loved the atmosphere surrounding his calling. The locker-room
mentality, which he claimed some could never understand but
which had become essential for his happiness. The joking with
players, coaches and other scouts. The hot dogs served in media
rooms of junior rinks around the countryside and the fellowship
that develops on the road. It was not the NHL, complete with
comfy seats and black limousines. Perhaps, for an ardent fan of the
sport, it was that much better. "I love it. I couldn't be happier," he
claimed. "I would much rather watch a junior game than a pro
game because these kids play on emotion and intensity. They're
kids and they'll do anything they can to make it, night after night.
You never know what will happen from one moment to the next.
We're not only around the game, we're involved at the top level and
we get to watch the better part. What more could you ask for?"

———

In Lebret, the end was near. The Millionaires had withstood a last
charge from the Eagles and with about a minute left, a 6–4 Melville
margin resulted in ritualistic fisticuffs between the two teams. The
fans in the little rink flocked to the glass and pounded their fists at

the visiting players. Lorne motioned me down the steps. "Actually, it's been a surprisingly good game until now," he said.

On the way back to Regina, in the complete darkness of the prairie, he revealed that there hadn't been much call for him to attend the game. Not one of the players was of interest to the Edmonton Oilers—not one would get a second thought from any NHL team. Lorne said that he tried to see all Tier II junior teams at least once in a season, so the exercise had been helpful in that respect. More than anything, he seemed thankful for the chance to go to a hockey game and to be talking about his life spent in a thousand different arenas.

He had left the St. Louis Blues when the new general manager, Emile "the Cat" Francis, replaced the entire coaching staff following the 1976 draft. It was a draft that had seen the Blues select Bernie Federko, Brian Sutter, Mike Eaves and Mike Liut. All became accomplished players, but Francis wanted his own people in the scouting department. It brought to light the concept of loyalty, so prevalent in the game of hockey at any level. It is a principle that Davis has adhered to throughout his twenty years with the Oilers. The object of his unfailing admiration is the team's president and general manager, Glen Sather, one of hockey's most powerful leaders and arguably its most conscientious.

"Glen has always made us feel a big part of the team," Davis said. His face was barely visible in the half-light of the dashboard. "I feel a very, very important part of the Edmonton Oilers organization. Every year before training camp, before they step on the ice, Glen takes the scouts in and introduces us to all of the players and makes sure that they know there is someone to call if they are having trouble." It was as though Lorne was indicating that he felt needed by the Oilers. That was the quality that aroused his devotion. A loyalty to the team he worked for, even though he seemed to be on the fringes of their success. "Glen is loyal," he said. "Loyalties don't seem to mean much anymore, but I think it would be tough to work if there were no loyalties. I never knew Glen until I started working for him, but it was quite obvious to me that he hated everybody in every other organization. When you work for him, though, he'll stand up for you. He'll do anything for you."

Glen Sather has come to symbolize the Edmonton Oilers—the coach of four Stanley Cup championship teams in the 1980s and the mastermind behind a franchise that has won five, all told, in one of the league's smallest cities. He is proud and pugnacious, immaculately dressed. Sather has moulded the Oilers into a team of tradition that puts a premium on skill and speed. Each Edmonton squad is fast as Sather subscribes to the ideal of exciting hockey. "He won't change the way his teams play the game," Davis said. "I'm sure he'll end his career wanting his teams to play that way. Wouldn't it be great if every team was that way? It'd be a helluva game to watch, wouldn't it?"

———

"I've got all day to talk to you about Lorne Davis," Sather had told me in the moments before a game between his team and the powerful Detroit Red Wings. He hauled up a stool in the television studio of the Edmonton rink and began to tell stories of meeting Lorne Davis through his friend Father Athol Murray at Notre Dame College in Wilcox, Saskatchewan—a place he had considered playing as a boy. An offer came in from the Edmonton Oil Kings, and Sather scuttled his plans for Notre Dame but kept Lorne Davis in the back of his mind.

When he became a general manager with the Oilers, one of the first people Sather wanted to talk to was Davis. Lorne had been let go by the St. Louis Blues and was working part time for the New York Rangers while coaching with the Canadian national team. "So we got him," Sather said. "He came to us and he was overweight. Every year I've said to these guys you've got to have a medical with the players, but I could never get Lorne to go. After the twenty-first or twenty-second year he finally took the medical and it scared the hell out of him. He had high blood pressure, his cholesterol was wacko, and we had to put him on a diet. We probably got his life in order. He never cared about his health at all. All he cared about was hockey."

Sather has cultivated an intensely emotional connection between the people of Edmonton and their hockey team, a connection rooted in the concepts of family and trust. Everyone in the Oilers organization is seen as essential to the fabric of the club and any success that it has enjoyed over the years. Sather himself has found it difficult to leave Edmonton in spite of its recent struggles to survive in an NHL more suited to big, rich American cities. He has called it the most heart-wrenching aspect of his job, this need to stay while members of the family he has seen grow to maturity felt compelled to move on. It has happened with Paul Coffey, Mark Messier, Wayne Gretzky and a legion of others. In the end, he clings to the resolve of those who have remained and understands what each brings to the team, including scouts like Lorne Davis.

"The guys who own teams now have no idea what a team is all about and how it functions," he said. "It's tough to find guys who'll do the job that Lorne does—to drive all over the west. He puts on 15,000 kilometres in a month. You should travel with him for a while through the snowstorms in the winter. He's in the ditch all the time. It's incredible!"

The Oilers scouts all have Stanley Cup rings on their fingers. They can be seen in the team pictures at the end of a season when the precious trophy is won. Few franchises include the all too anonymous background workers at times of glory as the Edmonton Oilers do. Sather freely admitted that the credit belonged largely to the industrious men like Lorne Davis. "I don't do anything at the draft," he said. "I don't pick any of the players. I went to see Grant Fuhr in Victoria twice and in Windsor at the

Memorial Cup. He was brutal. When I went to see Paul Coffey
he was horseshit. I would never have picked Coffey. I relied on
them. That's all you can do."

The results have not always been favourable, but more often
than not Sather's faith in the scouts has been rewarded. Coffey is
one of the highest-scoring defencemen of all time, a remarkable
skater, and goaltender Grant Fuhr has gone on to win more than
four hundred games in NHL nets. Both have a legitimate claim to
hockey's Hall of Fame. "The scouts have been great," Sather said.
"They've been good friends."

On the subject of loyalty and servitude as it applied to the
trusted scouts, Sather bristled at any hint that they were somehow
subservient to those who managed the club. "Oh, I'd never call
Lorne a loyal servant of the team." He smiled. "He's been a loyal
partner."

———

The night advanced like so many others for the scout. Headlights
illuminating a highway through acres of the flat and fertile land.
Up ahead was the unfamiliar homestead in Regina. More comfortable and inviting was the rink he had left behind in minuscule
Lebret. There was the matter of his age—a year shy of seventy—
and the pension he would be forced to take at December's end.
"It's about time I quit," he said, much too quickly. The words were
the wrong ones and he knew it.

For thirty-three years, he had rolled down these roads and gathered what was stored in the sheds of the western plain. Players filled
his thoughts and his heart. The best of what he had seen from them
had been passed on to the fans. The quality of the product was
rarely less than Grade A. Now he wondered whether he could ever
successfully leave the chilly fields for the warmth that radiated from
his fireplace in the city.

"I'd be a pretty lonely man if I couldn't go to hockey games anymore," Lorne said, sounding like a farmer clinging to the land. "I don't know, I just get the feeling if I ever quit it completely I wouldn't last too long. I've seen that happen to lots of people. They get so old after they finish scouting."

His weight is down by more than twenty-five pounds and he's given up smoking and drinking, the result of the physical Sather insisted on. Lorne Davis didn't look anything close to his age. He talked about getting a tingle every time he walked into a rink, even though he knew it was unlikely that a real player would be there. I looked over at him and thought of all the seasons and all the harvests that he had toiled, and I could not imagine him anywhere but in the bleachers close to the ice with his lineup rolled tightly in his sturdy grip.

"Besides, I don't curl," he added. The fields had receded all too swiftly and the threatening glow of the town was upon us.

THE NATURAL

Andy Sullivan

The Big Bayman

(courtesy Pam Sullivan)

✧ THIS IS PART OF THE LORE OF the place they call "the Rock."
I first heard the story years ago during a research trip to St. John's
and historic Memorial Stadium, the most famous rink in Newfoundland. It was on that arena's hallowed ice that many of the
revered players from the island province had learned their craft. I
had only a passing knowledge of most of these local heroes; they
had been role players in the National Hockey League, and though
it was true that a few had flirted with stardom for some time, others had enjoyed only a fleeting moment in the sunshine of hockey's
major league. What was impressive to me, however, was the deeply
felt loyalty to the local boys.

In the bleachers that day, the names of Doug Grant, the old Red
Wings goalie, Alex Faulkner, another skater for Detroit in the early
1960s, and Joe Lundrigan, a Newfoundland native who had played
for the Maple Leafs in the 1970s, came to mind. None had been a
star in the NHL but they had been able to attract an enduring following at home in Newfoundland. The winter legends of this land
seemed enhanced a hundredfold by their comparative rarity.

There were also the current players, such as John Slaney of
Merrymeeting Road. He was a resident of St. John's and therefore
called a "townie" by the locals. Slaney had starred for the Team
Canada juniors not so long ago and had been selected by the Washington Capitals in the first round of the 1990 Entry Draft. Since
that time, the defenceman had been up and down between the
minors and a variety of NHL clubs in southern climes such as Colorado, Los Angeles, Phoenix and Nashville.

Darren Langdon, the most resilient of the modern-day Newfoundlanders to make it, was in his sixth full season with the New
York Rangers. A tough guy born in Deer Lake, Langdon had
more than three hundred games in the NHL to his credit and fewer
than 50 points scored to show for his trouble. Highly touted
prospects Danny Cleary of Carbonear and St. John's own Harold

Druken were still trying to catch on in Edmonton and Vancouver respectively.

I had expected to hear one of those names when I encountered a young married couple surveying the stands at Memorial Stadium that morning. Wayne and Laura Carew had come to town to search out the seats they preferred for the impending American Hockey League playoffs involving the hometown St. John's Maple Leafs. "Who was the greatest player you ever saw skate in here?" I had asked them out of the blue. They didn't miss a beat. "Andy Sullivan, without a doubt." The name was a complete mystery to me.

This Sullivan fellow played in the provincial senior league for a team called the Southern Shore Breakers. Wayne Carew was a teammate of his and swore to his brilliance. "Never played in the NHL but Andy could have been a star if he wanted," Carew claimed. His wife nodded her agreement. Andy Sullivan was the benchmark hockey player to them and it struck, I reckoned, a somewhat romantic chord.

Some say that Newfoundland's skating sons are loved better than most. It is a fact that the best of them made it all the way to the National Hockey League: Faulkner, Lundrigan, Grant, Slaney and Langdon. Then again, some folks are convinced that the best Newfoundland player they ever laid eyes on never saw the NHL at all. It turns out that he works at a fish plant in a place called, of all things, Witless Bay. And his case strikes me as more than a little curious.

———

Andy Sullivan was born into a fishing family in Calvert, Newfoundland, in 1961. In all, there were four sisters and eight hockey-playing boys. It is said that Andy Sullivan never played organized hockey until his late teens, instead skating freely on the frozen ponds of Calvert. Still, at the age of thirty-two, Sully (as he was known in these parts) cracked the lineup of the American Hockey League with the St. John's Maple Leafs. One step away from the NHL, he played alongside much younger men who were destined for careers in the big leagues, players like Yanic Perreault of the Los Angeles Kings and subsequently the Toronto Maple Leafs.

Sullivan turned out to be a last-resort replacement for a depleted squad. Lacking players as a result of injuries and a rash of call-ups to the parent club in Toronto, the local Leafs reached out to the Newfoundland senior ranks to fill their roster. Andy Sullivan was the first player to get the call, and a desperate coach named Marc Crawford, now the bench boss with the Vancouver Canucks, went out on a limb in November of 1993.

"We got into a predicament where we had to use somebody," Crawford remembers. "We gave Andy Sullivan his chance, and I'll tell you what: by the end of that first game everybody was saying, 'How come you never told us about that Andy Sullivan guy?' "

As we drive down the shore (or "up the shore"—it's said both ways in Newfoundland even though one is travelling south from St. John's), the mist shrouds the tops of the scrubby trees. Beside me in the van is Peter Hanlon, the director of communications for the Calgary Flames. Hanlon is in his early thirties and at one time did the same job for the AHL Maple Leafs. Before that, he had played senior hockey in his native province with the St. John's Caps. He knew the story of Andy Sullivan and had become the player's close friend during the time Sully skated with the Leafs. Home for a mid-season visit to his elderly father, Hanlon had agreed to introduce me to Sullivan—"the Wayne Gretzky of New-foundland," he calls him.

The route is the Southern Shore Highway, or "the Irish Loop," as it is more commonly referred to around here. Slicing through the fog of the mid-morning, we catch a glimpse of the coast every now and again. The two-lane road takes us through hamlets with such names as Donovans, Kilbride, Big Pond and Bay Bulls to the quaint village of Witless Bay, where Andy is to meet us at the fish plant he manages.

"There is still a mystique to Andy's situation because even though he had the opportunity to go and try it in the NHL, he decided not to, for his own personal reasons," Hanlon is saying as we make a left turn past the lighthouse at Witless Bay. "This guy could have played. He could have been there. There is a little romance in that."

I'm more than a little bit skeptical. This doesn't appear to be hockey country. It's early February and there isn't a flake of snow anywhere and no frozen pond in sight. Instead, the wind blusters across a rolling landscape of yellow grass. Little shacks are barely visible through mist as thick as skim milk. Beyond their front yards, the surf crashes against the craggy, black coast. Perched on small wooden stilts, an old fishing boat called *Baccalieu Guardian* seems to stand sentry for the weather-worn community comprising a couple of hundred souls—if that.

Remembering Marc Crawford's words, I wonder how anyone could have known about a terrific hockey talent from this place without being told. This was not a locale frequented by scouts on the lookout for the next Mark Messier or Raymond Bourque. This was not the frigid prairie, where an eagle-eyed bird dog might happen upon a swift-skating winger on the pristine slough. Nor was it northern Quebec, where hockey is akin to religion and outdoor rinks at every town's core brim with hearty defenders. In those places, the game is second nature to most, and one can expect to find a constant supply of players who just might make it someday.

Here we are in this outport village where the residents cling to the land like barnacles to a rock. We are standing outside, looking at a squat grey building attached to the water by a concrete pier maybe a hundred yards long. If Andy Sullivan's story holds water, he works at the family trade instead of playing the game for untold riches. It appears that Sullivan answers his calling here, at the Shaw-mut Fish Processing Plant.

"He's quite a shy fella," Hanlon hastens to inform me. "And he has a heavy accent that makes you think he's right from Ireland." Squishing over the mud and into the fishery, I grow increasingly curious. A distinct odour wafts through the door as we make our way in. "They call that a maggoty fish smell," Hanlon explains. "It comes from the crab that they prepare in the factory here." Hundreds of old wooden crates are stacked haphazardly on the property.

Up the stairs and through the panelled hallways, Peter and I find the manager's office at the back of the plant. There he is, pacing back and forth with his hands in his pockets and looking a bit like a deer caught in the headlights. A moss green crewneck sweater covers Sullivan's lean upper body. He's tall, about six foot two, and weighs a touch over 200 pounds, I estimate, with "a pretty standard haircut"—Hanlon's words. You can tell he's been sweating and fretting, wondering what all the fuss is about. He looks, at first glance, like he might be a player.

Andy Sullivan's record of play is a thing of beauty. Unlike those well-documented athletes in the Metro Toronto Hockey League or any number of more formal associations across the country, the winding road to prominence for a rural Newfoundlander of his generation is committed not to paper but to memory. It is more like listening to a tall tale by the roaring campfire than reading a chart of statistics.

So it is that Andy Sullivan, cornered in his office, nervously recites the path he's taken in search of his favourite game. "I had relatively little coaching," he begins. "And playing pro hockey, compared to what I had been playing, seemed a lifetime away. I never really gave it a whole lot of consideration."

A son of the Southern Shore, Sullivan first took to the ice in his native Calvert, a little farther up the road. Until he was fourteen, he played mostly on the local ponds, skating with his buddies in an

endless game of shinny. It was the freedom and the ice time that
mattered most. The score was rarely kept and valued only as a
source of bragging rights. "Once a year we'd rent the indoor ice,"
Andy recalls. It was a luxury to him, a place where hockey became
a little more formal and his dreams could roam free.

I notice that his skates and stick are propped in the corner. A
smallish bag contains his helmet, gloves and shoulder pads. Andy is
prepared for Thursday-night hockey that evening with the same
cast of characters that he's just talked about. It will take place at the
Brother O'Hehir Arena in downtown St. John's, just as it has since
1985. Peter Hanlon will play too—grabbing the rare chance to be
reunited with his former teammates.

"The more you watch him, the more you see that things seem
to happen for him," Hanlon exclaims. "The puck always finds its
way to him—he's one of those guys."

Andy Sullivan sighs and sweeps a hand through his straight chest-
nut hair. His eyes are brilliant blue and he looks remarkably like a
little boy as he shuffles his feet in embarrassment. "Go 'way, Peter!"
Andy says to his friend. His accent does indeed sound Irish to me.
"Things," for example, comes out as "tings." His friend is "Petter"
instead of "Peter." Andy has a gentle nature about him that is consistent with his lilt and, I imagine, his approach to life in general.

He goes on to tell of his first organized days in the Southern
Shore Junior League, a loose collection of teams from the coastal
villages where the coaching was friendly and familiar but about as
far as you can get from the cutting edge. From there it was on to
the big city, where Andy played in the juvenile association and then
in the St. John's Junior League with the Shamrocks.

Starting with the juniors in the 1980–81 season, Sullivan had
two years of eligibility left before his prospects to become a professional were undoubtedly over. Once a player is over the age of
twenty, he is no longer able to skate in junior hockey, and if he's
not drafted by some NHL team, the options are limited to the lesser

leagues and, in most cases, local senior hockey. It was at about this time that Sullivan, a torrid scorer and unparalleled leader for the Shamrocks, nearly got his chance. He was a great natural talent and was noticed by an observer who made it his business to watch the greatest hockey players in the world. Bob Cole was always on the lookout for a Newfoundlander who had the right stuff.

"Well, I thought we needed a connection to the National Hockey League," the Hall of Fame broadcaster explained. Bob Cole was looking over the hill in his backyard just outside Topsail, forty minutes the other side of St. John's. The constant rain dripped from his windbreaker as he pointed out Conception Bay, barely visible through the fog. His golden retriever rambled through the long grass and the sweet smell of cod tongues rose from the skillet on the stove a mere fifteen feet away.

"Maybe Hartford, one of the newer teams at the time, was the answer," Cole continued. "So I called my good friend Emile 'the Cat' Francis and I told him that I believed this young man had a chance to do something." Cole told Francis that Sullivan was big— more than six feet and with considerable power, about 220 pounds of it. "A very smart player, a very intelligent person, a very likeable person, a very strong person. A hockey player" were Cole's exact words to the Hartford Whalers general manager. He had sold Sullivan hard, and after years of watching him play was willing to stake his reputation on this "can't miss" local boy who would make all Newfoundlanders proud in the world of hockey at its highest level.

Emile Francis was building a new National Hockey League franchise in the early 1980s. The Whalers of the recently defunct World Hockey Association had been absorbed by the NHL along with the Winnipeg Jets, the Edmonton Oilers and the Quebec Nordiques. The Whalers were always eager to consider new talent that could help them rival the established powers.

With that in mind, Francis was inclined to take a flyer on Andy Sullivan, who was fondly referred to by St. John's fans as "the Big

Bayman." Francis promised Sullivan's travel to Connecticut and housing while the player attended the Whalers training camp. He also assured Cole that Sullivan would be looked after and extra attention would be given to his skating—an area of concern for Andy himself. Francis trusted Cole's recommendation implicitly and promised that he would be in touch.

"Hartford called. I told Andy that we had to go." Cole's memory of the incident was vivid. "I told him that we had to do something to see if he really had it. He was going to go, but I believe he started thinking about this going away to New England and not knowing anybody. He was working at his brother's fish plant at the time and was happy here."

As it turned out, Sully stayed in Newfoundland and passed up the best chance he might ever have to prove his talent in front of the most discerning judges in the world. "Eighteen years old and he'd never been in the hockey business. He wanted to stay home and good for him but I think he would have made it," Cole lamented. "Oh, how I wish Andy would have given himself a chance to get into the big stuff!"

We are walking across the floor of the fish processing plant. Eerily quiet in the off-season, the Shawmut fishery has been operating since 1989, buying 5,000 tons of raw materials and shipping them to markets in the United States and Japan. The product is crab. "Crab has generated more money for the fishing industry here than any other species over the last number of years," Andy says, matter-of-factly.

Fishing is in his blood. He has two brothers who troll the waters off the coast and another three siblings who work in the processing business with him. Before coming to manage this plant in 1996, Andy worked on the floor at a similar factory in Calvert, doing just about every job imaginable. There are stations along a silver assembly line where men and women will section the crabs—separate shoulders from the torso of the crustacean, hose it down and then send it off to another room to be packaged. In all, there are 320 people employed at this business, which will run full tilt from April to November. "On a daily basis we can process upwards of 200,000 pounds of live crab," Sullivan says, as if amazed.

When it came to his occupation, Andy Sullivan had always thought of himself as a man of the sea. The idea that he could make a living at hockey rarely entered his thinking. While on the ice he played at the game. His work was in the fishery and he was positive about what he was doing, day in and day out. When the offer from Hartford appeared, Sullivan balked. "I think it was a matter of confidence," he says, and sighs. "It goes back to having the confidence in my game overall. When I had the opportunity to go I was young and hadn't played a good calibre of hockey. I have always felt comfortable here. I have a fairly decent job in the fishery, which I enjoy, and it also gives me the opportunity to play hockey in the winter, so I guess I've had the best of both worlds."

Andy's way of judging himself in the world of hockey was refreshing. It's not the money that he's after or the prestige attached to making the grade in the big league. It appears that he's just happy to be able to play the game, but if he really is that good, what motivates him if not fame and fortune?

"I think it does come natural," Andy offers. "I just go out and play. I didn't come up through the minor hockey system or receive coaching at any level until I played senior. I was just going out and playing. Probably not playing any position—just shinny on ponds."

Sullivan went on to attend the Marine Institute in St. John's, but lingering within him was the heart of a hockey player. The love of competition sent him to senior ranks across the Island.

Andy played a couple of seasons with the Calvert Comets of the city league and followed that up as a member of the Stephenville Jets, a club that operated on the west coast of Newfoundland. St. John's had no senior team at the time and so he was forced to travel, but only within the province. Sully would fly out Thursday night, play a weekend series and then return on Sunday evening. The imported talent, including some former NHLers, received good money to play in a highly competitive provincial senior loop. Andy was compensated in kind, probably to a lesser extent, but was always the best player on his team.

They would battle against Port Aux Basques, which boasted the rugged Roberge brothers, Mario and Serge, both of whom had enjoyed brief flings in the NHL with the Canadiens and Nordiques respectively. Corner Brook and Grand Falls were also bitter rivals, and when St. John's returned to league play in the mid-1980s, Sullivan skated closer to his home in order to assume a starring role for the Caps.

It was a team that attracted Amherst, Nova Scotia, native Bill Riley. Riley was a bruising right winger who had carved out more than a hundred games in the NHL, mostly with the Washington Capitals, and at the end of his days in the league, the Winnipeg Jets. There were five more years playing with three different maritime franchises in the American Hockey League, where he became a prolific scorer and flamboyant entertainer at the next best level to the big league.

With Andy Sullivan operating down the middle at centre ice, Riley's Caps advanced to the eastern final in the Allan Cup playoffs during the 1986–87 season, as Newfoundland challenged once again for senior hockey supremacy in the country. The team from St. John's eventually lost to Brantford, but not without an enormous struggle. The roster of the squad representing southern Ontario was bolstered by a number of former NHL stars, among them one-time Bruins tough guy Stan Jonathan; Rocky Saganiuk of Toronto Maple Leafs fame; Stan Weir, who had played ten seasons in five NHL cities while posting more than 300 points; and Don Edwards, accomplished veteran of the Buffalo Sabres, who was outstanding in goal.

The whole experience proved that Andy Sullivan, a fish plant worker who had forgone a dream opportunity with the Hartford Whalers, could shine against some of the game's elite players. Those who watched it all happen came away convinced that he was deceptively great—perhaps unaware of his vast ability to dictate the flow of any game he participated in.

"He was exceptionally skilled," Peter Hanlon says. "To be honest with you, the first time I ever saw Andy Sullivan play I was a junior hockey player and they had to point him out to me. The first time I saw him I wasn't that impressed. The more you watched him, the more you knew his training was probably minimal, but he was one of those guys who just knew the game."

Hanlon's words suggested all the intangible qualities that make a hockey player special. He was telling me that this Sullivan character possessed those skills that are so difficult to teach. He was, perhaps, alluding to the character of a true athlete, the qualities one is born with. Like Wayne Gretzky's uncanny ability to see every other player on the ice, to know at any given moment not only where that player is but where he will travel. Hanlon was telling me that Andy Sullivan had the gift of a magic stick and an unswerving nose for the net.

After his three years as a star with the St. John's Caps, Andy was almost thirty and tired of travelling. He joined the Southern Shore Breakers, a senior team that played closer to home. He had done it all, been the Newfoundland scoring champ and won the coveted Herder Memorial Trophy as a member of the best team on the Island not once but three times. In his Breakers jersey—the one with a simple emblem consisting of the letters "SS" and crossing sticks above the ocean's waves—he became the favourite hockey star of an entire province. Simply "Sully," a sensation, with the name of his sponsor (Foodland) on the front of his sweater.

A brilliant player, however, cannot escape recognition in this country. Sooner or later, someone sees the chance to take every natural performer to centre stage and into the limelight. With the

onset of the 1990s, professional hockey found its way to Newfoundland, and Andy Sullivan of Witless Bay was forced to meet his
destiny head on.

———

The Toronto Maple Leafs are a team dear to the hearts of most
Newfoundland hockey fans. Native sons Alex Faulkner of Bishops
Falls and Joe Lundrigan of Corner Brook both cracked the lineup
of the cherished club in the 1960s and 1970s respectively. For
Faulkner it lasted a single game before he moved on to the Detroit
Red Wings. Still, the aura of the Leafs and the Island's connection
to the fabled team could not be denied. In addition, Bob Cole had
succeeded Bill Hewitt as the play-by-play voice of *Hockey Night in
Canada* with a special emphasis on Leafs telecasts. Every weekend
since 1980, Cole has made the trek to Toronto, tying Newfoundland to the NHL through this weekly pilgrimage.

After the nomadic wanderings of the parent club's American
Hockey League affiliate to such places as St. Catharines and New-
market in southern Ontario, Toronto's hockey management packed
up the "Baby Leafs" and sent them to St. John's to begin the 1991–92
season. They would play in the Memorial Stadium, a smallish
bandbox of a rink but one that was packed every night the team
played. The young coach was Marc Crawford of Belleville,
Ontario. He had won the Memorial Cup twice as a player with the
Cornwall Royals and succeeded as a grinding forward with the
NHL Vancouver Canucks for six seasons in the 1980s. After his playing days, the fiery Crawford had returned to Cornwall to coach
and manage his old junior squad before landing a coveted spot in
the Leafs organization.

The American Hockey League is a conflicted organization. On
the one hand it exists for NHL teams to groom young players, to nur-
ture the wealth of talent and property not quite ready for the "do or

die" world of the game at its zenith. But the AHL must also be accountable to the fans of the home city: they pay good money to be admitted to the second-best level of professional hockey. It is for that reason that the lineups of AHL clubs, decimated by their voracious big brothers in Toronto, Montreal, New York or any one of thirty major league franchises, must from time to time be propped up.

In the first year of the St. John's Maple Leafs existence, Crawford drove them to a Cinderella playoff run as they advanced to the Calder Cup final series against the Adirondack Red Wings. A veteran player and former Toronto Maple Leaf, Joel Quenneville, anchored the St. John's defence and acted as the assistant coach. He has since gone on to win the Stanley Cup as Marc Crawford's assistant in Colorado and today guides one of the NHL's premier teams, the St. Louis Blues. There is little doubt that Quenneville's savvy and experience contributed heavily to the stunning success of the team's inaugural year in Newfoundland. It should be remembered, however, that the war-wise senior statesmen are the exception in the American League. The emphasis is, and always has been, on the youthful and developing stars.

The team's third year, and Crawford's last at the helm before ascending to the NHL and a job with the Quebec Nordiques, was a difficult one. A quick glance at the final statistics for 1993–94 reveals that forty players got ice time. That's the equivalent of two full rosters' worth of personnel. Glen Stanford ran the hockey operations for the club and was constantly sending troops up to Toronto and bringing in others from the East Coast Hockey League to fill the vacated spots. A rash of injuries and a needy "big league" team created a revolving-door situation in Newfoundland. Great expectations had been created by that wildly successful first campaign, and because Memorial Stadium was small by league standards, it had to be close to full every night for the franchise to turn a dollar. This was no time for the fledgling professional hockey team on the Rock to falter.

"We were short." Stanford winces. He's taking a moment's breather in the Leafs downtown office before scooting over to the construction site of the new St. John's Civic Centre where the Baby Leafs will begin play next season. It's been difficult to keep Toronto convinced that the American League operation should stay on the Island—so isolated and inconvenient with regard to NHL needs. Stanford has fought hard to get the larger, more modern arena and has been a continuous force for the survival of the pro game in Newfoundland's capital. There was no chance he would let a thin lineup in November of 1993 slow his team's progress. He turned to Peter Hanlon, his right-hand man as well as a former senior player, and told him to be creative.

"Peter said why not get a local guy, it'll help put some people in the building. And that's what we did." Stanford's fingers stop drumming and he snaps them loudly, as if just finding the answer.

It was a move driven by two things: economics and sentiment. The cost of flying a replacement body into St. John's at a moment's notice from the ECHL was about $3,000. The player, unknown to the fans, may only play a shift or two and it was unlikely that he would leave any lasting impression beyond a shortfall in the ledger book. So why not tug at the heartstrings and see whether a local hero could create some interest? It mattered little that he wouldn't quite stack up against the younger and faster team members—he would be cheap and the fans would love it.

Crawford asked Stanford and Hanlon to identify the best senior players on the Island. He was looking for experience and someone who could spell off his remaining forwards for a shift or two. The coach was desperate and he needed someone immediately. "Without a doubt, Andy was the guy who came to mind right away," Hanlon says. "Not only had I played with him but I knew that he would be able to jump in and play the role that Marc wanted him to play. He was probably at an age where he was mature enough or experienced enough that he could deal with the pressures of the opportunity. He would also be able to excel with the opportunity."

Crawford had a history with senior hockey players. His dad, Floyd, had won the world title as a member of the 1957–58 Allan Cup champion, the Belleville McFarlands. Still, the Leafs coach was skeptical that a quality centreman could come out of a crab cannery in Witless Bay. He wasn't the only one with reservations. "When we first called Andy to ask if he would be available for Friday night's game, he hung up on us." Stanford chuckles. "He thought it was a joke and he told us to go to hell."

"When I got the call, I remember I was a bit apprehensive at first." Andy allows himself the hint of a grin. It had been his pal Peter Hanlon who had made the initial approach. "I thought he was just playing a joke. But he called back and I gave it some thought. I guess I had nothing to lose going down there."

He had already turned thirty-two, and that was well beyond the age of the majority of the Leafs. Sullivan noticed the generation gap when he walked into Memorial Stadium so that Marc Crawford could have a look-see at his newest recruit. "On average, they were ten to twelve years younger, but it was just the quickness of the game that struck me." Andy almost shivers at the thought. "They were all such great skaters, especially during practice, and that, you know, is when I think their skills really stand out."

Crawford was convinced that Sullivan could serve a useful purpose even if it turned out to work for a precious couple of minutes in each of the next few games. It was hard to get a reading from a first glance, but he could see that Sully had something. "He was a very unassuming guy. When you look at him you say to yourself, what does he have to offer?"

Glen Stanford had observed Andy Sullivan, off and on, for many seasons. He had been the rink manager at Memorial Stadium years ago and was in the crowd as the big centre powered the senior St. John's Caps close to the Canadian championship. He knew this local product was comparable to anything the Leafs had in their

1993–94 lineup. "He is very sturdy on his skates. He is very skilful around the net. If he has an opportunity to put the puck in the net, then he'll give you a good scoring opportunity. He won't muff it up. I think what Andy brought was something that was all around."

There was no way out for the reluctant hero. The Leafs needed a miracle to avoid a substantial drop in the standings of the AHL's Eastern Conference and they turned to Andy Sullivan.

———

There exists in the Island vernacular a peculiar but endearing way to describe a capacity crowd in any venue, whether it is for a sporting event or merely the local watering hole featuring a dynamite fiddler. "She's blocked!" The locals make it sound like "blacked" and they utter the description with such pride. In this wind-driven, hearty place, they come to see their own perform, above all others. So it was that Memorial Stadium was "blocked" for the Tuesday-night tilt against the rival Saint John Flames on November 30, 1993. Wearing his age on his back, Leafs number 32, Andy Sullivan stepped into the shimmering light. He was forced to confront all the wondering there ever might have been.

"Andy Sullivan *was* a fish plant worker," Bill Waters, the Toronto Maple Leafs assistant general manager, boastfully declared at the time. It was Waters's job to be responsible for the development club in St. John's. He had to answer to Cliff Fletcher, the top manager in Toronto, if something went awry. Waters was the one who had to explain why a part-time senior player who processed snow crab for a living was taking critical faceoffs. "He's a good hockey player and we signed him and we never regretted it." The hockey executive was as sure of himself as Daddy Warbucks ever was.

Sully skated with aplomb in his debut against the Flames— didn't look out of place in the slightest. Weaving a course through the centre of the ice, he thrilled the crowd with the rhythm of a loyal and native wonder. He passed expertly to players who flew around his flank. Sullivan found their sticks, tape to tape with rare exception, and the younger men warmed to him swiftly and completely. The Leafs beat the Flames with Andy assisting on a goal in that first outing. The crowd was absolutely wild and the headline in the St. John's *Evening Telegram* trumpeted "Sully Answers the Big Question."

The Big Bayman really was as good as the reports predicted. Crawford was ecstatic and saw in Sullivan a sort of soul mate. They were the same age and both loved the game, but Crawford had come from a situation where graduation to elite professional hockey came as a matter of course. Still, he could relate to the raw talent he saw in this older and naturally developed player. "As a thirty-two-year-old he became one of our better players in terms of understanding what needed to be done in order to be successful and in understanding team concepts," the Canucks coach said as he watched Mark Messier tour the ice at Vancouver's General Motors Place. He must have wondered at his own chances in life and the ones that had almost escaped the grasp of a talent like Andy Sullivan.

"He was a delightful guy. We could relate to one another," Crawford said wistfully. "It was great to see him enjoy the opportunity that he was getting and use it for what it was worth. He had no aspirations of going to the NHL, he knew that had passed him by. He was going to enjoy playing in the American Hockey League and he was going to enjoy playing as hard as he possibly could. He played extremely well."

In all, there were sixteen games in that first season of Andy's ascension to the wonderful world of the professional game. There might have been hundreds, even a thousand, if he had taken the chance fourteen years before. But it mattered little to him. The game was the thing. He kept his eyes open and learned to be a better player. "I really didn't go down there with intentions of trying to do too much," Andy says upon reflection. It's interesting that he describes the chance as going "down there," because he was moving up in the world in two senses. St. John's is north of Witless Bay and the Maple Leafs were, most assuredly, a step up from the local senior hockey he had been playing. Then again, Sullivan looks at things from a different perspective—something I had come to accept and appreciate in growing measures.

"I just wanted to go down and fit in and help the team. When I came in they put me at ease and told me to just go out and play the game and keep things simple. I'd find my way, I guess."

He more than found his way. Sully endowed his status as a shyly charismatic folk hero with every stride he took on Memorial Stadium's sacred ice. As a local, he could expect the devotion of the people, many of whom he knew personally. He might have been their linemate when he played for a team in Pouch Cove or coached their kid at his hockey school, where the young lads are known as the Eastern Flyers. He quite possibly worked alongside them at the plant. They knew who Andy was and what he represented. More importantly, they loved the way he played—as a natural, unspoiled by any system that too often threatens to shackle a wonderful hockey spirit.

"I think I've always had a fairly good sense of where the other guy was on the ice." Andy doesn't feel comfortable talking about himself. He just has a good feeling about hockey, unencumbered by any technical lingo. "It may have been my best skill more so than skating or whatever. With the type of game we play here, there are a lot of good players that do have hockey sense, and that's what makes it so enjoyable."

The St. John's Maple Leafs enjoyed renewal after Andy's first game that season. Players healed and some returned from Toronto to resume their roles in the hothouse that is the development process. Andy went back to the fish plant but made it plain he would be available when called upon. Soon he was back in Marc

Crawford's lineup, a trusted asset and a wealth of experience for an ambitious coach to count on.

There was a road trip to Adirondack in upstate New York, where the Leafs would play the Red Wings. The routine surrounding a professional hockey club away from home is complex yet unchanging. Team services directors handle travel arrangements and accommodations. They ensure that luggage and equipment are directed to and from the proper destinations quickly and without fail. The responsibility of the player is to simply get himself to and from the hotel room to the bus and to attend the team meal where meetings are generally conducted.

Peter Hanlon chuckles at the first time his friend Andy Sullivan took to the road as a professional player. It was so different from the days when he had loaded up a pickup truck and made it to his local games. In Adirondack, as is the case for every away game, the team gathers at a midday meal. It is generally a feast catered by the hotel where the team is housed—mounds of pasta and beef, milk and ice cream. On this day, Hanlon noted that Sullivan, the newest Leaf, was absent from the team meal.

He found Sully wandering into the lobby minutes before the bus was scheduled to leave for the rink. It turned out he'd been unsure whether he was invited to the gathering, as he really wasn't, technically speaking, a member of the team. In addition, there was the matter of money. Andy hadn't brought a lot with him and the cost of the smorgasbord might have been a problem. (Of course, the meal was free.) So he had opted to go to the local diner. "I decided to have the scallops," he told his friend matter-of-factly. "And they were lovely!"

It was that innocence and unspoiled way that drew Andy into the fold with increasing ease. As Christmas neared that first season, the Leafs congregated in their dressing room to exchange small gifts. Each player had chosen another's name from a hat and the presents were to be anonymously distributed. Andy tore the wrapping from his package to discover a set of three Tupperware bowls with his name on each. "It was for that standard haircut," Hanlon chuckles. "The boys gave him the bowls so that he could have three different looks!"

More than that, it was a sign of acceptance. The fresh-faced players felt at home with Andy in their midst, and although none of them hailed from Newfoundland, they valued Sully because of his connection to the place—his understanding of how important hockey was there. "The young aspiring players took to him right away," Hanlon remembers. "They had some fun with him. He gave it back just as good."

A mysterious aura surrounds the private quarters of a hockey team, just as in any sport. Those who are not an intimate part of the group—anyone beyond the players, including, on occasion, the coach—are not welcome beyond very restricted times. There are several instances where star skaters, arriving via a trade or free agent signing, have disrupted the intangible "atmosphere in the room" deemed to be so essential to a winning frame of mind. It is something every hockey player is mindful and wary of, including Andy Sullivan. His greatest relief, beyond demonstrating he could compete at the professional level, was being surrounded by the blanket of the Leafs themselves.

"Just being around the team and especially at that time of year was important," he stresses. "They made me feel very comfortable, and I think if you're comfortable with the team then you feel a lot more comfortable at the rink when you play the game."

There was still the matter of legitimacy. He felt driven to prove that he was more than just a body filling a sweater and a spot on the lineup card. In a sense, Sullivan desperately wanted to be something more than a novelty during his tenure with the Maple Leafs. He wanted to do what he did best, and that was to score goals and help the team prosper. Andy had watched the Leafs closely since their opening game at Memorial Stadium in the 1991–92 season.

"I thought, if given the chance, I may have been able to play at that level," he admits.

The newspaper prophets and local hockey observers had always trumpeted his amazing talent, and now that he had been afforded the unlikely opportunity with the cherished home club, they analyzed his every move. Everyone wanted Sullivan to be a success and they created a voracious appetite for a happy ending, one that would prove once and for all that there were excellent players skating at home on the Island.

The St. John's *Evening Telegram* carried a story leading up to Andy's first game that revealed exactly how high the stakes were. Hockey writer Brendan McCarthy laid everything on the line in a few simple words under the headline, "Sullivan to Suit Up for the Leafs." "It may be a decade too late," McCarthy wrote, "but Andy Sullivan gets the opportunity tonight to do what most Newfoundland hockey fans figured he was always meant to do . . . play professional hockey."

The enormity of it all must have weighed on Sully, and even though he delighted in the shifts he took during the first couple of games, a goal would be precious to him as Christmas approached. It might be the greatest gift he could give, not only to himself but to all the believers who had understood why he never took the road that might have led to stardom in the NHL and "away."

On December 23, 1993, a Thursday night on the Island in an overflowing Memorial Stadium, it happened. Andy put together a magnificent game against the Cape Breton Oilers and the house was all aflutter. The puck found him more often than not, and Marc Crawford was tuned in to the Big Bayman's frequency. The coach played him on a regular basis, double shifted him at times. Not too deep into the game, there was a sparkling pass from Ryan VandenBussche of Simcoe, Ontario, and Andy didn't come close to muffing it up. He buried it in the back of the Cape Breton net and sent the fans into a frenzied celebration.

The front-page picture in the *Evening Telegram* the next day expressed everything that had transpired on the ice and in the minds of all those who had witnessed it. VandenBussche was a dozen years younger than the man he had set up. There he was with his arm gleefully outstretched to embrace a beaming Sullivan. It appeared to be so simply genuine. Another goal in another game, just another day along hockey's road, but VandenBussche, and all his teammates, who flowed onto the ice in celebration, could understand that this was special.

"Sully Rocks the Stadium," the words screamed in bold black ink. Andy was one of the three stars in the Maple Leafs victory and brought the faithful to their feet for an extended ovation as he modestly took his bow at the end of the match. The club made a commemorative T-shirt with the newspaper photo silk-screened on the front and the date on the back. It sold like hot-cakes at Leafsport, the official merchandise store in the front lobby of Memorial Stadium.

Glen Stanford is organizing a tenth-anniversary celebration for the Maple Leafs at the Civic Centre when it opens in 2000–2001. He shows me the proposals for forty sets of tickets that will recapture the greatest moments of the Leafs professional hockey history in St. John's. One of the collector's edition tickets depicts number 32, Andy Sullivan, waving to the crowd on the momentous night he scored his first goal as a pro. "It was probably the loudest crowd and the loudest cheer that I've ever heard in that building," Stanford says with a Newfoundlander's pride and a little bit more. "And you're right. She was blocked that night!"

The beauty of Andy Sullivan's glory lasted a mere sixteen games during the 1993–94 season. His scoring totals reflected a substantial contribution for a player who was assumed to be nothing more than an extra body. Beside his name in the team's official book of statistics, three goals and six assists are recorded. Twenty-six of the pucks he fired at the net were on target and yielded a respectable scoring percentage of 11.5. In short, Andy had answered the call, but along the way he had created some faith and become an inspiration to those from home and "away."

Darby Hendrickson is a utility forward for the Vancouver Canucks—a sort of jack of all trades in NHL terms. He has good skating speed and works hard, which makes him valuable to his team because he can be used in a penalty-killing situation or when the opponent's top forward needs to be neutralized. At twenty-eight, Hendrickson is settling into his role, but as a first-year pro in St. John's, he recognized stardom from a much different perspective as he played alongside Sullivan.

"Well, it was neat." Hendrickson was talking to me outside the Canucks dressing room in Phoenix, Arizona. "You could tell the guy just loved to play hockey and obviously he loved being from there—a kind of local hero. To experience that situation was odd because I had come from such structured programs in Minnesota where I had played college and on Olympic teams. All of a sudden you have a guy who comes in like that and it was different. In some respects it was what minor league pro hockey can do. It just made you smile."

The effect of Sullivan's fleeting experience with the Leafs should not be underestimated or caricatured. This was more than a stunt by the local team to attract a few fans and peddle some merchandise. Nor did Andy fulfill the role of a fringe player as Todd Gillingham of Corner Brook did when he played for the St. John's Leafs over an extended period during the same era. Gillingham was a tough guy and a scrapper who saw limited duty, usually in situations that called for enforcement. His skill was not what the crowd had come to see. In that sense, Sully was special because he personified the natural talent that the faithful believed had existed on local rinks and ponds since the beginning of time.

For Sullivan, the satisfaction was immense, but ultimately he was unaffected by the attention. The greatest reward was not a

contract. (He balks at the question of how much he was paid; Peter
Hanlon reveals that it may have been $200 a game.) Nor was it the
adoration of the fans. No, the greatest gift of his time with the St.
John's Leafs was his status as "one of them," his inclusion in the fraternity of elite hockey players.

The management of the Leafs had a Christmas party that year,
and Andy, although he had only played a handful of games, was
invited. There were elaborate gifts at this function, and he stood in
the background as each member of the club stepped forward to
receive a deep blue leather jacket bearing the legendary logo of the
Maple Leafs. "It was a fairly big affair back then because they were
just in town a few years," Andy recalls.

He was bowled over when he was called, appropriately last, to
come forward and receive a team jacket of his own. For any kid
who ever played on a team, the leather-sleeved bomber with a crest
stitched over the heart has become the ultimate symbol of belonging. "I was never expecting to receive one because the jackets had
been ordered months ahead," he marvels. "By whatever stroke of
luck, I ended up getting one and I was quite excited about it."

———

Sully slipped into his life back at the fish plant secure in the knowledge that he had quietly capitalized on a rare moment in time.
Over the next couple of years he was called every once in a while
to "go down" for a game or two whenever the team was in need.
The Leafs management, including Bill Waters in Toronto and Glen
Stanford on the Island, allowed themselves to drift into a comfortable "rent-a-player" arrangement that afforded them a connection
to the fans as well as a surefire way to save a little money.

Marc Crawford landed a job with the Quebec Nordiques
and Tom Watt the former bench boss in Toronto, Vancouver and

Winnipeg, assumed the reins in St. John's. He also inherited the quirky and continuing saga of Andy Sullivan.

"I wasn't skeptical, because he had been there before." Watt is talking to me on the phone from his home in Saint John, New Brunswick, where he is the development coach for the Calgary Flames. "In every town you go to in Canada there's a guy who could have been. But in Andy's case I think it certainly holds true."

Watt, impressed by the aging player's fitness—Andy was, by this time thirty-four years old—used him in a variety of situations. He vividly recalls a desperate game against the Cornwall Aces; St. John's was down by two goals with less than a minute to go in the game. Instead of opting for younger and perhaps fresher legs, Watt dispatched Sullivan into the fray. In front of an empty net, his goaltender pulled for an extra attacker, and an apprehensive sold-out crowd at Memorial Stadium, the fish plant worker fashioned a little sleight of hand. He made a wonderful pass to set up Rob Butz for a goal. Then, with the Leafs down by a single marker, Andy remained on the ice and drew a critical faceoff back to Jamie Heward, who drilled it into the Cornwall net and knotted the game.

Tom Watt won university championships with the Varsity Blues in Toronto and engineered one of the greatest turnarounds in National Hockey League history in 1981–82, when he increased the point total of the Winnipeg Jets from 32 the year before to a respectable 80 at the end of a remarkable schedule. For his efforts he was awarded the Jack Adams trophy as the NHL coach of the year. Still, he seemed so proud to have sent Sullivan to the ice that night against Cornwall and to have witnessed a feat that spoke of inherent ability.

"The fans in St. John's were really ecstatic about that. I was asked later by the media why I had Andy out there. At the time it was strictly his experience. He just knew what to do." So impressed was Watt that he used Sullivan as frequently as he could. The playoffs loomed and the coach even hoped to place the centreman on the list of protected players, who would become available to the Leafs during the post-season chase for the Calder Cup, the one victory that the very successful AHL franchise in Newfoundland was still without. It nearly worked, but Cliff Fletcher, the general manager in Toronto, scuttled the idea.

"Of course Cliff came back to us and told us to hang on a second, you know we've got juniors coming down here in another couple of weeks," Glen Stanford recalls. "The coach at the time was not using it as a ploy to get a Newfoundlander in the lineup because we needed some people in the building. The stadium is fairly small and we were filling it pretty well every night anyway. It was a legit decision by a coach who thought that this guy could help us. But Toronto squashed that pretty quick."

The sad reality was that Andy Sullivan's window of opportunity had slammed shut. The professional game is reserved, at this level, for potential rather than proven ability. He was too old, and the rate of return on the investment the Leafs might make in him was not sufficient to warrant a further dalliance with nostalgia and heartwarming synergy with the fans of Newfoundland. Sully had had his day, and by the end of the 1995–96 season, the Leafs could use him no more. He resumed his job in the fishery and his life as a folk hero who played twice a week with his buddies.

———

Part of the reason Sullivan did not star in the NHL was a personal choice. The lack of confidence that he had feared as a young player with little training led him to hesitate when the Hartford Whalers extended their offer to him. Tom Watt believes Andy would have been an NHL player and a good one, but understands the barriers that prevented him from achieving a more extensive profile in the game.

"To go to the mainland even is tough for anybody," Watt reasoned. "But there's no major junior hockey in Newfoundland. To go to the mainland where the culture is a lot different, the language is different, and where you're known as a 'Newf' . . . I think it's pretty tough for guys to leave, and I don't know a Newfoundlander yet that, if there was work, wouldn't go home."

Bill Waters points out that more and more Newfoundlanders are taking advantage of opportunities to make the grade and get to an expanding National Hockey League. He says it's because there are an increasing number of high-level junior teams in Atlantic Canada. The Cape Breton Screaming Eagles, the Halifax Mooseheads, the Moncton Wildcats and a team in Bathurst, New Brunswick, associated with the Quebec Major Junior Hockey League, are signs that the vast search for talent is extending to players from the eastern part of the country.

This is something that Sullivan could not have tapped into when he was developing his skills. Nor did the St. John's Maple Leafs exist when Sully was playing shinny on the local ponds. He skated in professional hockey's hinterland, on the outskirts of any real chance to get to the fabled big time. Glen Stanford says, "If the American Hockey League had been here fifteen to twenty years ago when Andy Sullivan was young, maybe he would have ended up in the National Hockey League. It would have been very interesting if the St. John's Maple Leafs had come here in '81–82 and not '91–92. What would have happened to Andy Sullivan then?"

Vancouver Canucks rookie Harold Druken is the latest Newfoundlander to find his way to the NHL. "I know the legend of Andy Sullivan," Druken confirms while lacing his skates in the dressing room at America West Arena in Phoenix. "He was the guy I looked up to most as a hockey player when I was younger. I used to go down to Memorial Stadium and watch the games—he was my man. He was obviously good enough to play but he just didn't want to leave."

Druken was enjoying a bit of a roll, twenty games into his professional career. The Canucks were chasing a playoff spot late in the season, and he had contributed mightily by scoring with frequency and playing tenacious defence along with his Ontario-born linemates Matt Cooke and Brad May. "I just love this stuff," he said with obvious enthusiasm. There was nothing bashful about the curly-haired youngster who sat sweating in his locker-room stall. There was none of the boyish shyness that I had seen in Andy Sullivan.

Druken is part of a large family. His father has nine brothers and five sisters, all living in the same neighbourhood, and Harold's circle of friends when he was growing up consisted of his aunts, uncles and cousins. He played in the St. John's high-school league until he was sent away to preparatory school in the Boston area. From there, he was drafted by Detroit of the Ontario Hockey League and he starred for three years with the junior Whalers in Michigan before being chosen thirty-sixth overall by Vancouver in the NHL's 1997 Entry Draft. "You know everybody. You don't need any social skills or anything like that," Druken says of his childhood days in Newfoundland. "It's tough going away. It's tough meeting new people, but those are adjustments I had to make to become a professional."

The young forward has wondrous recollections of seeing Andy Sullivan play with the senior St. John's Caps as they battled for the Allan Cup in the mid-1980s. Druken was only a kid, maybe seven or eight years old, but he still retains an image, firmly fixed in his mind, of a great player with spectacular skills. "The whole building would be yelling, 'Andy Sullivan! Andy Sullivan! Andy Sullivan!' over and over again. Out where he's from, they play hockey on the ponds all the time. You could tell he knew the game inside out. He saw the ice so well."

Druken was ecstatic concerning his position in the NHL and hugely proud of being a Newfoundlander—still a rarity in the league. But he was not conceited about his fame or the obvious high esteem he had garnered back home. In his estimation, he still has a lot to prove, whereas some legends do not. "I'm sure if you went to Newfoundland and just interviewed people on the street they would say that, yes, Andy Sullivan was good enough to play," Harold says. "You've got me and Danny Cleary, John Slaney, Darren Langdon and those guys, but I still think Andy Sullivan sticks out in most of the people's minds."

On the way to see Sullivan play that Thursday night, Peter Hanlon and I made a couple of stops in and around the capital city of St. John's. We had lunch at Don Cherry's restaurant and sports bar, where all hockey fans in the town find themselves sooner or later. There were giant pictures on the wall of Johnny Bower and Terry Sawchuk, of Alex Faulkner and Doug Grant in their Red Wings uniforms. Bobby Orr had a place of prominence, as did Guy Lafleur and Frank Mahovlich, and a hundred other NHL legends kept them company.

But near the entrance, where one could not possibly miss it, was an enormous poster of Andy Sullivan as a Maple Leaf. In full stride and shaking the bonds of his pursuer, Sully broke away, undoubtedly heading for the other team's net and perhaps another chapter in his legendary story. Kitty-corner to the poster was a newspaper article in a handsome frame. *The Globe and Mail* sports columnist at the time was Gare Joyce. The headline proclaimed the nut of Andy's tale: "Baby Leaf Wonders What Might Have Been."

———

Sullivan's modest house sits in a subdivision on Cahill (pronounced "Cal") Road. His wife, Pam, comes across as somewhat less shy as she dons her boots and rain slicker so she can jockey the tenant's car out of a driveway cluttered by street hockey paraphernalia. She makes coffee and shows me a little scrapbook in which pictures of Andy with the Maple Leafs were displayed alongside family snapshots of Andy with his brothers, all wearing Calvert Fish Industries sweaters.

"The first time I saw him was in junior hockey and he was quite good," she mentions, a delightful twang in her voice. She takes me to the living room and shows me a pen-and-ink sketch she had commissioned from a local artist. It depicts Sully in his Leafs uniform. Pam had placed it right over the chesterfield, their one lasting memento of the instant he first played as a pro. "I was really proud seeing him play that night," she says as she gingerly lifts the picture off the wall for a better look. "I was so happy for him because he did it. He fit in quite well. Marc Crawford was very good to him. He gave him a chance and Andy played very well that night."

They have a six-year-old daughter, Claire, and an eleven-year-old son, Shane, who plays centre for the Eastern Flyers. Andy is the coach and the two of them are already up at Brother O'Hehir Arena getting ready for scrimmage. "Now, I don't think Shane loves it as much as his father," Pam tells me without a hint of regret. "Andy, all he had was hockey on the ponds. Shane doesn't have the desire that his father has or the love of it."

Pam first met Andy Sullivan when he came to St. John's to go to college. She has remained his biggest fan and knows he could have made it—could have accomplished anything he really wanted to. "It must be in the back of his mind all the time. Wondering if he could have done it. I'm sure he could have too. I guess it just wasn't meant to be."

Pam closes the scrapbook and puts it away, saying that Andy is embarrassed about these things being brought out too often. Apparently he never liked to fuss over them much. "It would have been great to see him play in the NHL," Pam declares. "I think it's more important to him now that people respect him here in New-foundland."

The rink that bears Brother O'Hehir's name is as stunningly simple as a hockey arena can be. One sheet of ice, three rows of brown bleachers on each side, a symmetrical roof that comes to a peak over the faceoff circle, and a frost that chills fans to the bone while forcing the players to step up the pace.

Little kids are buzzing around the hard white surface, and Sullivan is hopping up and down from one of the player's benches. "If you got no one to pass to and you get some free or clear ice, let's move with it," he gently reminds one of the youngsters. "When you got the puck, get your feet moving. Put your head up and look for the open guy."

The practice of atom-age members of the Eastern Flyers precedes Thursday-night hockey, where I will finally get a chance to see Sullivan play. Until I witness him in action, everything I have heard until now remains a bit of a myth.

One of the fathers, Rick Pearson, chats with me as the Eastern Flyers, winners of three divisions at the Lakeshore Tournament "up" in Toronto last year, clamour from the ice in front of the Zamboni. Andy shuffles behind them and disappears into the dressing room to transform himself from coach to player. "He came out of nowhere all the time," Pearson says. "Excellent with the puck and hands. He had very soft hands." I had heard Bob Cole say the same sorts of things out by Conception Bay. Now a little kid's dad is telling me that Sullivan is that much greater because he never left. "Andy gives a lot to his community and a lot to the Island. There are more and more players going away, and a lot of it is because of Andy Sullivan."

The ice resurfacing is nearly done and the reflection of the exhaust from the machine looks like so many clouds on the greyish blue of the pristine pool of frozen water. Pearson is still waiting for his son Steven to finish in the dressing room so they can make their way home. We are left alone in the rink in anticipation of the seniors who will soon burst from their workday costumes to become the players they secretly want to be. I'm starting to get it. Sully is the link, the real-life hero these people can see every day. Someone they can put a face to, talk to, and not just observe on some distant television screen. He's one of them.

"The knock against Newfoundland hockey has always been the coaching. He's an excellent coach." Pearson is an evangelist when it comes to Sullivan. "I can't say enough about Andy and what he's done for my young fella. My boy's been with him since he's been about six or seven. He's eleven now and he's just a great player." The lad appears and he's surrounded by the man's arm as they slip quietly through the side entrance and into the rainy night.

Sully covered himself with an aqua practice jersey and his pants, from his time with the Maple Leafs, rustle slightly as he pushes off the rubber mat and onto the indoor frozen pond. The socks over the shin pads are a mismatch: one is blue and white, the other black and silver. His skates are CCM Tacks, the standard for a hockey player for as long as I can remember. His white helmet is tipped low and meets his eyebrow. The chinstrap is firmly tightened. Well-worn navy blue gloves grip the stick and he keeps both hands on it, almost without fail.

Hulking Greg Smyth, a former NHL player with six teams who now lives in Newfoundland, sees me observing Sullivan and skates to a stop by the bench. "He's absolutely a hero," he says as Andy glides by us. "Put it this way. I believe when you say Andy Sullivan's name in Newfoundland, it's like saying Darryl Sittler's name in the Toronto area." Having said his piece, Smyth, an enormous defenceman who hails from Oakville but who fell in love with St. John's, chugs away.

Sully is a player. What convinces me is the way he relates to the puck. Receiving it behind his back without looking and never breaking his stride. Drawing it to the perfect position between his feet and out in front of his chin. It slides flatly there as he turns his head from side to side and records the whereabouts of his wingers.

Staring straight at one, he dishes the disc to the other. Suddenly left unattended, the fortunate skater deposits the gift behind a goalie who is unfairly but lovingly nicknamed "Leaky" Lake.

"He does something different every time he comes in. He may look to shoot and deke and you can't guess right," Dennis Lake laments. Lake has played a lot of senior hockey here and on the mainland and has at times been the backup for the St. John's Leafs. He still marvels at the Big Bayman. "I have no doubt he could have played if he had of got away when he was younger."

The night wears on, Andy playing every second shift, and the others become just like satellites orbiting his enormous presence on the ice. It's like watching Jean Béliveau, the calm grace of a player in complete command of the game. He slows and then accelerates in the wink of an eye, stops, turns and flicks his wrist—the puck chiming off the post. Unselfishly, he makes other players better by creating chances for them. Sullivan puts the puck where they're headed. It arrives just as they do. Meantime he is already off creating something else.

"Could have played and been a star in the NHL," says Jerry Williams, a little forward with his two front teeth missing. "Not only with one of the expansion teams. He would have been a star with one of the original six." I chuckle at Williams and his dancing eyes. It's not like I need any further convincing. Sullivan has the magic, the quality, that only the best have in their repertoire. It is impossible to take your eyes away from Andy. If you do, you are not really watching the game.

Some believe it is trite to say that home is where the heart is. As I watch the fish plant worker play hockey, I find myself wondering why that should possibly matter. He is exhausted an hour and fifteen minutes into the spirited game and, still standing, rests for a moment at the end of the bench, steam rising from his head and shoulders. Why didn't he take the chance? He could have made millions.

A little leprechaun of a player named Brian Mulcahy sits down beside me at the far end. "That's right. A good Irish name," he quips in a brogue so lyrical I can hardly decipher it. Mulcahy wrinkles his nose and smiles. "He's the best that ever played here, but he had a good job—running the fish plant and everything. He didn't need the money so he enjoyed it here. No sweat!"

The other players are not Sully's equals. Most are not even close, and yet they smile and shake their heads as he dances through their futile attempts to thwart his progress. He doesn't say much and there is no cursing. Andy Sullivan just plays, and I'm convinced he could go forever.

———

"There's something pure about Andy Sullivan," Marc Crawford told me when I was in Vancouver to see the Canucks play. The following week I would be travelling to the opposite coast, to Newfoundland and Sully's magic. "I mean, he played hockey for the right reasons, and a lot of times as pros we lose sight of that. It was nice to see a guy who played the game for the pureness of the game."

Maybe the case of Andy Sullivan isn't so strange after all. His is one of hockey's simple and most powerful lessons. When you're looking for heroes, it makes sense to look no further than your own backyard.

THE PIONEER

Angela James

Always Number 8

(courtesy Donna Baratto)

✧ ANGELA JAMES STORMED TOWARDS the American net. No one in the stands knew it yet, but this would be her last game with the Canadian Women's Hockey team. Driving alone with the puck, she carried with her the hopes of all women who love hockey, especially other players who were finding their place on the international stage. James was a superstar who, at thirty-four, could lay claim to being the greatest female hockey player ever.

The setting was the shootout following a scoreless ten-minute overtime in the final game of the Three Nations Cup in December, 1999. The club from Finland had been dispatched early in the tournament, before the final clash at Montreal's Maurice Richard Arena. For two of the three years it had existed, the Three Nations Cup had been captured by Canada, but it was always exceedingly close in the end.

The Americans were the Olympic champions, and that rubbed Angela James the wrong way. She had been cut from the Canadian Women's Hockey team that competed at the historic games in Nagano, Japan, where the first gold medal in women's hockey was handed out. It was widely believed that James could have propelled the silver medal–winning Canadians to the top spot had she and her magic scoring touch been with the team.

In December, 1999, Angela James had decided to retire from the national team, her Olympic dream unfulfilled. Her final words to her teammates in the dressing room before the game had been: "I've had a great time playing hockey and a great career. There just comes a time when you want to move on to other things, and that time has come for me."

Now there was just the matter of that one final shot. Her sweater billowing around her, James descended on Sarah Tueting, the U.S. goaltender. James dangled the puck dangerously and then drew it close—the dreaded deke nearly complete. Finally she slipped the puck into the net, scoring the winning goal.

Angela James bowed out on top. "It was a great way to end it," she told the reporters at the end of the day. It struck me at that moment that this player's magnificent exit left so much unsaid.

————

The evening is warm and a special shade of blue, that magical colour that can only be experienced in mid-April, between six and seven o'clock. It's the last breath of the season for most players, a time when in a nation of snow and ice, the great game is thankful for refrigeration and the opportunity of the indoor rink. In Toronto's east end, just up the busy road from the gathering swell of Lake Ontario and curious window shoppers at Kew Beach, winter sounds ring out: the shrill whistle and clacking sticks. Hockey noises.

"In a circle . . . this way, ladies!" The coach repositions the players at arm's length. A flock of skate blades stutter their way to a collective silence under the silver dome of the arena's insulated roof. "You guys are good! You know it! C'mon, let's go!"

With just a few words of encouragement, Angela James escapes the circle and then drags it behind her. Dressed in jet-black, she reminds me of a locomotive with her powerful strides, powering the pack of girls that follows close behind. Faster and faster they chug around the rink's extremity. Skaters of all shapes and sizes: tall and short, thin and hulking—some with long blond hair flowing from beneath their plastic helmets. Others with ponytails swinging to and fro. Breathless and panting, they chase the coach.

For her part, James flashes brilliant white teeth in an effortless smile. Her eyes beam behind gold-rimmed glasses. Turning her head from side to side, her large hoop earrings swinging furiously, she gauges the progress of her pursuers. From the nearly empty stands it is quite a sight: a wagon train of thirteen-year-old girls—a peewee team called the North York Storm.

It is the last practice for "the Storm" before the provincial playoffs the following weekend in Mississauga. There, the twelve best teams from across Ontario will gather and eventually declare a champion. Clubs from places like Ajax, London, Leaside and Belleville will join North York in the fiery atmosphere that has come to characterize women's hockey across the country.

The Game of Her Life, a television documentary co-produced by the National Film Board and the CBC following the 1998 Olympics in Nagano, estimated that 30,000 Canadian women and girls are now playing hockey. This is a far cry from the situation that existed for Angela James and her assistant coach, Geraldine Heaney, when they were aspiring players. Both played in the first World Championships for women, staged in Ottawa in 1990. Heaney has won five world championships and an Olympic silver medal as a member of the national women's team. James has won four world championships but was cut from the inaugural Olympic effort in Japan. Still, it is James, or "A.J.," as they call her, who is the drawing card for these girls.

"We heard Angela was the coach and we came solely because of her," says Gary Grubb, father of one of the players. His daughter, Laura, wears number 17 on defence and is in her fifth year playing hockey, but James is the first female coach she's had. Gary is also the team photographer and with his wife, Linda, is in the process of assembling the official yearbook of the Storm.

"There were sixty or seventy girls at each tryout," Grubb recalls, clicking away. "We saw an ad in the paper. 'Tryouts' was all it said, and that Angela James was going to be the coach. That's how the team came to be."

Meanwhile, James runs practice with smooth efficiency. She is constantly moving between the group of attackers, who are dashing from the boards behind the net and unloading slapshots on the goalie, to the other corners of the ice where her assistants are focusing on selected skills. Geraldine Heaney, a stellar defence player herself, is overseeing a squadron of rearguards as they nimbly traverse the blue line and fire pucks on the goal. Across the way, the third coach and only male on staff, Steve Redding, is working on breakouts. For a moment, James stops to concentrate on faceoffs at centre ice with Caitlyn Ruddy, the captain, and the team's smallest player, four-foot six-inch Katie Snowden.

"It was like Wayne Gretzky asking you to come and play," says Joe Ruddy, Caitlyn's dad. "We come in from Ajax for every practice and every game."

Ruddy volunteered to be the team's trainer. He reaches down now and grabs a plastic water bottle for an advancing forward in need of hydration. With a flick of his wrist the bottle tumbles three feet through the air and a gloveless hand makes the catch. The player removes her helmet and pushes back her long wavy hair. All this before chugging the water like a thirsty horse. "Oh, you're just so beautiful it hurts!" Ruddy teases. In a flash the helmet is back in place and the player charges back to the team in the middle of the ice.

"You guys, in the summer get a hunk of plywood and put it against your garage door or any old wall," James is saying to the players. "Take a hundred shots a day forehand. Then take a hundred shots a day backhand. It's gonna get better but you have to work at it. That's all there is!" With a wave of her stick, the skaters disperse, pausing only to collect a puck. Soon the sounds of slapshots peppers the frigid arena. It's like having twenty-five driveway players in the same place at the same time. Shot after shot, each harder than the last one. James circles, listening to the percussion she's orchestrated.

"We had to teach them how to win. They were used to losing, and that's a big thing to overcome," James tells me, resting at the boards. "Many of them were babied by their parents, but they've overcome that."

For a moment, A.J.'s eyes fix on one of the larger players. Carolyn Scott wears number 2 and acts as one of the assistant captains for the team. A big, powerful forward, she is clearly one of the more talented members of the Storm but has been playing for only three years. "Gotta get her under control," James remarks. "She's good but she hits too much."

A reference to the most obvious difference in the rule book between men's and women's hockey. In the game's female incarnation, intentional body checking is not allowed, something the powerfully built coach struggles with constantly. "It's a thing that girls have to understand. That they can be intense," she explains. "I don't mind if they hit a little bit. It's part of the game, after all."

Scrimmage time and the teams fly by with what seems to be startling speed. Carolyn Scott takes a breather on the bench and is eager to talk about James—the first female coach she's ever played for. "I think because of her experience and because she plays women's hockey at a high level, she influences me more," Scott says. "Men's and boys' hockey is a very different game. Male coaches tend to approach it that way. She knows *our* game. That's what I get from her."

The men in close proximity nod in complete agreement. Joe Ruddy, the trainer, recalls having to fetch something from Angela's black Oldsmobile Cutlass one night during practice. "The hockey pads, the pucks, the skates and sticks. It was like her whole life was in that car!"

Steve Redding sends another shift over the boards while James watches like a hawk from the other side of the ice. A big blond-haired man with METRO PREP on the back of his windbreaker, Redding is the only male in the rink sporting skates. During scrimmage he marvels at what James has been able to accomplish with the team in the short time she has been with them. "They all know her story, and for many of them she has been an idol since they can remember," Redding says, smiling. "She has forgotten more about hockey than I will ever know."

Little Katie Snowden is buzzing around the net now—Jen

Kramer, the team's largest player in pursuit. They call her "the Gentle Giant." The game is free of the intimidation factor, which can slow things down in a matchup between boys where physical play is paramount. Across the way, A.J. raps her stick on the ice and the pace intensifies. Gary Grubb snaps away as action shots jump out at him. His daughter pinches at the blue line and gets off a low drive at the goalie.

"I told her she'd be getting a hockey school all year," Grubb tells me. "To be on Angela James's team. Think of just who she is and where she's been!"

———

Long before Justine Blaney went to the Supreme Court of Canada and won the right for girls to play on the most skilled boys' teams in the country if they had the talent, Angela James was slugging it out on the streets and rinks of the inner city—not a traditional breeding ground for great hockey talent. Flemingdon Park, perched near the centre of the Don Valley, is full of high-rises and townhouses. In its day, Flemingdon was a model community emblematic of the rapid growth taking place in mid-1960s Toronto. By the '70s it had become a government housing project and, by all accounts, a rough part of town.

"There were wild things in my neighbourhood," James recalls. "Murders, drugs, you name it. It all happened where we lived."

She remembers as a schoolgirl going on a field trip to the police museum and being told of a famous murder case involving a man killing his wife and then stowing the body in a freezer. Angela discovered that the crime had taken place in her housing development, just around the corner from where she lived. "To me it was normal," she says, shrugging.

Her mother, Donna, was a single parent and raised the family of five children on her own while working as a bookkeeper and at the snack bar of the local arena. There wasn't much money and the equipment was hand-me-down, but there was a place to play just outside the front door. "She played road hockey with the boys," Donna Baratto says of her youngest daughter. "There was a whole group of them on our street and she was the only girl. From kindergarten on—she was playing with the boys."

James winces at the thought of her first foray into the game. "As the only girl, I started in net and I constantly got the tennis ball on the forehead," she says. "Then somehow I scrounged up some equipment so I had my own nets and stuff. The others would have to call me to come and play if they wanted the nets. My only condition was to be able to play forward. So that's how I got out of the nets. I was tired of those tennis ball marks on the forehead!"

Across the way there was an outdoor arena, but to reach it you had to travel through the hydro field and blocks of concrete jungle. Wearing her precious black and yellow hockey skates, which had been donated by a neighbour, Angela would walk the distance across the pavement. "There were little puddles of ice every once in awhile, which meant you could skate in short bursts," she says, grinning. "The rest of the time I would be grinding the blades." The skates themselves were so worn that the steel caps had fallen from each toepiece and protruded into the front portion of the leather boot. A.J. would jam her feet in anyway and wiggle her toes up under the jutting metal. "That was OK. I had a pair of hockey skates, and that was all that mattered."

———

Like her daughter, Donna Baratto seems at home in a hockey rink. Tinted glasses fail to hide her laughing eyes. As she turns to greet me at the Seneca College Sports Centre Arena where Angela is starting her summer skills school, this hockey mom turns from the boards, shivering slightly. "It's way too cold in here," she says. "Let's go to the canteen for a coffee."

Donna wraps her hands around the Styrofoam cup as if she's done it thousands of times before. "Her passion for hockey has been with her since she was very little," Donna says of her daughter. "I'd hoped she would pick swimming, to be honest, because no girl went anywhere in hockey back then."

In fact, Angela was enrolled in synchronized swimming but it didn't last very long because she had to make a choice between travelling on weekends to meets and playing road hockey with her pals at Flemingdon Park. A.J. chuckles at her experiences in the pool. She believed she had signed up for competitive swimming. She enjoyed the physical training at the outset of the program but wasn't cut out for the artistic side of the sport.

"I think I went in one competition and then quit," she muses. "As I recall, I forgot to put my nose clip on but I went through the moves anyway. I got a ton of water up my nose when I went under and ended up splashing the judges. I believe I came seventh out of seven people in the meet, so that was enough!"

But when it came to hockey, there was nowhere for her to go, it seemed. Nowhere for her to play hockey within walking distance of her home unless it was with the boys. The administration of the Flemingdon Park house league was strongly against allowing an eight-year-old girl into their midst and did so only after Donna threatened them with legal action. "I said I was going to take it to the Human Rights Commission even though it was just starting up," she says.

Although Angela got her wish and a chance to play that first year, it was an uneasy situation for the only girl in a league full of boys. Her skills were not the problem. Her gender was. "The very first year that she was in house league there was trouble," Donna recounts. "It's always the grown-ups who wreck it for the kids."

As it turned out, that first year Angela was the leading scorer for her team and in the league. Her mercurial climb began in the novice ranks but then moved swiftly through the atom level, only to wind up in peewee because she scored so many goals. Angela's success created jealousy, not felt by the other players so much as their parents. The president of the league's son was on her team and in his father's eyes was overshadowed by a girl. "She was outskating the boys," Donna says. "The president saw it and said, 'No more girls in the league, and that's final!'" Angela's mom thrusts her jaw forward and bangs her fist on the table as if to demonstrate the rigid attitude that prevailed in minor hockey during the early 1970s.

Angela smiles as she recalls her first days in organized hockey. "I was just like everybody else. Got in little scraps."

With her banishment from the Flemingdon Park house league, James was relegated to playing with the girls, if she could find enough of them to choose up sides. "There was only Annunciation in Don Mills," her mother says. "The Catholic church had a house league." A league, as it turned out, that had to compromise competitiveness because of a lack of players at all age levels. "They used to have three lines. First the seven- and eight-year-olds would go out," says Carol Law, a childhood friend and former teammate of Angela's. "Then after about two minutes they'd blow a whistle and the nine- and ten-year-olds would go out. Then it would be the older girls. You had seven- to fourteen-year-olds playing on the same team."

"I didn't drive. I didn't have a car," says her mother, shaking her head. "I would hurry home from work, throw a hockey bag over my shoulder, and we'd run down the street to catch the bus. All this when there was an arena right down the street. That's what really burned me. Now, if you want your daughter to play on a boys' team, they have to let her."

Countless trips on the TTC buses all over the city to get to what seemed like a thousand different skating rinks. Many times Donna

Baratto made the journey with her in what was to become a lasting partnership not between father and son but between mother and daughter, in pursuit of the Canadian dream.

"We didn't have a car or a lot of money or anything like that," Angela says. "We did have a ton of love in our house. My mom never let the children go without. She found a way so that we could have what we needed."

Clearly the most talented player in the Annunciation league, James moved ahead of the others quickly. It was on to ladies senior C for the hard-shooting youngster, but only for a year. Very quickly she made her way to the top level of women's hockey in Toronto, ladies AA. Her first team was the Toronto Islanders, and she was a star by the time she was fifteen. Two years later it was on to Burlington for three years. Then on to Agincourt and Mississauga and the North York Aeros, which had been formed from the Annunciation church league. She played with the Toronto Red Wings briefly in the 1996–97 season and then came back to the Aeros organization, where she remains to this day.

"Angela was aggressive, she was strong and she was not afraid to go into the corners. She had grit," Donna Baratto says firmly. "You watch hockey and you can tell the players who are intense and who really love the game. She was one of them. She kept competing to get better and better. As much as she was shy about it, I think deep in her heart she always wanted to be the best."

During the mid-1980s, while enrolled in the recreation management program at Seneca College in North York, James played defence for the varsity Scouts. Over the course of her tenure, the team won a silver and two gold medals in the Ontario College Athletic Association championships. James led the league in scoring for three straight years and was Seneca's Athlete of the Year in 1984 and '85. To this day, her number 8 sweater remains retired and hangs in an ornate glass case on the arena wall. The inscription under the captain's white jersey reads: "Angela 'A.J.' James. League Record Holder. Goals 80 Assists 48 Points. 128. 1982–85."

Angela James has been convinced of her connection to hockey since she first hoisted a stick in front of her townhouse to take shots on her sister. It was a life in hockey born on the asphalt streets of the inner city. "Because we grew up in the projects, the kids were always outside and playing hockey," Angela says. "It is, and always has been, my life."

———

At the Beatrice Ice Gardens on the campus of York University, the Thursday of Easter weekend means playoff hockey and the first of a best-of-three final between the hometown Aeros and the visiting Brampton Thunder. At stake is the Ontario Women's Hockey Championship.

Members of the Thunder's management linger outside their team's locker room. They shuffle their feet and mutter over being the underdogs heading into the contest. I ask them about the opposition, and one player in particular. "Angela James is a superstar, right?" The group of men survey each other's reactions swiftly and the leader speaks up. "I would say she used to be," he offers. "But there's no question she's been the pioneer."

Up in the stands there are maybe two or three hundred fans gathered in a single section of the rink. The Aeros are dressed in red uniforms with black and white trim, a maple leaf on each shoulder. The Thunder players are clad in white jerseys with blue and gold trim. It is Brampton's first year in the league, but they have Olympians like Vicky Sunohara and Jayna Hefford in their lineup. They too sport a reminder of their first allegiance—a small Canadian flag tattooed on the jersey over each player's heart.

The Aeros, a squad with a great history in the women's game,

counter with a veteran star on defence in the person of Geraldine
Heaney as well as the darling of the national team, forward Cassie
Campbell. This is their building, and a glance across the rink reveals
an impressive string of championship banners. Long known as the
Toronto Aeros, they have dominated the senior AAA ranks almost
uninterrupted since the late 1980s.

A trio of young girls is oblivious to the historical backdrop at
work in this crucial matchup. Maybe six or seven years old, they
march in a halting unison at the foot of the bleachers, holding plac-
ards with Brampton Thunder colours. Proudly raising a lightening
bolt, the youngsters are building on momentum. In the third
period, Vicky Sunohara has won a faceoff and scores on a low slapshot to Kendra Fisher's stick side. It makes the score 3–1 Aeros with
time running out. "Do it again, Thunder! Do it again!" the little
ones shout. In the stands above them, parents and friends stamp
their feet.

Across the aisle, a young couple is watching intently in Aeros
territory. The mother rests a three-year-old on her knee and whispers: "Let's go, Aeros, let's go!" The little girl is chanting along
when suddenly she sits up, signalling a certain player's return to
action.

Number 8 of the Beatrice team leaps over the boards as the
Aeros change on the fly. She takes two powerful wide-legged
strides in pursuit of the errant puck and violently rams into one of
her own players. As her teammate crumples to the ice, number 8
remains solid on her skates. She pounces on the disc and generates
full speed in the wink of an eye. Crossing the blue line, she cocks
the blade of her stick as if loading an archer's bow and drives a
booming slapshot right on the Thunder net, but the Brampton
goalie somehow manages to block it.

There is little doubt that James has been the most dominant
player in the annals of the women's game in Ontario. Seven straight
years, beginning at the outset of the 1990s, she led the Central

Ontario Women's Hockey League in scoring. In half a dozen seasons, the stalwart of the Beatrice Aeros has captured the most valuable player award. In more than a dozen appearances at the senior national championships, James has been selected MVP an impressive eight times. Even now, at thirty-four, she leads her team in scoring; the runner-up is not even close to matching her totals.

Margot Page coaches the fledgling women's hockey program at Niagara University in western New York. She was a member of three world championship teams for Canada in 1990, '92 and '94 and was a teammate of Angela James's. Page also played alongside James on the Toronto Aeros in the early 1990s and lined up on the opposite side of the ice when she was with the Hamilton Golden Hawks before that. It was Margot Page who observed from the broadcast booth as the colour analyst for CBC television during the first Olympic hockey tournament for women in Nagano, Japan, during February of 1998.

"She was the most threatening player on the ice," Page says emphatically. "She had the skill but she also had everything else. She had the speed and the physical prowess. You couldn't stop her because of that."

Watching James is like watching a huge cat on the prowl. Barely lifting her skates off the ice, she generates explosive momentum in an instant. While others seem choppy, she is smooth and steady. Her appearance is striking and, in this setting, formidable. Backchecking and chipping pucks to open territory, constantly on the chase, James is a dramatic presence. She is also the most solid-looking player on the ice. In a cast of characters where the average weight of each participant is 130 to 150 pounds, Angela James plays at 165. She relishes the advantage. "It's a physical game. That's what I was brought up on."

Against the Thunder in this close and crucial match, James takes faceoffs in the defensive zone, kills penalties and centres the power play's first unit. She churns constantly from the moment she leaps over the boards to the end of an extended shift. After one particular foray which has proven futile—her line has given up a good scoring chance to the opposition—she returns to the player's box, flings her stick on the ground and collapses in a heap on the bench. James is, above all, demanding of herself and will not tolerate inadequate performance.

"It wasn't just her skill level that set her apart. It was her competitive nature in the game that made her great," says Margot Page. "She was so fiercely competitive that you were scared to go into corners with her. You were scared to take a body check from her because you knew that she would be the one coming up with the puck and you would be the one getting hurt."

As the third period marches on, the stakes get a little higher between the Thunder and the Aeros, and the game gets rougher. A male referee and two female linesmen are letting things go and seem determined not to become factors in the outcome of the match by calling intrusive penalties.

Number 44 of the Aeros is Sommer West, a strapping forward just twenty years old who is one of the team's bright young stars. She's a disciple of Angela James's, a graduate of her summer hockey school who has been streamed into the junior national program. West plays in the same style: mixing it up at the boards with one of the Thunder's defenders, digging crosschecks delivered to the upper arms of her adversary, working the puck free as the Aeros go on the attack.

James likes what she sees in West. Above all a student of the game, the veteran is constantly evaluating the style of play she observes among the elite female players. "In women's hockey, we develop some really bad habits," she says, matter of factly. "Going by your check all the time. We're used to that big, wide swoop. We don't play a stop-and-start game." James seems to long for a game where physical superiority and the fear factor can make a difference.

A quick check of the season's stats for the Aeros reveals that Angela James leads in almost every category. She has scored 31 goals in twenty-four games and assisted on 17 others: 6 game-winning goals, 7 on the power play and 2 while shorthanded. Skip down to the team's overall record: of the twenty-five regular season games, the Aeros won twenty-three, with only one loss and one tie.

Less than half the third period to go and the action is furious. Three Olympians combine for Brampton's second goal, one goal away from the heavily favoured Aeros. A beautiful passing play results in Lori Dupuis converting feeds from Jayna Hefford and Vicky Sunohara. An air horn blasts from the Thunder's section of the stands and there is a rumble as feet stamp the aluminum bleachers.

Angela James watches the celebration from the bench. Although she loves the physical side of the game, she can appreciate the freedom that a lack of intentional bodychecking has afforded the women. "One thing that's good about the game is that you can see a lot of plays develop and the execution that results," she has said. "It's because people aren't getting hammered and the play is not stopping before it gets started. Perhaps there is more finesse and more system involved. I like that aspect."

The smallest details can and will determine the outcome in many confrontations. With approximately four minutes left, James finds herself stranded on a long shift. She traps the puck against the boards in Brampton's territory with her arms, drops it to her stick and begins the process of pinning the play in the Thunder end by way of her ferocious forechecking.

Minutes later, the Aeros are penalized and must finish the game shorthanded. A time-out is called and the coach entrusts Angela James with the task of winning the vital faceoff in the defensive zone.

She watches the eyes of the official. The instant the puck smacks the ice, James sweeps it to the corner behind her. It is as if she was the only player in the decisive zone. Geraldine Heaney clears it out of harm's way, the buzzer sounds and the Aeros have won the first in the best of three playoff games against Brampton. Off the ice, the home team is greeted by the leather-jacketed coaching staff in the tunnel to the dressing room. "Way to go, girls! Good one!" they all chime in, patting every back that trudges by. "Keep her goin'!"

Angela James marches from the ice with her visor and helmet tipped way back, a scowl on her sweaty face. She scored the second Aeros goal and played in every critical situation of the victory. A fan yells out from the background. "Way to go, Angie! Good game!"

For an instant, she looks up. With a little grin she stops to respond. "Thanks, but I was really no good tonight," she murmurs, then disappears into the privacy of the club's sanctuary.

A small flyer promoting the first playoff matchup has been printed on red construction paper and several copies of it litter the hallways in the bowels of the rink following the game. "SEE THE BEST WOMEN HOCKEY PLAYERS IN THE WORLD!!!" the headline screams. There are the logos of the Thunder as well as the Aeros and a roster of Team Canada players along with Olympic performers who have become feature attractions: Cassie Campbell, Geraldine Heaney and Amanda Benoit of the Aeros; Vicky Sunohara, Jayna Hefford, Lori Dupuis, Karen Nystrom and Laura Schuler for Brampton. Oddly, there is no mention of Angela James. None at all.

———

The women's game came into its own in the 1990s. The first officially sanctioned World Championships for women were held in Ottawa in 1990. The selection procedure that went towards building the national team was still in its infancy. With little in the way of an infrastructure, some stars almost slipped through the cracks. One of those players was Angela James.

"1990 was kind of funny," Margot Page remembers. "Originally, Angie wasn't chosen to come on the team and yet she was by far the best player."

The game was struggling with its rules. Many in the International Ice Hockey Federation (IIHF) wanted deliberate bodychecking, which was still part of women's hockey, to be eliminated from that first showcase event. The Europeans were behind the North American players in terms of speed and skill. Their only hope to stay close to the favoured teams from Canada and the United States was to use bodychecking to slow them down. In the end, the first world championships retained the physical element of the game but reluctantly so.

"I went to the tryouts and there was bodychecking. That's all I was, a bodychecker," James understates her talent. "My style was my style, and I didn't mind getting hit. I remember getting called in during tryouts that year, and they said they wanted me to calm down a bit. I agreed and stopped hitting but then people started killing me. They were hitting me hard, and I didn't understand what was going on. So I started to get a little discouraged. By the end of the camp they said I hadn't made the team."

Those in the know in Canadian hockey circles understood that growing pains would be part of the process for women's hockey as it skated into the international spotlight. Some players were given a second chance to be selected to the national team roster. "They said they wanted another look at me," Angela remembers with a smile. "A week later they called me back and said I was on the team after all."

Eight countries including Canada, the United States, Sweden, Finland, Norway, Switzerland, Germany and Japan contested the first championship. A national television audience watched the final game from the Ottawa Civic Centre and saw the Canadian players with pink uniforms and pink tape on the blades of their sticks. In the middle of it all and wearing number 8 was Angela James. "White pants. That was the worst," she says, laughing. "I was given a pair of size 52 pants, so I was trying to pull them up all the time."

It was evident from the very start that James was the dominant offensive factor in every match for Canada. She netted the initial goal in women's world championship history, led her team in scoring and was selected a tournament all-star as Canada claimed the historic first title with a 5–2 victory over the United States. "It meant the world to me," James reflects. "We never had anything like it prior to that. All I knew how to do was to play hockey, and that's all I wanted to do. To play in front of ten thousand fans— well, that was outstanding!"

Margot Page, a teammate of Angela's at the first World Championships, points to James's talent and skill, which allowed her to stand out from every other player. "I think Angela in her prime had the ability to go with the puck and scare teams," Page recounts. "Even when she started out internationally, when she decided to go with the puck, nobody could stop her."

Two years later, the global summit of women's hockey moved to Tampere, Finland. The momentum that had been established in Ottawa was all but lost as the glare of North American TV lights failed to cast many shadows in Scandinavia. Donna Baratto made the trip and watched the Canadians dominate the field—a group that included the People's Republic of China for the first time.

"We had our faces painted with Maple Leafs," says Angela's mom, proudly. "We had a ball over in Finland, even though on the way over my clothes went all the way to Singapore!"

Thankfully, Donna's clothes were returned to Canada, as were Ruth Schuler's, who also had hers diverted to Asia. Ruth's daughter, Laura, starred up front with Angela James for the powerful defending champions as they ran wild on the wider ice surface.

Even with intentional bodychecking now prohibited, the Canadians intimidated with speed and skill. They were never challenged, and the European crowds watched in awe as the women, clad in more appropriate red and white uniforms, defeated the United States 8–0 in the final game.

"It was the best team ever," James says about the Canadian team that won the World Championships in Finland that year. "I popped a couple of goals in the final game. But no-one was there to capture those moments. If they're captured it's a much bigger deal, as it was in Lake Placid in '94."

At Lake Placid, the final game for the championship pitted the Canadians against the Americans once again. At the end of the first period Karyn Bye had scored, giving the United States a 1–0 lead. For the first time the Canadians were not in complete control of the World Championships at such a critical stage. "That 1994 game was the first time Canada faced a challenge in the gold medal game," says Les Lawton, the Canadian coach. As they skated off the Yankee ice, the women in red and white knew that their undisputed hold on women's hockey supremacy was on the line.

In the second period, the Canadians raised the level of their game. Nancy Drolet fired a shot at the net and just as the American goalie Erin Whitten drew a bead on the puck, Danielle Goyette of St. Nazaire, Quebec, swooped by and got a stick on the passing disc. Redirected, it found the back of the goal and the Canadian women allowed themselves a cautious celebratory dance. Still, it was a tie game and the Americans could always rely on a friendly crowd. What they didn't count on was the ability of a certain Canadian forward to grab the confrontation by the throat and single-handedly point the way to another victory for her team. Angela James ventured into new territory when she turned the tide for the two-time defending champions.

"She just took the puck and drove up the right wing." Margot Page nearly jumps through the phone as she tells the story. "Then she deked the pants off the defence and went right in and scored. It turned the game completely around."

A viewing of the game tape reveals an astounding goal that gave Canada the lead for good in that decisive game. Geraldine Heaney, the veteran defender, started the play by emerging from behind her net to make a short pass to James on the right wing. In full flight by the time she reached her own blue line, number 8 passed her rivals as if they were inanimate. She raised the blade of her stick to feign a patented, booming slapshot, and in the process froze Kelly O'Leary, the only player between her and the American goal. "I always remember that because the defence looked like she closed her eyes," James says. "Then I just walked around her."

It was far from a walk. The play more closely resembled a bird of prey with wings extended, as James stretched to the backhand and seemed committed to a harmless fly by. Waiting and waiting until the helpless Erin Whitten was completely out of position, James struck with a perfect backhand, billowing the twine of the American net. It was 2–1 Canada. "It was one of those real turning points," Les Lawton says. "You could see the emotion of our team shift," Margot Page remembers vividly. "We suddenly understood that whenever she got the puck she could do something with it."

Minutes later, Heaney chipped the puck off the boards in her own end and James was after it like a hungry wolf. Gobbling it up at her own blue line, A.J. accelerated down the right wing and again left American players in her wake. Michelle DiFronzo dove at the attacking Canadian forward but couldn't dislodge the puck. Karyn Bye, a familiar combatant, chased James without success. Angela went to the backhand and as the goalie Whitten stretched out her pad, James lifted the puck into the net to give her country a commanding 3–1 lead. "When you're in that kind of situation you're in a different zone," James says. "It's like a juice, a running juice that you live off."

Canada went on to capture its third world championship with a

6–3 final score over the United States. "It was incredible to see Angie's reaction," Margot Page recounts. "She was pumping her arms. The interview on national TV afterwards was really cool."

On the ice for the last shift, she let her stick and gloves fly at the final buzzer along with the other Canadian players. Number 8 was selected as the final game's most valuable player. She had three world championships to her credit, and this one was the sweetest. Assistant coach Melody Davidson was there to embrace her. "That was the first time that I had coached her, but having been aware of her and having heard other people talk about her, I can say that the great maturing of her personally came in that game in that tournament," Davidson states. "She just stepped it up on the ice and took control."

At the 1997 World Championships, Canada struggled to win its fourth title in a row. The Finns were closing the gap and proved to be a formidable challenge in the semi-final game at the Kitchener Auditorium. By this time, the assistant coach from the 1994 team, Calgary's Shannon Miller, was in command of the Canadian squad. Angela James was a key member of her offensive arsenal. Miller's last words in the dressing room before the game with Finland were recorded by documentary makers shadowing the women's team who were bound for an Olympic appearance in Nagano, Japan, the next year. "Set the pace!" Miller shouted. "Redden [goaltender Leslie Redden], you're in net! Heaney, Campbell, on 'D' [defence]. A.J., you're starting. Let's go!"

Things did not go well initially. The Finns led 1–0 after a period. At the intermission, Miller addressed the stunned troops and questioned their commitment as a unit. Urging them to be better and to recall their place in history, the coach challenged the veteran players to rise to the occasion and set up a final showdown with the Americans who had breezed by the People's Republic of China in the other semi-final by a score of 6–0.

"C'mon, Ang, get it on net!" Miller screamed from the bench.

James delivered the shot with rising superstar Hayley Wicken-heiser picking up the rebound and depositing it in the vulnerable Finnish goal. Canada had drawn even with Finland. Eventually they persevered to win the game 2–1 and moved on to face the United States in the final game of the World Championships. In front of more than 6,000 fans, the largest crowd to watch a hockey game at the Kitchener, Ontario, rink, the aspiring Olympic gold medallists were to tangle with a team that had closed the talent gap substantially since the first World Champi-onships in Ottawa seven years earlier.

Shannon Miller relied heavily on James at crucial moments. Wearing a microphone for the filmmakers, she is heard to speak directly to number 8. "A.J., we gotta chip the puck past these guys, then beat them to it," Miller pleaded.

In a dramatic display of eye-hand coordination, James deflected a hard shot from the blue line past her old rival Erin Whitten to give Canada the lead. On close examination, Angela's stick was arguably over her shoulder at the time contact was made with the puck. While it is a skilled manoeuvre, the referee could easily have called it a high stick and therefore illegal. The goal stood, however, and Canada had pulled ahead at a crucial point in the game.

For the first time, a championship game went to overtime. Nancy Drolet of Drummondville, Quebec, broke the 3–3 tie and the home team's perfect record remained intact. With her arm around Geraldine Heaney, Angela James held up four fingers. The two understood that their solid record would allow them to travel to Japan as favourites. At stake in February of 1998 at Nagano was the first Olympic gold medal to be awarded in the sport of women's hockey.

———

With four world championships to her credit, it was Angela's belief that she would be a strong candidate to represent Canada and perhaps more importantly, women's hockey, as it made its debut at the ultimate level on a truly international stage. "It was all I had worked for since the announcement in 1992 that women's hockey would be an Olympic sport," she says. "Based on past performance, present performance and everything else I brought to that program, I should have been there." That she would not get to the Olympics would be her greatest disappointment.

Clues that she would not realize her dream began to develop at the 1997 World Championships in Kitchener when she was benched in the overtime period. During the Calgary training camp employed as part of the Olympic selection process, she was moved to the fourth line and taken off the power-play and penalty-killing units. "I thought I'd have to live with it because I was there to do a job," she says. "It was a month into camp, and I knew that something had gone wrong. I knew they wanted to release me for whatever reason. There was another five months to go before the games."

Geraldine Heaney had been Angela's teammate for years with the Toronto Aeros and had celebrated all four world championships with her friend. She is only two years younger but regards James as a mentor. In addition to being coached by James for a season at Seneca College, she is also James's assistant coach with the North York Storm peewee team. The history the two players shared brought them closer during the countdown to the Olympics.

"That summer we worked out together all the time," Heaney recalls. "When we went to Calgary we were workout partners. We hung out together almost all the time leading up to the Olympics." As time went by Heaney noticed James had lost some weight. Ideally, the forward played at about 170 pounds, but Heaney suggests she was down to about 150. Undiagnosed at the time, James had struggled with a thyroid problem that sapped her strength. "Just working out with her I noticed that she wasn't as strong," Heaney says. "I was lifting more weight than she was, especially with the legs. She should have been pushing much more than me, but I really never thought about it too much at the time."

Near the end, Angela James was called into Shannon Miller's office and, before a rolling documentary camera, was forced to endure a humbling real-life drama. A hockey player who had been at the forefront of the game as it emerged from virtual wilderness was left squirming in a swivel chair.

"I was told that I was in the grey zone. I asked what the grey zone was because I didn't understand. She said that players like Hayley Wickenheiser were up here and players like me were down there."

Less than a hundred days before the Olympics, Angela James was released from the team of twenty that would try to win that first gold medal for Canada. Of the twenty-eight players who had been invited to the tryout camp, she was the most accomplished and was obviously crestfallen at hearing the news. Storming out of the coach's office, James went into seclusion. Her regular monthly paycheque as a member of the Canadian team had been terminated. More importantly, her dreams of skating into Olympic history had been dashed.

"The one thing I said to the media was that a dog would be treated better," she says. "They just released me. No-one called, and I had been with this program for eight or nine years."

Officially, James had been cut because of a concern over her defensive play and also because the team wanted to include some younger players in its lineup. It was also suggested that, like Mark Messier who had not been selected to play for the Canadian men at the Olympics, James was a player who needed an inordinate amount of ice time in order to be effective. A star, yes, but not one that fit into the strategy for the upcoming hockey summit.

The younger players who were fighting for spots on the team

seemed impervious to A.J.'s disappearance. The same was not true for veteran performers like France St. Louis, who openly wept at the prospect of trying to win a gold medal without the acknowledged offensive leader of the team. Geraldine Heaney couldn't believe what had happened. "She might not have been the number-one player," Heaney reasons. "But she still should have made the team."

The fallout from Angela's dismissal was messy. She questioned her release with members of Canadian Hockey, the sport's governing body, but ran into mixed reaction and varying opinions with regard to an appeal process. Coach Shannon Miller and James were portrayed as enemies by the media. It was also reported that Angela had accused Miller of favoritism, something she vehemently denies having said.

"The whole lesbian issue came out," James sighs. "My appeal and the initial investigation into my release were overlooked. It was bad enough that I had lost my dream of going to the Olympics, but I was associated with being a big cry baby about the whole thing. I thought to myself: if this is the way I am going to end my career, man, am I going out with a blast!"

The Canadian team, without Angela James in the lineup, went to the final game in the Three Nations Cup against the United States as a prelude to the showdown in Japan. The Americans shut out the visitors by a score of 3–0 and exposed a weakness in the Canadian team. They lacked scoring depth. "They had few people who could score—Wickenheiser, Jayna Hefford and Danielle Goyette—but if those three were shut down, nothing else was happening," Margot Page had observed from the broadcast booth while lamenting A.J.'s absence. "She's the kind of impact player who can change the pace of the game. I don't care if you're talking ten years ago or this year, if you can get her on the ice, she's a threat."

Geraldine Heaney was beside herself as the trip to Japan

approached. Her friend was no longer with the team and she knew there was trouble brewing in the ranks. "In the dressing room she could have made the difference," Heaney explains. "I won't say that we would have won, but I will say that she would have made an impact on the team."

During the Olympic tournament Canada played with little impact against the United States, losing 7–4 in the last game of the round robin before facing the Americans yet again in the game that would yield historic prizes to the winning country. Angela James was back home trying to block it out. Her mother was devastated. At the recollection of her daughter's separation from the national team, Donna Baratto's eyes well with tears. "When she called me at work and told me, she was crying," Donna manages to say. "It took my heart."

In the final game at Nagano, Eric Lindros and Wayne Gretzky bit their nails and watched nervously in the stands as the Canadian women struggled to score. Gretchen Ulion had converted in the first period against a heroic Manon Rheaume in the Canadian net, and the Americans held the lead throughout. In the third, Shelley Looney extended the U.S. margin by another goal, and still Canada could not score. It wasn't until Danielle Goyette managed a goal that the spell was broken. But when Sandra Whyte deposited the puck in the cage vacated by Rheaume as a desperate Canadian measure, the U.S. victory was sealed. For the first time at a major international championship in women's hockey, the Canadian representatives would stand on the second level. Receiving the precious first gold medal and beaming with delight was Cammi Granato of Downer's Grove, Illinois. The captain of the United States team had honed her game in Canada and for years had been refereed by Angela James.

Only twenty-eight, Granato was half a dozen seasons shy of Angela James's experience but had battled the older player through four world championships and countless exhibitions. Granato had been there when James exploded for the two decisive goals at the 1994 Championships and watched in horror as her own team was completely deflated by the heroics of Canada's number 8. She had been matched against James's line over the years, but rarely had Granato been completely successful against the legendary figure. "It was in the big games that she seemed to thrive on delivering the goods," Granato remarks.

The admiration of an arch-rival, however, is often the most complete. "I respect her because she was the one player who was a thorn in our side throughout," Granato says. "She is fierce to play against. On the rare occasions that you would win a faceoff from her she wouldn't let you forget it. You'd take it across the back of the legs right away."

Granato does not understand how James could have been left off the roster at such a momentous juncture in the history of the game. "I didn't want to pass judgment at the time, but I certainly wondered why it had happened," Granato concedes. "I felt bad for her and could relate. If someone like her didn't make the Olympic team, then I knew it could happen to any of us."

Cammi Granato may have become the poster girl for U.S.A. Hockey, but she will never take the credit for changing the game and delivering it from obscurity. "We are pioneers, that's true," Granato says of the American Olympic gold medallists. "But players like Angela James from Canada were around and dominating before my group ever arrived. They paved the way, and we came in at the right time."

———

In the north end of Toronto, Seneca College's Women's Hockey School is just heating up. Summer draws to a close and the girls return to the ice as the last days of August are baking the city with a desperate, almost suffocating warmth. In the rink, the frosty air is

refreshing and the youngsters seem energized by a crisp reminder
of the winter season approaching. Four groups work on skills. The
coaches drill them on passing, peripheral vision, defensive tech-
nique and pinning on the boards. The skaters wear different
colours and emblems on their hockey sweaters. Representatives of
the Leaside Wildcats, the Etobicoke Dolphins, the Stouffville Stars
and the Mississauga Chiefs hustle by. One girl wears a baseball cap
pulled down over her eyes and a T-shirt that reads "Canadian Girls
Kick Ass."

"My name's Kate," the girl says. "I'm a centre, and you'll be seeing me at the Olympics someday."

Swooping around the pylons with effortless grace and obvious
power, is Kate's idol. Clad in a Team Ontario track suit and bran-
dishing a stick, which she uses as a pointer, Angela James is instructing while her flock remains transfixed at centre ice. Hockey school
is in session and it's time to get down to business.

James is not your typical hockey hero. She's a woman from the
inner city, the daughter of a black father and a white mother. And
she is relaxed and open about her same-sex relationship with a
woman whose name is also Angela.

"Most of my life is an open book." She laughs, catching her
breath at the boards. "Because I don't hide anything from them, I
think they appreciate me more."

In the stands, Angela James is the veteran player, the demanding
coach, the knowledgeable referee and the wise instructor all rolled
into one. In the last few minutes of the class, she explains the
timetable for her school. There are two on-ice sessions a day, physical training in the gymnasium and even a couple of hours of mar-
tial arts. "It teaches them discipline and respect," Angela says.
"They get out of control sometimes. After karate training they
come back on the ice a lot calmer and more willing to listen."

In addition, it's likely her old friend and teammate Geraldine

Heaney will make an appearance to conduct a class in some of the finer off-ice technical points of the game. Heaney is a maybe this year because she has been barnstorming the province with a travelling hockey school for girls, visiting towns from Sudbury to Sault Ste. Marie to Sarnia. "Women's hockey is growing, so it's very good," Heaney had reported. "In the smaller places the response to us is unbelievable. Kids have their parents drive two to three hours a day just to go to camp for the afternoon or the weekend."

James watches the kids file off the ice and into the dressing room. She brags about a certain girl who blossomed in the morning workout. "In the other session she was one of the younger ones and couldn't keep up," Angela says. "We moved her to the junior group and now look at her go!"

From one such observation she shifts gears to applaud the efforts of the young instructors who are, for the most part, members of the elite program with national team aspirations. James excuses herself for a minute and quickly sketches a diagram on her clipboard to remind herself of a drill for the afternoon.

I understand that Angela has to get to the dressing room and talk to the players before they assume the rest of their schedule. Knowing that she has accomplished so much in the game internationally and can still dominate on the ice, I wonder out loud if she harbours any lingering dreams for herself. Perhaps, I speculate, there is yet a chance to go to the Olympics later in her hockey life. James stops to consider and admits that there is a bad taste in her mouth because of all that has happened. She concedes that a certain bitterness remains. "I just can't shake it," she says.

She will not speak openly about any remaining hope of participating at the Olympic Games when she is thirty-six. I can't help believing that it is still there. She shakes hands and walks from the bleachers full of bravado. Humming the theme from *Hockey Night in Canada*, she claims she might like to be an announcer some day.

"I can give back more to the game at the grassroots level," she reckons. And then she hops downwards to the tunnel, where the children gleefully surround her.

Melody Davidson has an open mind when it comes to the tra-
ditions of hockey. She's the new coach of the Canadian Women
and took them to another world championship victory in 1999. To
her, performance has to do with resilience. It is a game where skill
and youthful enthusiasm are coveted qualities. Still, she believes, a
hearty spirit is required for a player to be of substantial talent and
lasting effect. That is why Angela James is significant. "She has
been there since the beginning and persevered through many
things," Davidson notes. "She has recognized her importance and
the importance of other people as role models. She's still there even
after being released from the Olympics. That's what being a pioneer is all about. You stay in the game regardless of the situation for
you individually and you stay in for the love of it."

The question applies to all trailblazers and pathfinders throughout history: Will those who have undertaken the exploration survive to reach the promised land? Why didn't A.J. fulfill her dream
of playing at the Olympics? The answer is too obvious. She made it
possible for all the players who looked up to her. That will be
Angela James's legacy to the game she adores.

THE COACH

Brian Kilrea

Killer

(courtesy The Ottawa Citizen; photo Pat McGrath)

✥ THE ACRID BLUE SMOKE OF half a dozen Don Tomas Cuban cigars billows from the doorway of a room deep in the bowels of the Ottawa Civic Centre. Just beyond the threshold, a few teenage boys clad in their light blue athletic underwear are hard at work with acetylene blowtorches and raspy files as they whittle and mould hockey sticks into goal-scoring weapons. They are apprentices learning a highly skilled trade, cloistered in the dank, rubber-floored hallway of a rink in the nation's capital.

Across the way, Brian Kilrea holds court before the game, his back leaning against the concrete-block wall and one foot resting on the simple three-slat wooden bench. The sixty-five-year-old coach of the Ottawa 67's wears grey flannels, a white shirt and black woollen vest; his blazer is hanging neatly on the back of a chair nearby. His wavy auburn hair has just a tinge of grey—the only sign that the greatest junior coach in Canadian history is approaching emeritus status.

Drawing deeply on his stogie, Kilrea faces everyone in the room. The assistant coaches, Bert O'Brien and Vince Malette, are there, as is the youthful owner of the team, Jeff Hunt. An ancient man named Garry "Stump" Craig, a goal judge, sits kitty-corner to his lifelong friend, enjoying Kilrea's largesse as he clips the end of his own precious cigar. This is a wonderful place, redolent of old-time hockey, and it is quite clearly Brian Kilrea's domain.

"Roger Neilson has bone cancer. Did you know that?" Kilrea remarks to no-one in particular. He is referring to the coach of the Philadelphia Flyers, a man he had warred against when Neilson was with the Peterborough Petes of the Ontario Hockey League. Advocates of different styles of hockey, the two rivals had battled heroically. But tonight Kilrea is expressing his concern for a comrade in difficulty. Roger Neilson, the former coach of the team that Kilrea's 67's would face tonight, was in trouble, and it was an unsettling reminder to Kilrea of hockey's trivial nature in the grand scheme of life.

The men contemplate an age-old rivalry. They argue about the injuries and the lineups, about which team is better and who might shine once the puck is dropped. They are insiders blessed with the knowledge and intuition only experience can afford. And Brian Kilrea is at the centre of it all, master of this room and all who enter.

A young boy in an Ottawa 67's cap and an oversized sweater wanders through the door. Looking no more than five years old, he wears a "barber pole" sweater in the colours of the Ottawa junior team—red, white and black horizontal stripes almost touching the floor—as he makes his way to Kilrea. The old coach leans down and extends his right arm to gather the kid close. The boy whispers in his ear: "5–3." Then he turns and scurries from the room with almost no notice taken.

"Who was that?" I ask Kilrea.

The coach exhales in a cloud of smoke and removes the glasses from his bulldog-like face. "That," he says, with gathering drama, "that was the Predictor." Kilrea goes on to explain that the child— the grandson of the team physician, Dr. Peter Premachuck, makes an appearance in the moments before each home contest and forecasts the score of the impending game. "He's done his homework," Kilrea adds. "He knows the teams and checks the standings. He's right a lot of the time." There is a glint in the old coach's eyes, just the hint of a grin.

———

"Killer" he was called in his younger playing days. Born in Ottawa five years before the onset of World War II, the son of a photographer, Brian has family roots in Northern Ireland. If you listen to him speak for any length of time, you'll begin to hear the singsong lilt in his voice. Three of his uncles played in the National Hockey League. Hec, Kenny and Wally Kilrea were at one point or another all property of the Detroit Red Wings. They became role models, symbolic of the kind of life their young nephew wanted for himself.

He was not a huge man, by hockey standards, but Kilrea was a hard worker and was signed by the Red Wings. In those days, players became the property of NHL clubs at an early age, and he was assigned to the junior Hamilton Tigers of the Ontario Hockey Association. Still, he spent time at the Red Wings training camp each fall and revelled in fleeting relationships with his heroes, great players like Gordie Howe, Ted Lindsay and Leonard "Red" Kelly. He remembers games of billiards and ping pong, general joking around and, most of all, a sense of togetherness.

Not talented enough to make the Red Wings or their top farm club in Edmonton, Kilrea was assigned to the Troy Bruins of the International Hockey League. Playing as a centreman, he spent four years in the Ohio town of 6,000. Against opposing teams in places like Cincinnati, Toledo and Indianapolis, Kilrea became somewhat of a star in the senior league. He was named Most Valuable Player of the team and led the club in scoring while securing a spot on the All-Star squad one season. It was in Troy that he acquired the nickname "Killer" because his pugnacious look reminded one teammate of a "baby-faced killer." The name stuck, and it's been his calling card ever since.

In the 1957–58 season the Red Wings called him up to act as relief after a rash of injuries. It lasted only about a week but he spent one thrilling shift playing on a line with Howe and Lindsay. Kilrea isn't sure to this day if he touched the puck in the ninety seconds he was on the ice against the Boston Bruins, but he is positive he didn't make a mistake. The chance to practise and skate with his idols in those few days is something he has treasured throughout his career.

Detroit took him off their list of protected players at the end of the next season in Troy, and he was free to sign with anyone he

wanted to play for. The Springfield Indians were an independent
team in the American Hockey League, which was one step below
the NHL. The Springfield, Massachusetts, team was owned by the
notorious Eddie Shore, a star and acknowledged "bad boy" during
his brilliant career with the Boston Bruins. Kilrea was scouted and
signed by Shore for what was considered decent money in 1959.
He got a $4,000 annual salary as well as a $500 signing bonus. On
top of that, Kilrea was promised $1,500 if he could stick with the
Indians past the last series of cuts.

The problem was, and Kilrea had been warned about this,
Shore was a possessive and domineering executive as well as being
a demanding, some say vicious coach. When he owned you, Eddie
Shore did just that and Kilrea experienced the negative side of his
owner's greed during the nine years he spent in Springfield. There
were rumours that NHL teams were interested in acquiring the productive centreman, but each time Shore made the price too high as
he jealously guarded the talent on his roster. Three Calder Cup
championships proved the Indians' supremacy in the AHL, and Kilrea skated alongside some talented players on their way to illustrious careers of their own. Defencemen Ted Harris and Kent
Douglas played for the Indians before winning the Stanley Cup
with Montreal and Toronto respectively. There was also a soulmate
in the rambunctious Don Cherry, who became a lifelong friend of
Kilrea's after both had gone into coaching.

"I've been thankful for Shore," Kilrea says years later about his
controversial coach and manager. "I'm not sure in the nine years
that I was there, however, that I was thankful."

What Kilrea accomplished in Springfield never led him to the
National Hockey League for any great stretch but it became the
foundation of his enduring role in the game. He observed Shore
closely and found him an astute businessman but more importantly,
a great on-ice teacher. Kilrea learned about balance and strength on
the rink as well as movement of the puck—two things that have

become hallmarks of his teams in Ottawa. As much as anything else, Brian Kilrea survived Eddie Shore, a coach who believed in fixing injuries and players by cracking necks as well as a few heads. Kilrea played for a long time beneath the level he might have been capable of, all the while shaping his future professional outlook.

"I didn't hate Eddie Shore for all those years," Kilrea told me. "I took what I learned from him and put the good to use and discarded the bad."

As he reached thirty years of age, Kilrea was still in Springfield, resigned to his fate as a career minor league player. Only rarely does the top level of professional hockey accept skaters of such an advanced age into the fold for what amounts to a first chance to prove their abilities. So Kilrea played on in the American Hockey League, demonstrating his lasting nature as a craftsman in the game. In his brief autobiography of 1993, he related the philosophy he held dear in subsequent years of coaching. "I just went back to Springfield every year with the hopes of being the best in the American League. But being there wasn't bad. We had some good guys on the team and we had a lot of fun. So I stayed put and enjoyed life where I was."

Labour trouble soured Kilrea's last year with the Indians. A handful of key players held out at the beginning of the season and forced Shore to pay them higher wages. The vindictive owner made it tough on the rest of the team by suspending the three star defencemen shortly after their return to the lineup. The reason he gave was their "indifferent play." In response, Kilrea, who was the players' representative, led a walkout and the Indians were shut down by a strike. The matter was eventually settled but Shore never spoke to Kilrea again.

The Indians were sold to Jack Kent Cooke of the Los Angeles Kings when the NHL expanded to twelve teams for the 1967–68 season. Red Kelly was the coach and talked Kilrea, his old acquaintance from Detroit Red Wing days, now thirty-two, into helping the team get started. Brian claims he might have been just as happy to stay in the American League to finish his career but wanted to lend a respected friend a helping hand. He ended up scoring the first goal in Los Angeles Kings history against the Philadelphia Flyers in a 5–3 victory. In fact, he scored two goals and added an assist in the game, which marked his return to the NHL after a decade's absence. Through twenty-five games with the Kings, Kilrea managed 8 points before a knee injury forced him out of the lineup and subsequently back to Springfield.

His NHL career over, Killer finished the season with the Los Angeles AHL team. He then went to Vancouver of the Western Hockey League and back to the American League with Rochester. He spent a season with the Tulsa Oilers of the Central Hockey League under the direction of the late coach John McLellan, who used Kilrea as a liaison with some of the younger players. "My time in Tulsa might have got me started in coaching," wrote Kilrea in his autobiography.

Injuries to his ankle and back sent Kilrea home to Ottawa at the end of the 1968–69 season. It looked as though his playing days were finished. In the summer months he made a successful attempt to get into shape at the training facility of the football Ottawa Rough Riders and accepted an invitation to finish the next season with the Denver Spurs of the Western League. Kilrea played well and was offered a "no cut" contract for $15,000 to play the next year in Denver. It would have been the biggest pay of his playing career but he declined because he had already accepted a job in the restaurant business back in Ottawa. His retirement from hockey came after only twenty-six games in the NHL.

It was a life in the minors. But Kilrea has no regrets about his playing efforts. He learned the game and won championships under the watchful eye of Hall of Famer Eddie Shore. A brief fling with the Detroit Red Wings resulted in the dream of skating alongside his heroes, Howe and Lindsay. He scored a landmark goal for a fledgling franchise upon his return to the big leagues. Most important to Brian Kilrea was the hard work and effort he put into an honest trade. The accolades and fame escaped him but not the appreciation for the talents of legions of players who populate the game at all levels. The dedication of his book speaks most forcefully about what matters most to Killer, even now: "To the many players who've toiled in obscurity," it says.

———

The Ottawa Civic Centre overlooks the Rideau Canal and is part of a bizarre structure linked at the hip with Frank Claire Stadium, where the Rough Riders used to play. It was completed as part of the centennial project in the nation's capital in 1967. The interior of the 10,000-person arena is remarkable in that one side of its grandstand is dwarfed by the other. On the penalty box side the ceiling overhangs the ice and tilts towards the centre faceoff circle. The bleachers for the football stadium are directly overhead and, when both a hockey and turf battle occur at the same time, the football crowd is, in effect, sitting on the roof of the rink.

On a rainy night in early December, Brian Kilrea is in his tiny office just off the rink's concourse, at work on the lineup for that evening's game. He pores over a ledger and sizes up Peterborough, a longtime rival of Ottawa's in the Ontario Hockey League. He faces a whitewashed corkboard wall that's blank except for old-fashioned moss-coloured luggage tags pinned to it. On each tag is scrawled the name of a player, and the coach has arranged them in formations of forward lines and defence pairings. They appear as squadrons of five, as he prepares to confront the Petes on his home ground. He's completing the lineup card he will submit to the office officials, after confirming the players who will not get a chance to compete this time.

"That's the toughest thing in the world to do for me as a

coach," he says. "Boy, when you tell a kid, sorry, he didn't make it, that's difficult."

I survey the working space he has occupied for most of his coaching life. There are few mementos on the walls. A framed poster from the Metropolitan Museum of Art entitled "Monster Cigars" dominates. On Kilrea's desk is a picture of his wife, Judy, and a small TV set with boxes of videotapes piled haphazardly on either side. "Videotape reinforces what you've already seen and remember," Kilrea scoffs. "Mistakes are best corrected as soon as a player comes off the ice."

He can be an abrupt man, some might say matter-of-fact. Others contend that bullshit doesn't wash with Killer. He is in his twenty-second year coaching the 67's, having begun in 1974 after learning the ropes in the Ottawa minor hockey system with tykes, atoms and peewees. His final apprenticeship, while working full-time in the restaurant business, was with a group of midget-aged players—he directed them to a surprise victory over a touring Russian team with very little time for preparation. Combative and competitive best describe Kilrea's style as a player and coach.

Glossy pictures clipped hastily from magazines are plastered on the wall behind his desk, covering the area from floor to ceiling, as in a young teenager's bedroom. Each of the images is of a polar bear. There must be dozens of them taken from the pages of *National Geographic*, real estate calendars and other sources. "What's with you and polar bears?" I blurt out.

Kilrea looks up from his writing and swings around to look at his collection, breaking into a full-fledged smile. "You think of Canada. You think of north. Strong, powerful, tenacious—to me that should be the Canadian animal," he declares. "I love polar bears!"

I think of all the years he has been at the helm of this franchise. Kilrea *is* the Ottawa 67's. The totals are impressive: two Memorial Cup championships; nineteen of the twenty-one seasons have produced more wins than losses. As I write this, Kilrea has recorded 865 victories, by far the greatest sum in Canadian junior hockey history. He surpassed Ken Hodge, who amassed 741 wins over twenty-two seasons of hard work in the Western Hockey League a couple of years ago. Four times he has been the Matt Leyden Trophy winner as the Ontario Hockey League's coach of the year. Trophies and plaques could wallpaper every inch of this office, yet instead they collect dust in some dark closet.

There he is, scratching a few notes with his left hand before making his way downstairs for the pre-game ritual. Kilrea opens the cigar box and stuffs a half-dozen brown tubes wrapped in cellophane into the inside pocket of his jacket. The gold Zippo and Kilrea's keys jangle as he crams them into his grey flannels. "This is where you don't want to forget nothing," he says. "Heaven forbid I should have to come back."

The walk begins. The same route before every game, it starts in the narrow hallways of the hockey club's administration office. A pizza box lies on the front counter. Kilrea is telling a story. "Funny how some kids are," he warms up. "We've got a guy on our team named Ian Jacobs. He's a native kid. He was just sitting there on the bench during a game one night. All of a sudden this song with beating drums comes over the loudspeaker. BOOM . . . BOOM . . . BOOM. 'Coach,' he says, 'sounds like they're playing my tune. Maybe you should put me out there!'"

The old coach chuckles and his eyes dance as we continue past the team photos, which line the reception area in chronological formation. Kilrea takes no notice of the "kids," as he affectionately calls them, but his words convey a strong sense of family, as if every player portrayed is still present in spirit. "Maybe the National League's a little bit different but I don't think it should be," he reckons. "I think there's a lot of times when humour and laughter take over. You have to have that kind of atmosphere."

Moving quickly now, he almost tows me behind as his cronies

are waiting along the path through the stands. I linger a little, fascinated by the faces reflected in the pictures of Kilrea's graduating
classes. The alumni include Michael Peca, captain of the Buffalo
Sabres; Bobby Smith, the classy centreman who broke in with
Minnesota; Chris Simon, a rugged left winger now skating for the
Washington Capitals; steady Andrew Cassels of the Canucks; and
goalies-turned-broadcasters Jim Ralph and Darren Pang. In the
portrait of the 1975–76 team, the captain has a huge head of dark
curly hair—they used to call it an "afro" back then. "Burrhead was
a beauty," Kilrea says, then marches on.

———

Doug Wilson is now the director of professional development for
the San Jose Sharks and lives in northern California, thousands of
miles from his Ottawa home. Already forty-one but looking as if he
could still play with the ease and fluidity that marked his sixteen-
year NHL career, Wilson brings the intelligence and experience of
an accomplished defenceman to his job.

With the Chicago Blackhawks and later the Sharks, Wilson
scored nearly a thousand points and played in seven all-star games.
He won the Norris Trophy in 1982 as the NHL's best rearguard
while patrolling the blue line and generating much of his team's
attack—some say the most demanding job in all of hockey.
Throughout his days spent skating on NHL ice, Wilson was also a
player representative and active in the meeting rooms of the game.
He was president of the National Hockey League Players Association the last year he played for San Jose. Currently, in addition to
his scouting duties and evaluating the Shark's talent base, Wilson is
developing a plan for assisting retiring players with their post-
playing career opportunities.

Wilson is not like Brian Kilrea on the exterior. Neat and well-
dressed, the former defenceman carries a certain cool reserve. On

the subject of his junior coach, however, he is emphatic and effervescent. "I think the thing about Killer is that he was our friend, he was very close to us and we had tremendous respect and trust in him," Wilson said. "We could laugh and have fun, but when it came down to time to work, we would go through the wall for him. That's a rare talent for one person to have."

Kilrea's approach to the game is not complicated. The principles of hard work and discipline are the building blocks of his philosophy. "I love it," he had told me when I asked about the rigour of on-ice practice. "I'm hard when I'm on the ice. I may even kick a player off the ice," he related. "Our team's rules are what they are. If a player doesn't like them then he can go play with a different team that has different rules."

Skating is the key. Doug Wilson remembers the wind sprints that signalled the conclusion of most training sessions in his junior days. "We skated and skated," he sighed. "There was never any complaining and whining. We trusted him and respected that he was right. We probably needed it or deserved it. He got our attention."

Devotion to Kilrea's tactics soon followed. Much of Wilson's professional talent rested with his mobility as he was faster than most of the bigger young men playing at his level. From the Ottawa blue line, number 7 scored 295 points in the 194 OHL games he played from 1975 to 1977. Blessed with a blistering shot, Wilson became the anchor of the team in Kilrea's early years as coach. As a reward for his accomplishments, his sweater has been retired and hangs from the rafters of the Civic Centre.

Doug Wilson does not languish in an endless recitation of statistics or personal highlights. Something more lasting than the wins and losses, or the trophies won, marks his admiration for Kilrea. The former NHL great reveals a refreshing understanding between player and coach, a time-tested union too often fraught with artificially created distance and omnipotent rank. "He treated us like men with fairness and honesty," Wilson says. "We were a very tight-knit group of people. One thing about Killer that has never changed is how he treats his people. Loyalty is an important thing."

The defenceman and the coach honed their mutual understanding on a road trip one season to Niagara Falls. Wilson's close friend and teammate Larry Skinner was injured and unable to play but had permission from Kilrea to accompany the team on the overnight journey. The bus left on Saturday for a big Sunday afternoon game with the Flyers. Upon arrival in Niagara Falls, the coach called for a curfew—standard procedure the night before an important match. When he did his usual bed checks, Kilrea discovered that Wilson, who was the team captain, and Skinner were still absent. Leaving a note on the hotel room door, he planned to fine Wilson $25 for insubordination and to send Skinner home to Ottawa on the early morning bus.

The offending pair returned not long after and got the news of their proposed punishment from the coach. Kilrea expressed his disappointment with their behaviour and dispatched them to their room. Ten minutes later Wilson returned to see his coach and cut a deal. He said he would pay double the fine if the team lost against the Niagara Falls club the next day and nothing if they were able to win. Kilrea accepted the deal. Almost as an afterthought, Wilson announced that Larry Skinner would stay the course and return home with his teammates following the game. Kilrea ended up admiring the captain for protecting his friend.

The game went Wilson's way from the outset. Kilrea later said that Wilson came to the rink "with dynamite in his eyes!" He scored two goals and added two assists, not to mention engaging in a fight with one of the more intimidating Flyers. Skating by the bench at the end of the contest, with the good team from Niagara Falls soundly beaten, Wilson declared his account settled.

"The Larry Skinner incident was one of those times we made a bad decision," Wilson admitted later. "But standing up for a teammate was something Kilrea had instilled in us. We made a deal and then went the extra mile to not let him down. Those are qualities that are important to Killer because I think he lives his own life that way."

———

For his part, Kilrea remains devoted to Wilson all these years after the defenceman has left his charge. He recalls the lesson learned on the Niagara Falls road trip with nostalgia and more importantly, cherished understanding of its significance. "Fine, it was over," Kilrea says, dropping the hint of a smile and looking straight ahead. "You have to remember kids will make mistakes."

The volunteers are already gathering in the lobby of the Civic Centre. Card tables are being erected so that women and men of all ages sporting red and white 67's ball caps can flog 50–50 tickets. The proceeds go to the Ottawa Heart Institute. As Kilrea appears they all wish him well for a game still nearly two hours from the opening faceoff. The navy blue, teal and purple seats speckle the empty arena. "Go get 'em, Killer," someone yells. The coach— unstoppable now that he's on his way—waves without looking and allows his face to crinkle with delight.

After a quick hesitation, his hand ruffles the hair of two youngsters in wheelchairs waiting for him at the landing by the first section of bleachers he passes. "Looks like my other buddies are a little late today," he says, feigning scorn for the regulars who await his appearance before every game. He has a certain amount of superstition built into his life, and the tardiness of the fans is a bit disconcerting. He pushes on. "That looks like the easiest way to go," he motions to the most direct passage to the gaping entrance at the other end of the rink where we are headed. "But I always have to take the same route." Kilrea veers to the right.

He winds his way through the middle of the stands, walking

over the narrow concrete between the rows of plastic seats. He has the focus and concentration of a schoolboy balancing on an imaginary train track. It's as if we're skipping school. "I've been able to not have a job for life," he almost giggles. "Because I don't think hockey is a job."

Kilrea then turns sharply to the left and straddles the rail guarding against a drop of about seven feet to ice level. Pushing off with his arms and the accompanying jingle from all the metal in his pocket, he jumps to the floor and looks up with hand extended so that I can follow. Suddenly, I feel as if we've hopped the fence and we're about to invade a forbidden skating rink for a midnight game of shinny.

We go through the entrance where the Zamboni machine will appear to resurface the ice, then down a dark hall where two teenagers are taping the blades of their sticks outside the dressing room. One of them is huge and bulky with an oversized upper body and the slightly bleached hair that's currently in vogue. "Hey, show us the pump for that chest," Kilrea roars, without stopping. He ducks to the left and into his coach's room. Hangs his jacket. Flicks the Zippo. Eases into modest recline. "I don't find it hard to relate to them because I use a language they understand," says Kilrea. "Sometimes there's a few foul words in there. Whatever it is, they understand it. They know when it's a day of fun and a day of seriousness."

———

"He's a piece of work, isn't he?" Bobby Smith remarked. The general manager of the Phoenix Coyotes was on his cellphone from the airport in Boston, where he was about to catch a plane for Philadelphia and his team's next game against the Flyers. They were proving to be dominant teams in the Western and Eastern conferences of the NHL respectively.

I had called Smith at his office in Arizona and left a voice message, hoping to cull his thoughts about days spent under Kilrea's tutelage in the late 1970s. The Calder Trophy winner as the NHL's best rookie in 1979 with the Minnesota North Stars, Smith had always been regarded as one of the league's most intelligent players of his era. A big, smooth-skating centre, he had gone on to win the Stanley Cup with his second team, the Montreal Canadiens, in 1986. There was no question that he had qualified as one of an elite group of players to compete at the NHL level, as he scored more than a thousand points in almost exactly the same number of games.

There were rumours that Smith would become a medical doctor at the end of his playing days, but that was an urban myth of sorts because he had taken only a few science courses at university. I remember his devotion to the cause of literacy in Quebec after encountering him at various fundraising functions. Indeed, I targeted Smith for my first television interview after arriving in Montreal. Assigned to cover a Canadiens practice as a cub reporter on my initial television assignment in the fabled city of hockey, I knew Smith would make things easy because he was so articulate. I wasn't disappointed in the least.

He had returned my call this day after only a few minutes. Checking his voice mail and eager to get the word out about his favourite coach, the rising hockey executive called back twice because the connection cut out temporarily.

"He has a huge influence on those kids," Smith said, in reference to his own mentor. "I would say particularly the ones who have moved away from home. From age sixteen to nineteen you see more of Brian Kilrea than you see of your own father."

Although Smith lived at home when he played for the 67's, he found himself over at Brian and Judy Kilrea's watching sports on television with the team's other players on a regular basis. The guys would lie on the floor—heads propped up by pillows—while Killer lounged in his favourite chair and Judy Kilrea distributed chicken wings or popcorn. "As much as Brian is the mentor, Judy is a big part of it too," said Smith.

Kilrea told me once that the team was the most important thing to him. No individual player was more important than the collective whole, the well-rehearsed unit with each part performing a specific function like a well-oiled machine. At the same time, he told me: "When I get behind the bench, winning is everything— 7:30 to 10:00, I'll do anything to win."

"I think that he would say the kids matter most. It's not winning the Memorial Cup, it's the kids' individual prospects," Bobby Smith countered. "Brian realizes that he has a responsibility to these young kids to see that they become as good as they can be as individual players. He has always made the players play a player's game so that they would have the opportunity to improve as far as their ability could take them."

This is borne out in the style of play the Ottawa 67's have come to adopt since Kilrea's hiring in 1974. They score goals and play a skating game, unwilling to fall into a defensive style, which is less risky but sometimes more forgiving to a less skilful squad. "We didn't dump it in or get it deep," Smith said. "You didn't get benched for losing the puck at the other team's blue line. He lived with mistakes, but you look at the track record of the guys who have gone through Ottawa and gone to the NHL and it speaks for itself."

The success rate of graduates from the Ottawa 67's program has never been questioned. The former Kilrea juniors populate many NHL rosters and have done so with distinction. Bobby Smith freely admits when he joined the 67's as a seventeen-year-old he could barely compete at the Ontario Hockey League level. By the time he left he was the most coveted junior at the NHL draft and was immediately the top scorer for his first professional team, the North Stars. "There's no question that Brian Kilrea is the best coach I've had," Smith said. "Technically Jacques Lemaire was better. Bob Gainey was a very good coach. But I wouldn't have been the first draft choice overall and I wouldn't have played fifteen years in the NHL had I not had Brian Kilrea coach me for three years when I was a teenager."

Smith picks up the phone and talks to his old coach on a moment's notice at least once a week. He asks his advice and has even employed Kilrea as a consultant when the Coyotes were preparing to select junior players at the big league draft. A fledgling hockey executive learning the ropes from his favourite teacher, Smith has never forgotten the lasting effect of a thorough education. "Teenage boys that come through there and then leave at nineteen or twenty are better people for it," Smith concluded.

It turns out there are to be two pre-game addresses to the Ottawa 67's in the tense moments before they skate out to face their rivals this night at the Civic Centre. It is usually the private prerogative of the coach to motivate, cajole, instruct or harangue players before they enter the battle. Some prefer to yell or scream and beat the drum. Others drift to boards at the end of dressing rooms and make spaghetti-like diagrams with black erasable markers. Still others have been known to engage in question-and-answer sessions with their players in an effort to create a democratic atmosphere of understanding.

Ten minutes before faceoff, a man of about forty strides confidently into Kilrea's room with his hand extended and a grin plastered across his face. Mark is hailed by the coach and hugged with great fondness. As it turns out, he is from Smiths Falls on the rural outskirts of Ottawa and is mentally handicapped. He has been a fan of the 67's most of his life and makes the pilgrimage to the "big city" to see his favourite team a few times a year. On every occasion, Kilrea accepts him to the inner circle and discusses the fortunes of the team as if Mark was, in reality, the fretful general manager come to pay his quarterly visit.

Tonight Mark has a theory on how to most effectively dispatch the Petes. "Killer, the boys have to go hard from the opening faceoff

and never let up," he intones. It is the basic tenet of hockey that each
player takes for granted. Instead of laughing, Kilrea rubs his chin and
puts his arm around Mark's shoulders. "I like it, Mark. I like it very
much," he says in affirmation. "Now the best thing for you to do is
to go in and tell the boys yourself. They should hear it from you."

Mark marches to the room across the way without hesitation.
We listen and Kilrea never cracks a smile, preferring to watch the
glow at the end of his cigar in silence. "Now listen, boys!" we hear
Mark shout. "Go hard as soon as the puck is dropped and never
give up!" In response, yells of agreement flow across the hallway.
The players hoot and holler in a primitive sort of fight song. Mark
bursts into the room and waves a triumphant fist at Kilrea. The
coach returns the gesture and promises his friend a couple of autographed sticks to take back home. His first message of the night has
been successfully delivered.

The locker room is carpeted wall to wall in deep pile maroon.
The "barber poles" are arranged neatly on two sides with skates
tied and sticks in hand as Kilrea arrives two minutes before they
leave for the ice. He leads Bert O'Brien, Vince Malette and myself
into the dressing room but only he is allowed to speak. The place
reeks of sweat and the stench of stale equipment, which has
invaded, it seems, every crevice of every hockey pad there. The
coach begins to pace in silence while staring at his shoelaces.

"They'll bang it out," he finally says, in reference to Peterborough's team. "Make sure we don't give them anything." The players nod their heads in unison. Then comes a nugget, a gem from
Kilrea's time-tested repertoire. "He who works the hardest, works
at the opposite end." In an instant, the players are on their feet.

"Let's go, boys!" Seamus Kotyk, the goaltender, leads the way
and the rest follow in single file. It's over the rubber mats and into
the light of the arena, where teenage cheerleaders greet them with
red pompoms. They stand at attention while a youth choir sings the
national anthem and 6,000 or so fans sheepishly hum along.

Kilrea is like a caged animal behind the bench, prowling up and down. Resting his elbow on his knee, which props up his chin for only seconds at a time. He mutters and taps players on their shoulder pads. They fling themselves over the boards at the slightest signal he sends their way.

These young men and the hundreds who have gone before them are the coach's legacy. Not the one-goal victories or the championship banners but the kids, as he calls them. "What they give you is all they've got every night," he said earlier. "It's fun to see them go out and play and it's even more fun to see them improve, and you do."

They are quite a collection, these teenagers who rattle the boards and dash up the ice like fully grown men. Mark Bell is a mammoth centre who stands six foot three—a couple of inches taller on his blades—and weighs well over two hundred pounds. A star in the making, Bell has been drafted by the Chicago Blackhawks and is bound, after this game, for the camp of the Team Canada juniors, who will soon compete in Sweden at the World Championships.

In the penalty box is Miguel Delisle, another hulking forward who has already engaged in fisticuffs with T.J. Eason of the Petes. Delisle will be eligible for selection at the next NHL draft in June. His black eye and contentious manner suggest he's hoping to attract the attention of teams who need muscle. Glancing up at the ceiling banner, which proclaims Brian Kilrea as the winner of the junior record 742 games, Delisle declares, "Killer's the best coach ever. No question about that." The penalty gate swings open. His penance over, Delisle bursts from the box and rams into an advancing adversary before charging to the bench and Killer's words of wisdom.

Lavente Szuper is the backup goalie. A native of Budapest, Hungary, Szuper came to the 67's in 1998 as an import. He proceeded to post a 2.33 goals against average, which became a new benchmark for the franchise. Still, he finds himself struggling to acclimatize in a strange country. Earlier, in deciding which players would participate in a series of community service spots on local TV, Kilrea had added Szuper's name to the top of the list. "We need a goalie," he told Doug Drain, the 67's director of communications. "Besides, he's adjusting to the Canadian game and a new country. This'll help him express himself."

Kilrea, it seems, has few favourites. He cares about all the players under his watchful eye, like a border collie shepherding in the most meaningful direction. The captain, Dan Tessier, is of particular note. He's leading the way in the first period. He nicely sets up defenceman Luke Sellars for the game's first goal. Then the diminutive centre receives Sellars' pinpoint pass and whips it by Mike Pickard in the Peterborough net as the home team goes up by two. Dan Tessier is a Kilrea favourite. "He passes the puck great and he's not scared," said the coach. "He's not a big guy and that's why he never got drafted. But you would like to see him get a chance."

Tessier is twenty years old and running out of time. Not being drafted is the equivalent of the cold shoulder from the National Hockey League. It's a surefire sign that the boys in the big league don't think you belong. Still, the native of Orleans, Ontario, is an OHL all-star, the acknowledged leader of his team—both in scoring and in spirit—and has other options. He's a student at Cité Collégial in Ottawa, a French-language institution that offers a police foundation academy. Tessier is in his third year and if he can't walk on to an NHL roster or play in Europe, he'll be a cop. That's just fine with Brian Kilrea. It's all part of the process. "I've got some kids who chose another route," he said. "Everyone isn't going to play the game. That's why you have to instill confidence in them to do whatever it is that they do best."

Kilrea's graduates have gone on to be great NHLers but also lawyers and firefighters and one is even a member of the Ottawa police SWAT team. Some have raised families and stayed in the area to coach local atom teams with great success. All of this makes him happy. Dan Tessier is still holding out hope that he will make it in hockey. He is secure in the knowledge that his coach is with him no matter what. "I know that Killer is going to do everything in his power to help me out," Tessier says. "I'm sure he knows how much I am producing out there for him and the team. He respects that. He's doing his job to try and help me and help everyone on the team. But there are twenty-five guys and I understand it's not good to concentrate on just one."

For his part, Kilrea remains open to the magic of the unexpected. It is his capacity to recognize value in all human endeavour that helps Kilrea's classroom venture beyond the boards of the rink and the hockey arena itself. "It's not just the guys who can claim to have been a 67 and now play in the National League," he offered. "I know they would all like to walk through the door that leads to the pros. Not all of them can. Still, they got their education here. They got their start here and they've settled down here."

Bobby Smith recognized this long ago. He is one of Kilrea's crew who has gone on to enjoy a wonderful and continuing career in professional hockey. He is certain that his old coach respects and admires what he has accomplished not only as a player, but also in his more recent pursuit as the general manager in Phoenix. Smith does not, however, feel he occupies a more exalted place in Kilrea's heart because of this and he used a contemporary example to illustrate. "He will be equally as proud of Dan Tessier if he doesn't make it, as he will be of Mark Bell who most certainly will," Smith said. "He looks at those two guys as being equally successful and he's proud of the influence he's had on both of them."

Defenceman Luke Sellars has taken a penalty at the conclusion of the period and the Petes have seemingly capitalized. A high stick, however, disallows the powerplay goal and the 67's escape with a 2–0 margin at the end of twenty minutes of play. Kilrea

follows his team into their dressing room and strides forcefully to
the board to illustrate a point.

"Don't stand here," he lectures, directly at the wall he is facing.
"We let them come through here twice." The team is silent—all
eyes turned to the front as they sense the coach is not pleased in
spite of the lead. "We took a bad penalty. We had the play and
then, Luke, you wreck it by f—ing around with a guy in front of
the net!" The offending defenceman, Sellars, has been singled out.
Kilrea finally turns to face the players and walks quickly towards the
door. Over his shoulder he asks Sellars, "Have you got your own
legs on today?"

"I don't know, coach," Sellars mumbles, as the others chuckle.

"I don't f—ing know either 'cause all of a sudden you can't
skate!" Kilrea is gone. His point resonates.

"He'd know the guys that had tough shells and could take some
real razzing or teasing in front of the other players," Ron Davidson
was saying. Davidson was on the phone from his office in Hailey-
bury, Ontario, as he prepared for a double murder case, which was
about to go to trial in a couple of weeks.

Davidson had just been confirmed as the crown attorney for
the District of Timiskaming, an area in the north of the province
that includes places like Temagami at its southern extremity and
Kirkland Lake, a famous breeding ground for hockey players. A
centreman with Kilrea's 67's during the 1977 season, Davidson had
gone on to graduate from law school at Queen's University in
Kingston and chose "the other door" that leads away from professional hockey. He had played with the National team for five years
and at the Lake Placid Olympics in 1980. There had also been a
hockey tour through Europe—Sweden, Switzerland and France—
for four years after that.

Now, ensconced in the legal life, the former skater clings to
the lessons of his coach, whom he calls the ultimate mentor. "You
forget all of the various technical instructions that coaches give

you and the little impacts that they have along the way," Davidson reasoned. "What you remember is how they moulded you as a person and how they made you appreciate that hockey is more than a game."

The Ottawa 67's that Ron Davidson played for went all the way to the Memorial Cup, only to lose to New Westminster in a tight game. He had been going through memorabilia in his basement and discovered the stick he had used in that tournament. It stirred all kinds of memories about his experience with Kilrea and the Ottawa junior team, and the impact it had on his life. Maybe it was Killer's approach to people and his efficient method of motivation. Perhaps, more important, was a thorough understanding of what it takes to reach young players. "It was his way of communicating very quickly and in a positive way," Davidson recalled. "Everyone came to believe that we were the team to beat that night."

This is, by far, the greatest challenge for the coach. To create and foster an atmosphere by which the players come to believe they are the better team and in turn, to have them perform to their full capabilities. It's commonly referred to as "getting the most out of your team." It's not an easy task and many approaches designed to achieve it are bound for certain failure. Kilrea, according to Davidson, had the magic formula.

"Brian never said a lot but he would convey a message to you as a player that the team was on that night," the crown attorney remembered. "All of a sudden he'd say something like 'You know, we're swarming them, we're all over them!' He'd tell the team it was having a great game even if it wasn't. He might be watching the game and out of the blue would talk glowingly about a great play we made or applaud someone's great effort. All of a sudden you felt like you *were* on that night."

Some coaches make players feel good about who they already are and others break them down, forcing them to become reliant on the authority figure, who then moulds them into the kind of player he wants them to be. Kilrea is part of the former group. Davidson remembers playing with a certain amount of pressure and being asked to perform to the best of his capabilities but he was struck by how little stress there was. "If you were reaching your potential and giving it everything you could, he understood that," Davidson said. "He understood that certain people had talent and that certain people had limitations. He would bring out the best in the players and he would make you feel good about the way that you performed and the way in which you were contributing to the team."

Humour has always been a useful tool for Brian Kilrea. Davidson always believed it was Kilrea's way of relaxing the team in difficult situations. But never, in his estimation, did the coach seriously belittle a player in front of his peers. Instead, like a wise professor, Kilrea poked fun at a favourite student to make the classroom less tense. It allowed for greater performance.

"When I played, the guy he could tease best was a guy named Jeff Geiger," Davidson said. "We'd put a real string of wins together towards the end of the season, and the streak was sort of in jeopardy because we were down by about three or four goals to Sudbury at home and we had been hit by a flu bug. After the first period we were down 4–0. The game could have been a complete write-off and guys were feeling sorry for themselves. They were all hanging their heads between their legs and Brian came into the room and he wasn't throwing garbage cans or whatever it was that a coach would typically do. He says, 'You know, guys, a lot of you have the flu and you've been hit really hard by the bug. I've got a lot of respect for the guys who will go out there and play even though they are sick. You've got to like a guy like Jeff Geiger. Jeff, come up here and stand in front of the other fellas. Jeff came up to me before the game and told me he was sick. But goddammit, he went out there and proved it!'"

Davidson laughed through the receiver and could still picture

Geiger wilting as the room went wild. Kilrea relieved the pressure and the team went on to tie the game against the Sudbury Wolves and keep their unbeaten string alive. "He could have come in there and pointed at guys, singled them out," Davidson summarized. "Jeff was having a bad period, and by teasing him, Kilrea turned the situation in his favour."

Here was a busy lawyer, happy to reminisce about his favourite teacher, a man who had influenced him deeply. But there was work to do—that murder trial to prepare for—so he held back. He asked for his old teammate Doug Wilson's phone number in California so he could continue the discussion of Brian Kilrea at greater length when he had a little more time.

"I just loved the guy," Davidson said, before returning to his law books. "You are dealing with kids who are in some of the prime years of their lives. They are in school. A lot of coaches say these are the most difficult years and yet these are the years when he takes them and they excel under his guidance and direction. They grow from boys to men under that kind of direction."

Kilrea finally directed the Ottawa 67's to a Memorial Cup triumph in 1984, a decade after he had assumed the reins as coach. The mid- to late 1970s saw some very good teams, particularly in the era of Bobby Smith, Doug Wilson and the prolific scorer Peter Lee. The team had only one appearance, though, in the Memorial Cup tournament, which brings together the best junior teams from the Ontario Hockey League, the Quebec Major Junior League and the always competitive Western Hockey League. At the cross-country showdown of the most promising talent in the country, Kilrea's team had come up short in 1977 against Ernie "Punch" McLean's Bruins, who were playing on familiar ice in Vancouver.

Seven years later, the historic chase for the Memorial Cup convened at Kitchener's Memorial Auditorium. From Quebec came the Laval Voisins along with a marvel named Mario Lemieux; the WHL was represented by the Kamloops Junior Oilers; and the host

Kitchener Rangers brought star forwards John Tucker and Wayne Presley to the equation. Lemieux's team was a non-factor in round-robin play while Ottawa and Kamloops moved on to the sudden death semi and the right to play the Rangers, who had dominated Ottawa 7–2 in the first meeting between the two clubs.

The 67's beat Kamloops 5–2 in spite of a key injury to the team's stellar defenceman Brad Shaw. In the final, a big eighteen-year-old forward named Adam Creighton took over and Ottawa romped to the championship with a 7–2 drubbing of the Rangers. Despite the crowd's taunts, his boys triumphed, and Kilrea must have marvelled at their resilience. Adam Creighton dominated and was chosen as the All-Star centre in spite of Mario Lemieux's presence. The coach had scored his biggest victory behind the bench.

That same season he had coached the Team Canada juniors at the World Championship in Sweden; he had been selected based on the mid-campaign performance of his outstanding Ottawa team. Included in the lineup were his club's best three defencemen: Brad Shaw, Bruce Cassidy and Mark Paterson. The goaltending was good because of the presence of future NHLers Ken Wregget and Allan Bester. Skilled forwards Russ Courtnall (right wing) and Kirk Muller (left wing) provided the scoring punch but there was a notable no-show. Although Kilrea paid Mario Lemieux a visit, Lemieux, who was about to become the record-setting sniper of Laval, chose to stay with his club team on the advice of its owner. Kilrea had no hard feelings because he understood the player's personal aspirations to shatter team and league marks for scoring in his draft year. Canada wound up fourth at the tournament, the only time Kilrea has been the coach.

The period following the Memorial Cup in the spring of 1984 marked a watershed in the behind-the-bench career of Brian Kilrea. He had been approached by and accepted a position with the NHL New York Islanders as the assistant coach to Al Arbour. The understanding was that Arbour, quickly becoming a legendary figure in coaching circles, was getting set to step down and assume more management responsibilities. Within a year or two Brian Kilrea was to be the coach of the team that had won four consecutive Stanley Cups at the outset of the 1980s. The team included future Hall of Famers Mike Bossy, Denis Potvin and Brian Trottier as well as perennial stars like Clark Gillies and John Tonelli.

"Everyone goes and they want to have a challenge," Kilrea reflected on the experience, which lasted two seasons. "I hadn't been looking to go because I had had other offers and turned them down. But this time I guess it was right. So I went. When I got there, I really enjoyed the players."

He watched in awe as the superstars still with the Islanders responded to every demand made by coach Arbour. "Al Arbour ran a practice and they did whatever he wanted, no questions at all," Kilrea recalled. "Whatever the rules that were set, they were abided by. If there were curfews they were adhered to. They operated as a group."

Kelly Hrudey was a young goaltender with the Islanders during the two years that Kilrea was coaching in the National Hockey League. He played behind another Hall of Famer named Billy Smith and was a product of the WHL Medicine Hat Tigers, where he had been coached by tough ex–Flin Flon Bomber "Paddy" Ginelle. "I always felt like I could talk to him," Hrudey remarked of Kilrea. "But what was odd about it was that I had never had a coach like that before so I didn't know for sure. I always thought that he was too good to be true."

Kelly Hrudey and many of the younger Islanders had never witnessed a coach like Brian Kilrea. Many of them had come from the west and heard positive stories about Killer in that he was a strict but fair man who treated the players with respect. "It was better than fiction when I met him," Hrudey maintained. "I didn't think that it was possible that a coach could behave that way and have success. With him it worked fine." But Kilrea's approach, which was based on knowing and understanding the needs of players as human beings, was proving a foreign commodity in the NHL.

The Islanders had always maintained a distance between management and players. Al Arbour did not socialize, even with his superstars. Kilrea did. He played in a bowling league on Tuesday afternoons with the players and their spouses and was a key member of the championship team alongside forward Greg Gilbert and Hrudey's wife, Donna. The general manager of the hockey team, Bill Torrey, quietly informed Kilrea that this was something Al Arbour would never do.

The players warmed to the new member of the coaching staff. One Christmas a bunch of them finished their carolling at the Kilreas' Long Island home. Brian and Judy invited them in for refreshments—more songs were sung, apparently deep into the night.

"What a thing! The New York Islanders, out here singing carols!" Killer's eyes lit up at the thought of it. "The management didn't think it was good. They told me that Al Arbour had never had a player in his home. He wouldn't have wanted that. I said to myself that he was missing something because these are the guys that have to play for you."

Hrudey suffered the wrath of Arbour for his participation in the Christmas festivities at Kilrea's house. It was made clear to the impressionable netminder that this was not how coaches and players related at the NHL level. "Al Arbour called me Santa Claus for two weeks after that," Hrudey chuckled. "It was because I was carolling and having a great time and also because I went to the assistant coach's house. To top it off I played poorly against the Pittsburgh Penguins soon after. To go one step further, a player Al really didn't like at all, Mike Bullard, scored a hat trick. I was doomed!"

It didn't work for Kilrea as it was supposed to in New York. Al Arbour stayed on the job and it soon became obvious that the accomplished junior coach from Ottawa would not assume full control with the Islanders. At the end of the 1986–87 season, a team banquet was held, and Kilrea was asked by the players to sit with them, instead of at the head table with management. He gladly did so and informed his wife, Judy, that they should pack their bags. They were going back to Ottawa.

In retrospect, Kelly Hrudey was mystified by Kilrea's failure at the highest level of professional hockey, considering his ability as a teacher and his intuition where people were concerned. "I don't know if he was out of place but the theory he believed in was," Hrudey concluded. "In the NHL, you couldn't be close. You couldn't have any compassion for the guys. It was all business and you had to distance yourself. At least, that was the theory everybody was working on. Who knows? Maybe Brian was the one who was right."

———

At the end of the second period a dark mood grips the Civic Centre. Festivity has turned to frustration in the stands and in the catacombs where Brian Kilrea and the Ottawa 67's lurk. They cling to a one-goal lead over a team they know they are superior to. The score is 2–1, and the coach is pacing in front of his silent players.

"We're guilty of not looking," he announces. "Look at your man!"

He fiddles for a moment at the board on the wall. A fan whirrs, cooling the players gathered around. Turning to face them after a few moments of incomprehensible drawing, Kilrea looks up and holds the gaze of every individual in the room. "Hard work is the key," he says. "You'll have to match them inch for inch. Good teams win third periods." On cue the goalie stands and leads the rest to the door, like infantry marching to the front. The general and his staff follow.

"I'll talk to you later," I whisper to Kilrea.

"Perfect," he responds with a pump of his fist.

In the years following the NHL experience with the Islanders, Kilrea settled into the job that was meant for him. As manager and coach of the Ottawa 67's, he moulded a team that came to reflect his values of hard work and effort. "I like being hard on them because then they learn that it's not just a cakewalk," he said. "If they could run their own ship then they wouldn't be worth a darn because everyone needs discipline—the good player or the player that's going to go to school. You need discipline to keep up your marks whether you are going to be a lawyer or a doctor. It's the same for a hockey player. You have to be disciplined in your time and your approach to the game. Sure, you may not like it all the time, but you'll respect it in the end."

In the end, he could not keep every player that skated for his team, could not find a way to connect with each one and drive them to their ultimate potential on and off the ice. Good teachers admit they cannot reach every student. "I've told someone who wants to walk off the ice that he should remember the door swings one way. If he walks off he won't be coming back," Kilrea warned. "If I lose interest in a guy then I may as well trade him because I don't know if we'll patch it up."

Chris Simon may have been one of those players. The big forward from Wawa, Ontario, is an Ojibwa and currently plays for the Washington Capitals of the NHL. He won a Stanley Cup with the Colorado Avalanche in 1996 and is one of the more imposing forces in the game, engaging in a rugged and intimidating brand of physical hockey. In 1991, after three full seasons with the junior team in Ottawa, Brian Kilrea traded Simon to the Sault Ste. Marie Greyhounds two games into the new campaign.

"He got to the point where he lost a bit of control," Kilrea remembered. "He gained weight, couldn't keep it down. He got hurt, and he wasn't doing the things that he should be doing to get himself in better condition. I called Ted Nolan because there wasn't anything else I could do for Chris."

Ted Nolan, another native, was the coach of the Greyhounds at the time, where Kilrea believed Simon would be better served. "I thought if I could get him back to the Sault, which is closer to Wawa, he could be better off," Kilrea explained. "His dad could go back and forth and he could get himself straightened out."

It worked but not without time and effort. Nolan reached Simon on a level that Kilrea recognized he could not. The draft choice of the Philadelphia Flyers responded to the change of scenery with 44 points in the final thirty-one junior games of his career. He had an excellent playoff season and became part of a large package of players who were traded by the Flyers organization to the Quebec Nordiques for the highly coveted Eric Lindros. Simon has always credited Brian Kilrea's trade with his ability to succeed.

For his part, Kilrea remains satisfied that he did the right thing for Simon. Even though Simon went on to play for a rival team, the traded player made something of his life. "You see this big tough kid who has turned his life around. Now he's a National Leaguer and a friend," Kilrea said, with obvious pride. "Matter of fact, he invited me to his wedding."

Michael Peca is the captain of the Buffalo Sabres and one of the best defensive forwards in all of hockey. A winner of the Frank Selke Trophy in 1997, Peca was traded from Sudbury to Kilrea's 67's during his second junior season of 1991–92. A winger with the Wolves, Peca was a moderate point producer who was able to blossom offensively once he got to Ottawa. Kilrea gave the left winger a new position and added to his duties by making him one of the leaders of the team.

"Killer seemed to think that centre was my natural position and that's where he played me," Peca said. "I played with Curtis Bowen and Grant Marshall and he gave us a lot of responsibility. We were the second line at the time and he put us in a lot of key situations in every game. It allowed us to develop."

This is central to Kilrea's coaching philosophy—the notion that the players must assume responsibility for the outcome of their hockey careers and down the road, their lives in general. As a teacher, he refuses to manipulate the young men in order to reach personal goals. His approach is reflected in how he thinks about people and the joy he draws from hockey, which is much more than the final score. "This is not a calculated game. It's not a game won or lost because the coach can plot the best defence or the best trap or the best whatever," Kilrea said firmly. "They just come to the rink and go. They don't care about anything but going out and playing well."

Kilrea believes that enthusiasm is harnessed when players are forced to take responsibility by an interested coach who breaks down barriers so that potential can be reached. "Such as Peca, now that you mention him," Kilrea remarked. "He's out there playing as a left winger with a right-hand shot. He was playing the left wing on the fourth line for awhile. When we got him we told him to go and play at centre. The next year we knew we had a starter on our hands."

Peca remains deeply loyal to Kilrea. He has been coached by exceptional tutors of the game—winners of the Jack Adams Trophy as NHL coach of the year, Pat Quinn and Ted Nolan. Peca admires them all but calls the Ottawa 67's leader the best he has been associated with. "At that point in my development it was so important for me to have him as a coach," Peca emphasized. "I think he genuinely cares about you beyond being a player. He takes a lot of interest in the kids' lives, the schooling, the way they behave and everything else. It enables you to mature as a young man, which translates into allowing you to become more mature as a hockey player."

I travel the rink in the third period of the game between Peterborough and Ottawa. Sit in the penalty box for part of it and watch Kilrea from across the glistening white ice. I watch him across the skate marks and through the buzzing players—the crushing bodychecks, which shake and rattle the boards. He paces up and down behind the bench, watching his players. Tapping them on the shoulders, sending them into the fray, or leaning down, pointing to some trace of a play that occurred moments ago and talking urgently into a player's ear.

Sometimes, like a protective bear, Kilrea gets up on his haunches and roars at the referee. His eyes flashing, his rage directed at some injustice to his kids. The expletives resound across the rink. Suddenly it stops and the game continues, with Ottawa starting to pull away.

Miguel Delisle bursts from the penalty box. He had been in there again, for an extended period of time. "Take care, Miguel!" yells the penalty timekeeper as he flings open the gate. "He's been in here so long we're on a first-name basis. We've even been giving him Juicy Fruit!" Delisle wears a black eye as if it was an Olympic medal and crashes the boards, finds the puck and helps set up a third goal by the home team. The score now stands at 3–1 for Ottawa.

I make my way through the concourse where they swill beer and wolf hotdogs. A strange-looking puck-like mascot is cuddling little kids and shaking a big white paw at anyone who comes his way. Vendors are yelling, music is blaring, fans ooh and aah, which causes me to stop and crane my neck towards the ice. In fits and starts, I make my way to the far corner and the owner's box, where Jeff Hunt is hunkered down on this and most other winter Friday nights.

In the front row of a narrow and lofty space, the thirty-five-year-old owner of the Ottawa 67's is on pins and needles, not to mention the front of his cushioned seat. He took over the team at

the beginning of last season when it was at the bottom of the
league in terms of attendance. Before his arrival, Ottawa juniors
were drawing about 2,200 fans per game to the Civic Centre. The
club had the worst attendance record in the Ontario Hockey
League. This year attendance is up to 6,200 on average; the next
closest is 4,300.

In his first year, Hunt's team had by far the best record in the
OHL's regular season, and in spite of losing to the Belleville Bulls in
the playoffs they had won the right to host the Memorial Cup
tournament at the Civic Centre. Ottawa got to the final against the
Calgary Hitmen of the WHL and in a wild finish, claimed their first
championship since the 1984 season. For Hunt, an entrepreneur
who had not so long ago been in the carpet-cleaning business, the
first season was a blockbuster hit with a storybook ending.

"In this community, he *is* hockey," Hunt says in reference to
Brian Kilrea. "As a new owner coming in, the only hockey credi-
bility that stayed with the team was him. That allowed me to focus
strictly on the business and the marketing of the team and know
that the hockey side was well looked after."

Looking over the jubilant crowd as they celebrate quick goals
from Ian Jacobs and Vince Grant to make it 5–1 for the home team,
Hunt represents hockey's new breed. He's one of the executives
who understand that the national obsession has become entertainment by necessity. This rink, like many others, has begun to resem-
ble a pinball arcade with all the bells and whistles. There are
cheerleaders and a rock 'n' roll band in one section of the rink.
Giveaways, contests and merchandise on sale in every one of the
Civic Centre's nooks and crannies. So rare is the chance to hear the
sharp shout of a player as he craves a pass from his winger. Almost
extinct is the crack of the puck as it leaves the blade of a stick propelled to the net by a wicked slapshot.

Not lost on the young owner, however, is the wisdom of his
coach and the connection to a more established hockey heritage he

represents. "It's one of those things that grows with time," Hunt reckons. "I think initially the players are just scared of him. It's not devotion, but it develops into devotion."

Hunt interrupts the discussion to lean forward and watch helplessly as Peterborough scores a goal against Lavente Szuper, who has taken over for a flu-ridden Seamus Kotyk in the Ottawa net. Hunt slumps, shaking his head, but still seems satisfied because the game is almost over. He has done his homework. "Ottawa went to the OHL finals two or three times in a row and lost. Someone else always got to go to the Memorial Cup. Some people attributed that to Killer and his teams choking in the big games," Hunt explains. "But he gets them there in spite of the team. He gets every ounce of effort and success that's possible. He gets more than other teams who are better blessed. He can get them there."

In a way, Kilrea has become Hunt's trusted guide to the mystery of junior hockey. I recall that it was the owner who sat closest to Killer in the coach's room before the game. The younger man remained silent, puffed on a cigar and seemed to absorb the atmosphere as if he were a curious undergraduate attending a tutorial by a famous professor.

Now, as the final siren goes and Kilrea's team wins again, Jeff Hunt smiles and turns to exit the hockey theatre where he's the proprietor. He offers a final comment on the role of Brian Kilrea.

"Devotion is what you do when you don't have to do it," Hunt says. "Anywhere we go, guys drop in and the alumni comes by. Not just the big shots who are playing in the NHL and doing really well but the firemen and the guys who drive two hours out of their way just to go down and say hello to him before a game. That to me is devotion. They all respond to him on the bench because he demands it. But you think when they leave that would be the last you'd see of them. It's not the case. They keep coming back."

In the end, his 866th victory secure, Kilrea repairs to his room across the way from his players. He has a few beers, another cigar and people drift in. The talk is of the game and of hockey in general. Teenagers in drenched shirts laugh and joke with a man who is almost a half-century their senior and still their friend. The coach is only slightly reflective. "The generation gap is the gap that I'm afraid of," he says, staring across the hall to the dressing room. "When I don't have time to listen or to help a kid, then the gap is too big."

Dr. Peter Premachuck arrives with his grandson Paul. The Predictor cannot hide his glee as he scurries to hug Killer. The coach surrounds the little boy with welcoming arms and I recall the score of the game: Ottawa 5, Peterborough 2. If you count the disallowed goal, the five-year-old was bang on with his forecast of a 5–3 victory.

"Things always work out for the best," Kilrea had said before the opening faceoff. "I'm a great believer in that."

THE VOICE

Bob Ridley

He Tells the Tigers' Tale

(courtesy Bob Ridley)

❖ I HAD BEEN LOOKING FOR A play-by-play man in western Canada, someone I could call The Voice. Dennis Beyak, who calls the Toronto Maple Leafs games, steered me in the right direction. "Bob Ridley's your man," Beyak said, without a moment's hesitation. "He's been calling Medicine Hat Tigers games on CHAT radio since day one. All the way back to Lanny McDonald."

It sounded perfect. Beyak, of course, knew the score because he had been a television commentator with the Edmonton Oilers and was a native of the Prairies. In his previous hockey incarnation he had also managed in the Western Hockey League with the Seattle Thunderbirds and the Saskatoon Blades. "Rids, they call him," Beyak went on. "Really nice guy, gets so excited when he's at the microphone. Trevor Linden knows him really well."

The whole thing was starting to come together. Medicine Hat was the perfect setting—not too big and not too small. A city of about 50,000 tucked into the southeastern corner of Alberta, minutes from the Saskatchewan border and devoted to hockey. The Tigers had always been a junior franchise of some distinction and were playing their thirtieth WHL season. The Hat's team had been competitive from the get go, featuring the likes of future Hall of Famer Lanny McDonald and sniper Tom Lysiak. They had played a rugged brand of hockey popularized by Bob Gassoff and while they didn't win it, they challenged for the Memorial Cup in junior hockey's heyday in the early 1970s.

In the 1980s it only got better for Medicine Hat. A series of good goaltenders and players like the rangy forward Trevor Linden took them to consecutive Canadian junior championships in 1987 and 1988. A young Barry Melrose, who piloted the Los Angeles Kings to the Stanley Cup final in 1993 against Montreal, was at the helm in Medicine Hat when the Tigers surprised the powerful Windsor Spitfires and captured their second crown. Throughout its three decades, Medicine Hat's team had enjoyed a notable cast of characters.

Bob Ridley was the heart of the story. Ridley and others like him deliver the game play-by-play to the home front without benefit of pictures or computer-generated graphics. The images he creates with words bring the game right into the living room, the diner on Main Street, the cattle barn and, most magically of all, the kids' bedroom. The radio drama, fading in and out on a cold Canadian winter's night, is most people's immediate connection to their team and favourite players. It's hockey's version of the fireside chat, a throwback to a time when imaginations ran wild and the sport was larger than life.

Nowadays, every time the Toronto Maple Leafs play, they do so on television. Eighty-two times a year, at home and on the road, in Montreal or in Phoenix, they look pretty much the same as they did the night before. Rarely do viewers get any sense of the game taking place in a strange and distant place.

On Sunday nights throughout my childhood I would retreat to my bedroom not long after supper was over and the dishes cleared. I remember the old General Electric AM clock radio on the nightstand and my father's knowing glance as he switched the light off after tucking me in. I was fooling not a soul. One Sunday, the Maple Leafs and Blackhawks were in Chicago for the final game of their weekend set. Toronto had won at the Gardens the night before and now they were in the city of Al Capone to try to tame the Hawks for a second straight night.

Foster Hewitt was the voice. His delivery came across high-pitched and urgent from the huge American metropolis. The roar of the crowd crackled across the airwaves, as the swashbuckling home team dashed into the Leafs' end zone. The signal on CKFH weakened from time to time—almost always, it seemed, when the big gunners like Bobby Hull and Ken Wharram unloaded on Johnny Bower or Terry Sawchuk in the Leafs net. After some frantic fiddling with the knobs, Hewitt's commentary would return to me. "Keon has the puck at centre ice . . . Moose Vasko heads him off. . . ." Desperate for the score, I'd sweat it out, alone and with the covers pulled over my head, until: "No score with eight minutes left in the first! You're listening to Toronto Maple Leafs hockey."

Inevitably, I would fall asleep with Hewitt's play-by-play in the background. Bob Pulford, Ron Ellis and the rest of my favourite players skated against the Chicago gangsters with the same right-eousness as Eliot Ness in the *Untouchables*. I always left the action lulled into slumber not by any sense of boredom but instead by the conviction that, in my dreams, the heroic Leafs would always pre-vail. Hewitt made them seem that good, his descriptive accounts as valuable to their fortunes as the speed of any right winger.

The radio play-by-play man becomes an extension of the team. He has a captive audience at home and provides a lifeline for the devoted fans whose general happiness in the coming days depends on a win, a narrow loss or, at the very least, a valiant effort.

———

"Just describe what's happening," said Rod Phillips, the radio voice of the Edmonton Oilers. "That's the challenge of the job. That's the fun part of radio. To paint the picture of what's happening." Phillips has spent twenty-seven years doing the Oilers broadcasts. During his tenure he has never missed a game and has covered more than 2,500 contests, including five Stanley Cup triumphs. By his voice, Albertans listening to twenty-four stations in smaller cen-tres like Cold Lake, Peace River, Wetaskiwin and Stettler have learned of the exploits of Wayne Gretzky, Mark Messier and all the great Edmonton players. Always, he has made them sound like vir-tuous crusaders—even during the dark times when they were los-ing. "We don't have a mass audience from coast to coast with fans backing different teams," Phillips argued. "Our listeners are Oilers fans. That's what they want to hear and that's what we give them."

It sounds, on the surface, like being the mouthpiece for the team. But there's another way to calculate the value of each club's broadcaster—one that reveals the connection between the game and the people who patronize it. Phillips was born in Edmonton and raised in Calmar, thirty miles southwest of the Alberta capital. He wrinkled his brow, considering his unwavering devotion to the Oilers over the years. "You can never be part of the team," he explained. "There are the coaches and twenty-three guys that are the team. But we're about as close to the team as the fans are able to get."

A messenger to carry the story home. Rod Phillips and others like him in the ranks of NHL broadcasters enjoy a substantial and diverse audience. The Edmonton Oilers are followed throughout the province, and Phillips is somewhat of a celebrity in Alberta. But I was looking for a less familiar voice. One that reached fewer ears but was intensely loyal to a faithful core of fans. I was searching for the only voice a particular hockey team could count on to get the story back to safety from across enemy lines.

"Bob Ridley's the one," Dennis Beyak had assured me, and it made sense. Ridley, I was informed, did it all for Medicine Hat's team when he was in the booth in Brandon, Manitoba, in Spokane, Washington, or any of a dozen rinks in the west. Indeed, he'd been the play-by-play man for their entire history—a combination of devotion and continuity that was extremely enviable.

"Oh, and one other thing about Ridley," Beyak added, almost as an afterthought. "He drives the team bus, too." This story was rounding into shape, like finding the right frequency on the radio.

———

At eleven o'clock on a Friday morning, the Medicine Hat Arena is all but deserted except for an enormous gold passenger bus stationed by the back entrance. It had been delicately and expertly inched into position over the crunchy white snow. "It's a Prevost

H355," the diminutive driver is saying as he lifts the door to one of two cavernous storage lockers built into the belly of the vehicle. "It's a charter and she'll cruise at about 110 to 115 clicks an hour. At least, that's what we're supposed to say."

Looking full of mischief, Bob Ridley whistles a little tune as he checks out his rig. It's cold but he's wearing a white short-sleeved dress shirt and a blue sweater-vest with his necktie done neatly in a half-Windsor knot. He has a full head of wiry grey hair and gold-rimmed glasses. The bus bears the name TOTEM on both side panels. It's the same word that's been stitched into his vest.

The boys are arriving—one by one—from inside the rink. Dragging their feet over the snow and with black equipment bags hanging from each shoulder, they proceed in silent, slow motion. Jay Bouwmeester is only sixteen and one of the hottest prospects in all of hockey. A big blond defenceman, Bouwmeester hails from Edmonton and is learning the ways of the west on the Tigers' bus. "He's going to be a good one," Ridley states.

Bouwmeester nods on his way aboard. "Hey, Rids," he salutes the driver.

"Good to have you back, Jay," is Ridley's response. He's referring to Bouwmeester's solid performance at the recent World Junior Championships in Sweden, where he starred for the Canadian team in a bronze medal effort.

The rest of the Tigers clan is loading up all that a hockey team needs to make it self-sufficient over the next sixteen hours. Four players tote a big black box, which contains wads of tape and tools to work over the hockey sticks until they are just so. Another couple of skaters handle the bundled sticks. Trainer Dale King and the physical therapist, Rick Carter, gingerly tiptoe another packed trunk to the threshold of the cargo bay. "Medicine Hat Tigers. Please Handle with Care" is the message written neatly in black marker on the top. "Your skates depend on it." The staff handles the sharpening machine with surgical expertise.

More bags follow—Ridley himself is lugging a couple of large briefcases up the stairs to the other side of his cushioned seat on the far left of the vehicle. His radio equipment is inside: all the wires, microphones, notes, statistics and recording machines he'll require once the Tigers get to their destination. On this day, they are headed north to Red Deer via Calgary, in order to play the first of back-to-back games with the Rebels. By Western Hockey League standards it's a short trip. Five hours of driving there . . . play the game . . . drive the five hours back and be ready to take on the same team the next night in Medicine Hat. To me, it sounds like a marathon.

The goalie, number 30, is Kyle Kettles of Lac du Bonnet, Manitoba. He is quirky but good, having played well at this year's WHL All-Star Game in Kelowna, B.C.—one of very few Tigers on the roster. Wearing a toque and sporting an overcoat, he's decided to travel in the tie and jacket that coaches prefer as road attire. Kettles chucks his bag underneath and waltzes aboard, armed with a couple of pillows and a sleeping bag. Over his toque he's forced his Discman's earphones and, oblivious to the others, he quietly finds his window seat in anticipation of some solitude. "He's a neat guy," Ridley says in a sort of running commentary. "You should see him warm up just before they go on the ice. He flaps his arms like a giant bird getting ready to take off. It's pretty bizarre!"

Arriving last are the coaches. The boss, Rick Carriere, and his assistant, Randy Wong, are all business as they adopt the ritualistic positioning common to most hockey teams on the road. Carriere, looking like a Marine with a brush cut and starched white shirt, bounds aboard and parks himself in the first seat over what will be Ridley's right shoulder. Wong, a younger and smaller man, slips into his spot across the aisle.

This is the signal that the Tigers are prepared to travel. Ridley secures the barn doors on the storage compartments and checks the tires on all eight wheels. "You need at least a number 2 licence," he explains as he dusts off his hands. "That, and I have to have a medical every two years in order to drive the bus."

Before he ascends to the driver's seat, the vantage point closest to the road on this two-tiered luxury liner, Bob Ridley squints into the clear blue sky and sweeps his foot lightly over the snow crystals, which match the colour of his hair. It's a great day to make the trip and the open highway has him in a relaxed state of mind. "If the roads don't look good, we just don't go. We'll play the game later," Ridley offers. "You can always play the game but you can never replace the kids."

When your cargo is the young people who play hockey, you've got a special level of trust. The driver of this bus is fifty-four with a wife, a son and two daughters of his own. The twenty-one players who sit behind him are confident of his concern for their well-being. The boys are between sixteen and twenty years of age and full of hope—each generation of Medicine Hat Tigers as important as the previous and as ambitious as the next. The younger ones sit in tandem, the veteran players take solo seats near the rear washroom.

Bob eases himself into the hydraulic driver's seat and adjusts the cushion. He checks the mirrors, then turns the key, and the diesel engine roars to life. His freckled hands grip the steering wheel, which looks to be two feet in diameter, showing off the two giant-sized gold rings from the Memorial Cup wins by the Tigers in the late 1980s. "You guys ready to rock 'n' roll?" he barks. Some of the teenagers have already tipped baseball caps over their eyes on the way to a game-day nap. Ridley silently answers his own query, releases the brake and swings bus number 805 towards the Trans-Canada Highway.

It is three hours from Medicine Hat, in the east of the province, to the Stampede City. Just before reaching the outskirts of Calgary, Rick Carriere has scheduled a stop for the team's midday meal. In Strathmore, the Tigers will fuel up for the game at Red Deer's glossy rink, the Centrium. They'll also meet to go over certain tendencies of the Rebels—on the power play and when they are shorthanded.

This fifty-six seater is a luxury for the Tigers. Back when Bob Ridley first joined the fledgling team from Medicine Hat at the outset of the 1970s, they had an old grey military troop transporter that was a lot like a school bus. It was tough making those long journeys to Brandon and cold beyond belief. The Tigers management experimented with chartering for awhile and then they decided after a couple of years to buy their own vehicle. It was an ancient silver Greyhound. "It had about a million miles on it but they didn't know who was going to drive the stupid thing," Ridley chuckles. "They asked if I could relieve the hired driver a little bit to help out. I had operated some farm machinery, so I said sure. Obviously I was kind of snookered because they thought I did such a good job that I've been doing it ever since."

He has a model of the old bus in his house on Higdon Avenue in Medicine Hat. It was painted with a wide orange stripe, and "Medicine Hat Tigers" was printed neatly in huge black letters on both sides. "We called it the Iron Lung," Bob says, with some lingering fondness. The bus was retired a few years ago and now its likeness is mounted on a plaque, a commemorative gift from an earlier edition of the Tigers. "To Bob Ridley. For Being There When We Needed You," reads the inscription.

"The shitter smelled so bad," recalled Kelly Hrudey, a goalie for the Tigers in the late 1970s and early '80s. "It took us an hour to get used to the smell." Still, the Iron Lung became a special place for Hrudey, who went on to star for the New York Islanders, Los Angeles Kings and San Jose Sharks through fifteen NHL seasons. "It was perfect for me," he reckoned. "Even though you are in a small and confined area with twenty-five other guys, you actually get an opportunity to have some time to yourself. I'd look out the window and think about hockey and the game."

There is plenty of time. A few hay bales are left stranded in the fields. Dusted by the snow, they recede in the wake of the bus as it makes the turn off Deerfoot Trail and proceeds north on Highway 2 bound for Edmonton—Red Deer being somewhere in the middle. The light is fading now and the silhouettes of hockey players are framed against the deepening azure sky. The Medicine Hat Tigers are a very young team with nine sixteen-year-olds in their lineup. They are in last place in the WHL's Eastern Conference, having won only thirteen of the forty-four games they've played, but they have tremendous potential.

Berkeley Buchko sits in the back of the bus, the senior Tiger in age and experience, wearing a white shirt and tie, black horn-rimmed glasses. Buchko's travelled this highway for four seasons. "After you're on the road for a week, you can start getting sick of each other," he deadpans. "I mean, it's just like family. You love 'em and you hate 'em."

Berkeley is a twenty-year-old centreman who has not yet been drafted by an NHL club. The captain of the Tigers will almost assuredly not get a chance to be part of a championship team but he's weathered more storms and learned more than anyone on the Medicine Hat bus, with the exception, that is, of Bob Ridley. Buchko says, "He's been around a long time and that kind of experience helps the young guys."

Red Deer is not far off now. A few seats to the front, Denny Johnston of Rosetown, Saskatchewan, is scrambling to get out of his travelling clothes and into the jacket and tie he's brought along in a suit bag. "We've had a couple of close calls when he's had to jam on the brakes," the seventeen-year-old says when asked about Ridley. "But he's a mighty good driver and we feel safe with him."

Johnston's words startle me a little. Watching Bob Ridley focused on the road ahead, the damp and glistening blacktop stretching to the horizon, I reflect on the heavy responsibility he carries. Young and talented players have faith in his ability to get them to this and every game.

In December, 1986, a similar bus carrying the Swift Current Broncos to a game against the rival Regina Pats swerved off the road in bad weather. The accident cost the lives of four players—Trent Kresse, Scott Kruger, Chris Mantyka and Brent Ruff—and left the Broncos and the Western Hockey League in shock. The community of Swift Current rallied around the young franchise, which survived to win the Memorial Cup less than three years later.

It is an incident not lost on Bob Ridley. He never takes his hands off the wheel, nor does he avert his eyes from the seemingly endless road ahead. Bob does not dwell on the possibility of a mishap, preferring to treat the whole process as a rite of passage for the players. He is there to be an experienced guide. "Many of the guys come up to the spot beside me and chat. You get to know these people inside out, what makes them tick," he explains. "These guys spend hours and days and months on the bus together. I think they are better people for it. It helps them develop character and gives them a feel for what it takes to be a successful hockey player because you can't just play at home. You've got to play on the road too."

Trevor Linden of the Montreal Canadiens, a native of Medicine Hat, rode on Ridley's bus in the late 1980s. He was an essential part of the two Memorial Cup championship teams before being drafted second overall by the Vancouver Canucks in the spring of 1988. Linden's eyes lit up when I mentioned Ridley and inquired about his worth to the Tigers. The star player laughed when I explained I'd be taking a round trip to Red Deer with the team. Linden stressed that the real litmus test was a much longer voyage. "For example, we'd be in Brandon on a cold and stormy night," Linden recalled. "Bob would do the play-by-play of the game, then he'd load up his Thermos and drive us back to Medicine Hat, which is a twelve-hour ride. We'd get to the high school, he'd stop and drop us off and that would be the end of his day. Of course, we all slept in the back of the bus or did homework, and there was Bob all by himself driving."

The neon lights of the local A&W and the Esso station signal the proximity of Red Deer and the awaiting Rebels. Chris St. Jacques, a Val Kilmer look-alike, is swaying to the beat of "Shiny Tunes #4" blaring through his headset. There are players here from several provinces and from the United States and the Czech Republic as well as Slovakia. All of them must have parents in distant places, no doubt concerned about their well-being.

Rick Carriere is going over some last-minute notes before the bus pulls into the Centrium. He has run the hockey operation in Medicine Hat for the past three seasons and is counting on his planning to come to fruition as the young players mature. Now forty, Carriere played in the WHL with the Saskatoon Blades before a short career in the Eastern Professional Hockey League. A graduate of the University of Alberta, he skated for one of hockey's great collegiate mentors, Clare Drake of the Golden Bears, while earning a degree in education. Carriere considers himself a teacher and knows his role in these kids' lives has a certain amount of gravity. He also knows he couldn't succeed without Bob Ridley.

"When I got to Medicine Hat I found out what a great individual he was, not only as a human being but what a great bus driver he was also," Carriere says. "It's a big asset to have the comfort of knowing that you're going to get to the game every time."

Bob Ridley reverses the purring Prevost down the ramp at the Red Deer rink. The warning beeps pierce the silence as the boys await their release and the nervous routine of the dressing room. They arrive for the game well fed and well prepared. It's a necessity if they are to perform to their potential. Someone who cares has brought them here and is about to continue the telling of their story before transporting them home again.

"Kids are naive and don't know what can go wrong. It's the

parents who entrust Bob with their children," Kelly Hrudey had told me. "That's why you know he's good because so many parents have had faith in him over the years. They know that he's going to get those kids home safely."

The pace is frenetic and it's still an hour or so until game time at the glistening Centrium. A smaller version of the Saddledome in Calgary, the rink seats about six thousand, with room to expand into the luxurious open concourses. There are pale green seats and banners, proclaiming the arena as a world-class facility for more than just one sport. The 1995 World Junior Hockey Championship was held here. Another big year was 1994, when the Centrium hosted Skate Canada International as well as the curling Briar.

The Tigers quickly grab their equipment bags and hustle down the hall to the locker room. Bob Ridley abandons the bus in the garage by the ice machine's entrance, but only for a few moments. He snags those two black briefcases and half runs to the staircase beyond the Rebels dressing room and the office of their coach/manager/owner, Brent Sutter.

From there, Bob huffs his way up three sections of steps underneath the stands until he emerges in the upper concourse. Still moving, he turns the corner by the pizza concession and climbs the concrete bleachers until he arrives at the door to the press box just underneath the steel girders of the Centrium's roof. Flinging open the door, Ridley rushes to the countertop that overlooks centre ice. The bags are placed down, unzipped and emptied of their contents in a matter of seconds. Ridley unravels the spaghetti-like wires of microphones, phone lines and headsets and plugs them into a black metal box. Soon, a series of flashing green and yellow lights are dancing on the front of the commentator box. He's getting a level as he dons the earphones. "Test . . . test . . . test," he chants. "You're listening to Tigers hockey on New Country 1270 CHAT."

After a quick call to the station back in Medicine Hat, Bob extracts a stack of statistics from one of his bags. They are the game notes prepared by the Rebels public relations staff. Included in the package are the lineups of the two teams that will take the ice tonight. He also has charts on everything from the scoring leaders in the Western Hockey League to the schedule in the weeks to come. There is an injury update along with a numerical roster featuring each player's birthday and his hometown. All of it becomes valuable information to Ridley as he builds his homespun commentary on the impending game.

None of the notes are his own and he has not read them in any great detail. I watch as he takes the staple out, fingers through the papers, and then tapes them securely to the blank white wall on his left. There must be twenty sheets of typing up there—almost impossible to decipher. "I just tend to make it up as I go along. They call it 'winging it.' That's how I was brought up in the industry," says the graduate of Calgary's Mount Royal College. He has a diploma in broadcast arts and has worked for years as the sports director at CHAT radio and television in Medicine Hat. "If I was to make a bunch of notes I'd just forget what they said and so I just kind of go with my background, plus the fact that I know what these kids are all about, and I take it from there." Knowing what the Tigers are all about has come, at least partially, from spending all those hours on the bus with generations of young players.

Suddenly, Ridley is reminded of his next pre-game duty. Grabbing his portable tape recorder and stick microphone, he hurriedly leaves the broadcast booth to get to the garage. Bus #805 has to be started up and repositioned outside in the windswept parking lot at the back of the rink. It will get bitterly cold, and the pre-heater has to be engaged. On the frostiest of evenings, Bob will keep the vehicle idling during the entire three hours it takes for a typical hockey game to unfold. He has learned to leave nothing to chance.

———

Stopping by the media room, I grab a quick coffee and doughnut, thankful for a moment to chat with Kelly Hrudey, who has made the trip from his home in Calgary to watch his former team play. The young and excitable broadcaster for Rebels radio is there as well. Cam Moon played briefly in net for the Tigers in 1989–90 and subsequently in Saskatoon with the junior Blades. Wide-eyed and effervescent, Moon is climbing the ladder in the broadcasting world, having graduated to Red Deer a couple of years ago following a three-year stint calling play-by-play for the Nanaimo Clippers of the B.C. junior league.

"It may worry the odd person," Moon ruminates on the subject of Bob Ridley's workload. "I mean, people must be wondering if this guy gets any sleep at all."

Moon is keenly aware of radio's vital role in junior hockey, particularly in the west. "It's the only link that there is to the fans when the team is on the road." He has come to understand how influential the hockey broadcaster can be in a hockey-mad centre in the province of Alberta. "I'm sure Bob Ridley is considered part of the family for most people in Medicine Hat," Moon suggests. "They refer to him on a first-name basis whether they know him or not. They feel they know him, you see, because they've heard him on radio."

Moon is about to excuse himself as he is in the middle of preparation for the pre-game show. He and the show's host, something that Bob Ridley does not have the luxury of, are in the process of assembling the starting lineups and will soon conduct a call-in contest awarding various prizes to the winners. The money's not great but it's play-by-play and it's the Western Hockey League, possibly a small step away from the NHL and the big time. Still, Cam Moon says there's more allure to this whole scenario than just the hope of moving on. It's what keeps Bob Ridley going too.

"It means he's proud of the Medicine Hat Tigers and he's proud of the city of Medicine Hat," Moon concludes. "It's important in

this league that play-by-play people are proud of their cities and of
their teams. I'm sure if Bob wasn't proud of both of them that he
wouldn't have been there that long."

Kelly and I go looking for Bob and are told that he's down by
the Tigers dressing room. Styrofoam coffee cups in hand—they
seem to be mandatory for access to hockey's inner circles—we proceed through the bright hallways underneath the grandstands. Players in cutoff underwear are passing pucks back and forth on the
slippery concrete floor.

Thwak . . . thwak, and then the hissing sound as the jet-black
discs travel distances of maybe ten yards between receptive
wooden blades. The nimble centreman, Ryan Hollweg, a trans-
planted Californian, is naked except for boxer shorts bearing the
Stars and Stripes. Muscular and sporting tattoos on both shoulders, he's playing a mind game with the Rebel players who are
just down the line, pelting tennis balls against the wall in order to
refine their reaction time and dexterity. There is intense activity
as the young hockey players gradually build momentum to the
opening faceoff.

We are invited into the Red Deer coach's quarters to exchange
a few words with Brent Sutter, who assumes every major position
in Red Deer's junior hockey universe. Sutter is one of six brothers
who made it to the National Hockey League from the tiny town of
Viking, about an hour and a half northeast of here. He played a
total of eighteen seasons, at the end of his career with the Chicago
Blackhawks and before that the New York Islanders, where he and
Kelly were teammates. In his second year of retirement, he has
managed to purchase the Red Deer franchise at a reported cost of
$3 million. He is commited to ensuring the continued health of
hockey in this region of the province.

He talks about the bus rides of his youth while playing for the
Lethbridge team. "We didn't have a shitter on our bus," Sutter
scoffs at Kelly's complaint about the old Iron Lung. "In fact, we

pissed out the window more often that not. If we lost, there was no choice because the coach sure wasn't stopping!"

———

"You're playing 500 in your last three games and that certainly has to give you a lift heading into this weekend's series with Red Deer." It's as much an encouraging statement of fact as it is a question. Ridley has the microphone thrust towards the coach, Rick Carriere, and is conducting the self-contained pre-game interview, which will run as CHAT's pre-game show immediately before the puck drop. "Yeah, we've got Red Deer this weekend and Kootenay next weekend, so we feel they are very important for us," Carriere begins to respond. "We want to come up with a big effort tonight and go home with some momentum for the game tomorrow."

It is a wonderful scene—the bus driver, a shorter earnest man, in quiet conversation with the beleaguered coach of a struggling team. They stand among the tattered spare nets in the bowels of a rink a long way from home. Still, this little dialogue will help to reassure the fans, five hours away in The Hat, that things are looking up for the Tigers. The pre-game pep talk is just around the corner and so Ridley wraps it up. "All right, looking forward to it. Have a great game against the Red Deer Rebels," he offers to Carriere. "Thanks a lot, Rids," are the coach's final words into the microphone.

Carriere ushers his friend to the broadcast booth before making his own way to the dressing room. "You know, I've never actually heard him do the play-by-play," Carriere admits. "I'm always on the bench, you know. Maybe I'll have to get it recorded or put an ear piece in so I can listen during the game. I do know this," the coach continues. "It's been a tough year for us and he's been there all the way. He helps me through game after game. Always thinks of the positive things and better times."

"Got any snow at home yet?" Bob is making the connection with Mike the technician back at the radio studios in Medicine Hat. He is comfortably seated to the far left of the booth, awaiting the national anthem in Red Deer. It's a good house, maybe 4,500 to 5,000 fans in the building. With a coffee cup in his right hand, he makes a little wave with his left to the official scorers and public address announcer seated beyond a small Plexiglas window in a room just like his. He's waiting now because the interview with the coach, taped earlier, is running back home.

Downstairs, Medicine Hat's team is assembling outside its dressing room. In single file and clad in white sweaters with orange and black trim, the players stride to the chute that leads to the ice. Goalie Kyle Kettles is at the front of the Tigers pack. Stitched to his chest is the head of a Bengal in full roar. I am reminded of Ridley's words as Kettles begins to flap his giant padded arms in some weird warm-up routine. The others stand back just a little, seemingly unaffected by their netminder's display.

Just across the way, the boys from Red Deer appear in a parallel formation. Sinister getups make them look a little bigger than they really are. A dominating black and blood red are the colours. On the front is the huge crest of the team: a sort of skull and crossbones fashioned in bone white by combining the fleshless mug of a steer over two intersecting hockey sticks. The rink darkens and the players begin to move. The show is about to begin.

"Four commercials every period, eh?" Bob's getting the format straight for the umpteenth time this season. "Hey, Mike, that's all right. What the heck, gotta pay the bills!"

The national anthem is under way. A young woman faces the mammoth Canadian flag at the north end of the arena and sings beautifully. Bob is standing with his headset on. The arm holding the microphone is tipped slightly skyward as he takes a sip of water and swishes it around. He's getting ready to describe three hours of on-ice drama without a script and without a break. He's confident he can make it sing. "I just hope they're ready because I am," he declares. "Hockey's a fast-action sport and in junior hockey there's always something happening, even if you have to make it up a little bit sometimes. There's always something taking place out on the ice."

Trouble is, the lights are up and the referee is drawing the opposing centres to the faceoff circle to begin the game, but CHAT's broadcast is just getting to commercial after the packaged interview with Rick Carriere. The timing is going to be off and it looks as if eager listeners back in Medicine Hat will miss the action commencing on the ice below.

The worst nightmare for a radio broadcaster ensues. The Rebels are like hungry wolves. Spurred on by a vocal throng, they attack the Tigers' zone. No more than fifteen seconds elapse but Kettles is under siege in the south end. Flailing around with even more animation than the warm-up I had seen moments ago, the goaltender is desperately overmatched. Colby Armstrong of the Rebels flips the puck in and the red light beams for Red Deer just 17 seconds into the first period. The crowd cheers wildly while, upstairs, small beads of sweat gather on Bob Ridley's forehead as he notes the goal scorer and the assists on a thin white piece of paper placed in front of him.

Finally, he begins to broadcast. "All right, we're under way with the action here at the Centrium, and already the Red Deer Rebels have scored," he admits across the airwaves. "We had Armstrong coming in hard from the left side and cruising through the crease. He did his damage against the Tigers goaltender Kyle Kettles. The Medicine Hat Tigers are off to a tough start at the Centrium tonight."

Description is so essential to Ridley's role in the radio theatre. He must allow the fans to envision all that has transpired—in this case, as a postscript. "I try to deliver the message of what's happening on the ice," he says. "Try to provide as much entertainment as I can and be as accurate as I can."

In that vein, Bob Ridley warms up to the game once he is finally on the air and in full command. Elbows on the counter and with the single lineup sheet in one of his paws, he leans out over the ice and swings his head back and forth. Lips moving constantly, Bob's voice has a definite edge to it, not high-pitched but metallic in texture. The words come at you like bullets in a rapid-fire shooting gallery. "Chris St. Jacques, Ben Thomson, Ryan Hollweg. They're kinda like the buzz-saw line out there for the Medicine Hat Tigers."

The game proceeds at a fast pace and the young players make few mistakes. Whistles signalling off-sides and icing are a rarity in the early stages of a game, meaning that Bob keeps talking—there is barely a second's break in his non-stop commentary. A quick check of the indicators on the commentator's box reveals that Ridley is pushing the limits of the microphone. Seven small lights flash lime green at the lower end of the range to crimson at the top levels. Bob is in the red most of the time.

"Actually, I've kind of tempered my style a little bit," he claims. "At one time I was a screamer. It's a high-tempo game. It's an emotional game, and unless you try to be emotional yourself, I don't think you can deliver a message."

He's really into it now as Jay Bouwmeester starts to lug the puck with increasing intensity. The big defenceman is smooth and skilled and obviously one of Bob's favourites. The kid draws a penalty midway through the period and Ridley leans back to refer to one of the sheets taped to his wall. Never skipping a beat, he comes up with a story to tell—a little context for this particular situation. Bob informs the fans that the phenomenal Bouwmeester scored his first junior goal just last year when he was called up as a fourteen-year-old, and it was right here at the Centrium in Red Deer.

"Maybe he can connect again on this power play," Ridley wishes aloud over the air.

He's a supporter of the team and perhaps believes that they can detect his urgings from their positions on the ice surface seventy-five feet below. Rids is with them again, just as he was on the bus. Now his words are pointing the way to the net and to a tie game with the enemy Rebels. "You gotta have fun with yourself and within your heart," Ridley explains. "I think that fun will carry back to Medicine Hat and the people who are listening."

The Tigers start to make strides with the man advantage. Ridley is up, out of his seat, moving his right hand and the pen it's clutching to the beat of the action. Resembling an orchestra conductor, the play-by-play man's words become like staccato notes foreshadowing the impending crescendo. "Bouwmeester . . . tees it up . . . rebound . . . they scooore!!!"

Virtual silence in the building as the Rebels slump and the Tigers swagger. From where I sit, Ridley's verbal arrows have pierced the air and I'm certain they must have heard him without the aid of radios back in The Hat. It's that loud and, as he delivers the blow, Bob leans way back in his chair and allows himself a little pump of the fist and a satisfied smile.

Splitting his attention expertly, Ridley neatly notes the scoring play and simultaneously describes how it happened: "Hollweg for the Tigers getting the rebound. He goes top shelf and the Medicine Hat Tigers have tied up this hockey game!" For Hollweg it is the eighth goal of the season. Paul Elliot and Jay Bouwmeester have drawn the assists. All of a sudden, tonight's broadcast has legs.

———

At Ridley's home, there is a rogue's gallery of the players he has come to know over the years. Young men, some on their way to hockey greatness, mingle with others who remained in Medicine

Hat and pursued less glamorous lives. He treats them all with an abiding reverence. In turn, Bob's treasures reflect their gratitude towards him.

He directed me towards a picture of speedy Boston Bruins forward Rob DiMaio, one of the Tigers graduates he felt closest to. A team photo shows a red-haired, younger Ridley in the front row beside goalie Pete Peeters, who went on to play with distinction for the NHL Flyers, Bruins and Capitals. The wall is filled with testimonials. The inscription on the portrait of former big league defenceman Al Pedersen, who toiled in Medicine Hat between 1982 and 1985, reads, "To Bob, The Iron Man, Thanks for the Memories." He's called "The Iron Man" because he drove the Iron Lung and made them into local heroes. It's something they'll never forget.

If there is a caricature in the world of hockey, he appears in the form of a man called Lanny McDonald. There he is on Bob Ridley's wall in a Calgary Flames uniform, holding the Stanley Cup horizontally over his head at the Montreal Forum. McDonald's mouth is wide open in exaltation, the lower part of his face framed by that famous prairie duster of a red moustache. He looks like a tiger who has just captured his prey. Now a member of the Hall of Fame and one of the great right wingers of all time, first with the Maple Leafs and later in his career with the Flames, McDonald starred with the inaugural Medicine Hat teams of the early 1970s.

"Even as a raw-boned kid out of Craigmyle, Alberta, he was outgoing and personable, a leader both on and off the ice," Ridley said of McDonald. "He brought his heart and soul to the game and you couldn't ask anything more of an individual than that."

Lanny McDonald is still in hockey, an executive with the Calgary Flames and one of the most popular Albertans ever to play the game. Given where he's been and all of the adulation he has received, you might expect he'd have a less-than-vivid recollection of the man who called the play-by-play for his junior team. But

McDonald delighted in a discussion of Bob Ridley and the marvel of the man's folksy charm, still going strong thirty years later.

"Bob is everything. He does it all. He drives the bus, he's the play-by-play guy and he's the biggest fan," Lanny emphasized. "He says hello to everybody that he possibly can during the broadcasts and he is the biggest cheerleader of all. He just cares so much about the Tigers. It's like they are part of his family, and really they have become that after all of these years."

When I think of the time he spends on the road with the kids, days and weeks on end, tens of thousands of miles every season, watching generations grow and move on, I can understand Bob's connection to the franchise. He's the one constant, the one person who never left. Instead, Ridley remains as a living history of this western city's obsession with its hockey team. "More than anything else he had this care for the game. It was so genuine," Lanny said, through that delightful moustache. "You know his voice would go up . . . Whoa!!!" The great player rocked back and howled like a coyote. "It was like he was living every second that was being played out there himself and letting everyone else know all about it too."

Medicine Hat's greatest success in junior hockey occurred in the late 1980s nearly twenty years after their entrance to the Western Hockey League. While McDonald, Tom Lysiak and the Gassoff brothers, Bob and Brad, went to the Memorial Cup tournament in 1973, they could not overcome the powerful Toronto Marlboros and the Remparts from Quebec City. The Marlies, coached by George Armstrong, won the Cup at the Montreal Forum with an awesome display of offensive weaponry.

In 1987, Medicine Hat travelled to Oshawa, Ontario, to play in the three-team final against the host Generals and the Longueuil Chevaliers of the Quebec league. A member of the Tigers squad that had lost in 1973 was behind the bench for Medicine Hat this time. Bryan Maxwell was redeemed with a surprising 6–2 victory over the Generals. Medicine Hat's own Trevor Linden, solidifying his reputation as one of the brightest junior prospects in the country at the time, scored two goals for the underdogs.

Ridley showed me the picture of the jubilant '87 Tigers on display at his house. There was Linden surrounded by his teammates, all of them sweating profusely and whooping it up as they grasped the spoils of victory. Beside the shot was another photo, this one of Linden in full flight as the captain of the Vancouver Canucks. "To Bob—a class act and a true friend," the salutation started. "Thanks for hauling me around Western Canada safely. Your friend, Trevor Linden."

Linden starred again for the 1988 Tigers, who repeated as Memorial Cup champions. He remains one of the most important hockey personalities in Bob Ridley's life, not only because he was essential to the Tigers' fortunes but also because he was from Medicine Hat. Linden and another veteran NHL performer, Murray Craven, became home-grown icons. "Their first pair of skates were bought there. They first stepped on the ice as two-year-olds in Medicine Hat, and that's what makes them very special," he reckoned.

It is Linden though, who endures as the quintessential Medicine Hat Tiger in Bob Ridley's mind. Twice a Memorial Cup champion, he led the Canucks to a Stanley Cup final appearance and forced a seventh game before bowing to Mark Messier and the New York Rangers in 1994. Linden has also played with Team Canada on several occasions, including the Olympic Games, where he scored the tying goal in a dramatic and ultimately losing battle with the gold medallists from the Czech Republic and their superhuman goalie, Dominik Hasek.

Trevor Linden's influence, however, extends far beyond the ice surface. Linden has served as the president of the National Hockey League Players Association and been active in advocating for the rights of his fellow players. In addition, he won the 1997 King

Clancy Memorial Trophy as the NHL player who best exemplifies leadership on and off the ice and makes a noteworthy humanitarian contribution in his community. It is the same award won by another famous Medicine Hat Tiger, Lanny McDonald, in 1988 when he was with the Calgary Flames.

"He is an outstanding individual. In my estimation, Trevor could, sometime down the road, be an outstanding coach at any level because he loves the game so much," Bob told me. "Trevor brought a lot, not only to the franchise in those successful years, but also to the Western Hockey League. All the players that ever played against him would attest to that because when you went up against Trevor Linden, you went up against a pretty dynamite hockey player."

He's now considered a veteran and struggling just a little with the Montreal Canadiens. Linden reminded me, when I met him at the Molson Centre one day, that I had "wimped out" by not travelling with his beloved Tigers on a longer swing to Manitoba or British Columbia. Growing up in Medicine Hat, he had always wanted to play for the Tigers, the dream having been fixed in his consciousness as an impressionable youngster. Sometimes when he's swirling around Montreal's rink in the historic sweater of "les glorieux," he can still faintly hear Bob Ridley's voice.

"I grew up listening to him so he's one of my favourite play-by-play guys," said Linden, while sitting at his stall in the Canadiens' dressing room. "For me it started as a very young boy. As a five-year-old I remember lying in bed listening to Bob Ridley bringing the Tigers hockey games home, listening to him on the radio night after night and usually falling asleep after the second period. Having a chance to play for the Tigers of course meant that Bob had a big influence on me."

Linden, who is one of the more articulate NHL players, credits Ridley with helping him to overcome a pronounced shyness towards the microphone. He learned how to be interviewed because the man on the other end of the mike welcomed the players as human beings. Most found it impossible not to express who they really were when answering his questions. "I remember players would go up and stand and talk with him and tell stories just to pass the time." Linden was thinking of the old Tigers bus. "I did my first interview with Bob, and I was extremely nervous. But he kind of helps you along."

Barry Melrose was a first-year coach with Medicine Hat when they stunned Windsor to win their second Memorial Cup championship in as many years. It was 1988 and at Chicoutimi, Quebec, that the Tigers came from behind on a late goal by Mark Pederson to overcome the Spitfires by a 7–6 score.

Melrose himself had played for Winnipeg, Toronto and Detroit in his hard-working NHL career and left Medicine Hat to continue learning the coaching craft in the WHL with Seattle, in Adirondack of the American Hockey League, and eventually in the NHL with Los Angeles. In 1993 he helped Wayne Gretzky and the Kings past the Maple Leafs in a wild seven-game series and on to the Stanley Cup final, won ultimately by the Montreal Canadiens.

"Winning the Memorial Cup was just as exciting as beating Toronto in game seven," Melrose stressed from his home in Grand Falls, New York, where he works as a hockey broadcaster for the American television networks ESPN and ABC. I had run into him at the NHL All-Star Game in Toronto and mentioned my interest in Bob Ridley's story. Melrose shoved his card into my pocket and declared, "I would love to say a few things about Bob Ridley."

This kind of allegiance was becoming a pattern where Ridley was concerned. No-one I had approached was anything less than effusive in his praise of a person who seemed, on the surface, to fulfill a minor role in one of hockey's strongholds. "He was probably the most underrated member of the team that won the Memorial Cup in 1988," Melrose declared. "We all forget the work ethic that a man like Bob Ridley has. It's really hard to know where to start. He was the bus driver, radio broadcaster, equipment hauler, friend, confidant . . ." Melrose was just getting going.

He remembered jumping on the ice and hugging Ridley, who had scrambled down from the broadcast booth to join the on-ice celebration after the cup was won. Also valued by Melrose were the discussions on long trips back from games the Tigers lost. It is amazing to Melrose that NHL teams now employ, in his words, "seven or eight trainers, three or four public relations guys, five or six assistant general managers and four or five assistant coaches." In junior hockey, Melrose recalled, a few devoted souls like Bob Ridley sustained the entire organization.

"Every team has unsung heroes and behind-the-scenes people who work eighteen hours a day," he concluded. "Bob could have left Medicine Hat a number of times and moved onwards and upwards. But he loves the small town. He loves his job and he loves the people there. I can remember watching only one away game on TV and that was the Memorial Cup. Other than that, Bob Ridley brought the games home."

————

A dozen years later Ridley's still telling the story of the Tigers' latest battle. Time passes in Red Deer but Ridley's enthusiasm does not. There are commercial breaks and updates from around the WHL to handle, all of it done by a jack-of-all-trades, a one-person information network. I can imagine the Tigers fans two to three hundred miles away hanging on his every word.

"Here's a quick glance at the out-of-town scoreboard for Kitchen and Light Gallery, where friendly service and customer satisfaction are number one."

Bob goes on to run down the latest scores from Swift Current, where the Broncos and the Brandon Wheat Kings are in a scoreless tie. Another game is going on in Prince Albert. There, the home-

town Raiders are down 1–0 to the Saskatoon Blades. As I close my
eyes and listen, sitting beside him just over the ice, the proceedings
take on a magical quality. The players become faster and stronger
and the hits a little more crushing. Ridley makes things more vivid
by letting his voice rise and fall in roller-coaster fashion.

"Here comes Chris St. Jacques . . . Little Mister Dynamite himself hits the line . . . unloads with a shot!" Ridley waits for a second
or two, even though the play is complete. "Good save in there by
Shane Bendera. Gobbled up by Bendera, and the buzzer sounds to
end the first period."

He handles the intermissions by himself, pulling in a former
junior player. Rids reclines in his chair and folds his arms over his
belly. A constant smile, easy questions—he's more like a raconteur
than a probing radio interviewer. Although he's genuinely curious,
there is nothing about Ridley's approach to suggest he would ever
allow his interview to become an inquisition.

"You always look for the positives, not the negatives, not the
losses," he had told me earlier, with great conviction. "You look for
a great play, a great save by an outstanding goaltender, or whatever.
If there is some enthusiasm generated on the ice by a young rookie,
that's a good thing. You're always looking for those sorts of things
to make it sound positive."

It made sense. What point was there in telling a story of doubt
and probable defeat? The prospect of victory, faint as it might be,
was much more appealing, and the hope that he could generate
with his voice was undeniable. His goal was to make the listeners
imagine they were there at the game, in all its excitement. This,
I recalled from my youth, was what made the marriage of radio and
the game work. I'll never forget going to Maple Leaf Gardens for
the first time after listening to Foster Hewitt on CKFH and finding
that the whole "live" experience was missing a certain something.
I now understand that it was the descriptive commentary that lifted
the proceedings off the ice and into my imagination.

The game in Red Deer between the visiting Tigers and the
Rebels has provided Ridley with fodder for an entertaining broadcast. His work is easier on this night because Medicine Hat has put
up an exceptional fight, coming back three times to tie the score
and send it to overtime locked at three apiece.

"All right! The Tigers are determined to win this one. Like
I said, they're taking no prisoners!" Bob begins the extra period as
the team's biggest fan.

The overtime produces plenty of chances for both sides but the
goaltenders are stupendous. Maybe all that pre-game flapping paid
dividends for Kyle Kettles because he is tested and responds to several close chances by Red Deer.

"And there goes the buzzer to end the game! It's a 3–3 tie and
certainly a positive start to this weekend for the Medicine Hat
Tigers!" Bob utters his final piece with a Cheshire cat grin plastered on his face.

"What do you do now?" I ask him.

"Well, I pack up and head for the bus," he says, matter-of-factly.
In the time it takes to blink, he has the headphones off and is
stuffing them in one of the briefcases.

The players gather in the hallway outside the dressing room,
their hair still wet and gelled just so. Some have been joined by
their families—moms, dads, grandparents and cousins—who have
travelled from various parts of the province to see them perform.
Bob is loading the bus with equipment bags, a couple of dozen
pizza boxes and a case or two of Gatorade. The Tigers will be
rolling minutes after the game. It's five hours non-stop to The Hat;
the estimated time of arrival is 3 a.m.

It has already been a long day for Ridley, but it has also been a
happy one. The draw with a very good team has him in a satisfied
state of mind. There is clear sailing on the highway, the trace of
unfrozen moisture reflecting a soothing orange from the headlights
and the stars sparkling bright in an unclouded western sky. The

driver's stoic face is illuminated by the myriad coloured dials and gauges that he monitors from time to time.

The players have devoured the post-game refreshments, and the noise level subsides noticeably about an hour out of Red Deer. Legs are stretched across the aisle, heads are resting on pillows pushed up against the windows of the bus. Chris St. Jacques ("Little Mister Dynamite himself") has just finished a short chat with Bob on the stoop to the right of the driver's seat and makes his way back to the middle row to rest in the spot across the way from his friend Denny Johnston.

Kelly Hrudey, a former Tiger along for the ride, has assumed the spot vacated by St. Jacques and begins to reminisce. "Those trips to Billings weren't very much fun for you," Hrudey recollects. "In the dead of winter and snowbanks literally halfway up the side of the bus and those two-lane roads. I don't even know what highway that was any more in Montana."

"That's why we called it the Turkey Trail," Bob responds. "It was just a narrow trail all the way down there. You'd meet a semi and the mirrors would touch. That's how close it was! I was quite happy when the franchise moved elsewhere."

They chat for half an hour or so. The conversation includes stories about a former player named John Hilworth who was such a gifted mechanic that he fixed the air conditioning on the old "Iron Lung" during a trip to Calgary years back. On another occasion he repaired the Zamboni machine at the arena in Medicine Hat which had packed it up midway through the first intermission. They also recall twenty-two-hour trips to Seattle in blinding snowstorms and players who never made it for whatever reason. Ridley has an easy answer for every morsel of Medicine Hat Tigers trivia that Hrudey can't quite put his finger on.

"I think when you consider sports franchises and what they have to offer, one of the things that you always look for is the history of the team," Hrudey says, flopped back in his seat. "People make the history. It's the games and the people and what happened. I don't know how much longer Medicine Hat's going to be around. Maybe they'll be around two more years or fifty more but I don't think there's going to be anyone more important to that franchise than Bob Ridley."

To describe Ridley and his contribution to the team, it's important to know that he has missed only one game in his thirty years, when he was on a curling assignment covering the world-class Silver Broom. It has become the one minuscule blemish on his impeccable record of devotion to this franchise. How much longer will he make it his life? "As long as I feel good about the game and still feel healthy, I'll just keep puttering away at it and do what I do best," Ridley figures. "It's just the passion of the game. Players have got it. Anyone that's been involved for a long time is still involved because of the passion. That feeling of wanting to watch the kids develop, to wish them all the best as they continue on towards a playoff spot."

A logging truck is parked by the side of the road as the twinkling lights of Medicine Hat appear at 2:45 a.m. The Tigers roll past it, and Bob Ridley's delivery is right on time, as always.

———

Under a crescent moon the following night, those who aren't at the Medicine Hat Arena for the game huddle around the radio. At the Legion hall they congregate in the Crown 'n' Anchor room with the radio on.

"Good evening, everyone," Ridley's voice chimes. "Welcome to Tigers hockey on New Country 1270 CHAT. Back-to-back games for the Tigers and the Red Deer Rebels."

A father and son are enjoying a couple of beers and listening to the action. Brian Varga played with the Tigers eighteen years ago and rode the bus with Ridley. "I think he's a Medicine Hat icon," Varga says. "The legend lives on. He's just been great."

Brian's son, Dustin Varga, looks more like a rock star than a fan of WHL hockey, but he knows the deal where Ridley's concerned and chooses a fitting metaphor to express his understanding of the play-by-play man's appeal. "If anything, he's the one that keeps them driving. I know my grandma loves him. All the people around can't wait for him to come around and interview them."

"Over 4,200 fans looking on here," Bob boasts over the radio. I wonder if he's embellishing just a little—after all, he's already admitted that he looks for the positive and tends to make a few things up as he goes along. Then I remember he told me about the Tigers unveiling their new sweater at the game that night. A third jersey had been designed to commemorate the team's thirtieth anniversary. "It's a sell-out crowd here," Rids crows.

The Arena in Medicine Hat is not like the state-of-the-art Centrium in Red Deer. It's more weathered and speckled with seats of a brighter hue. Ridley's booth dangles directly above the crowd and his perch is isolated from the rest of the press quarters. Over his shoulder, just barely out of his arm's reach, hang the banners for past Tigers victories. The orangey-red Memorial Cup banners are there; he can see them out of the corner of his eye . . . always.

The place is indeed sold right out. The home club dashes over the ice in their new black getups. A Tiger in full flight is emblazoned on each player's chest—a ravenous, perhaps desperate-looking Bengal, befitting a team in Medicine Hat's present circumstances. So many young players have yielded so few results over the course of this difficult season.

I wonder, as I search the faces of the fans, if Bob Ridley's appeal extends to the people when the team plays at home and is accessible, in a very real way, to the residents of this smallish city. I discover that, as a group, they are devoted and diverse. A little girl sits

quietly, her long auburn hair hanging luxuriously over the neckline
of her Tigers team jersey, her mother's arm draped across the back
of her chair. They watch the game intently, swivelling in tandem to
follow the play. Old men in CCM caps lean forward whenever the
favourites enter the opposing zone. A guy with an earring in his
left lobe and spiky locks dyed ash-blond is shoulder to shoulder
with his buddies. They all wear shirts bearing the Tigers logo.
When the play is on, they do not fool around.

Behind the bench struts Rick Carriere, fuming because his
team is trailing by quite a margin. "You guys have done f—all this
period," I hear him mutter to no one in particular. "C'mon boys,
chase the puck!" shouts one rabid fan as the Tigers languish at the
Rebels blue line, hardly resembling the predators they are named
after. I wonder what Rids is saying to sugar-coat this game.

Roberta Kelly sits near centre ice, wearing the almost invisible
headphones of a Walkman. Right beside is her husband, John, also
tuned into the radio. She works at the Dairy Queen on the main
drag and he's employed on the line at the Goodyear Tire and Rubber plant in town. Together, they follow Tigers hockey and can't
imagine it without Bob Ridley's commentary.

"The night shifts are so boring," John explains. "To listen to
Ridley makes the night go a hell of a lot better. It's the real deal
because the boys get all pumped up when the Tigers score. You can
hear the tire builders cheering." I can make out Bob's voice very
faintly when John takes off the headphones to talk. "Meadow
Muffler and Brakes—your number one choice. Located on
Kingsway!" He must have just finished an update during a break in
the action.

"It isn't a game without Bob Ridley," Roberta chimes in. She
explains that she's seen him at the grocery store and the drive-thru
at the Dairy Queen. Ridley has a family and, for the most part, is
just a regular guy, according to her. Still, she wants to make it clear

that when he gets on the radio he's something more than your average citizen. "He brings a sense of sport to Medicine Hat," Roberta explains. "He brings Red Deer here. He brings Seattle here. He brings Spokane here. It's important. It's hockey."

For all his encouragement and care, he cannot make them win this Saturday night. The Tigers play like a last-place team and score only near the bitter end of the game against Red Deer. The final count is 5–2 and in the weekend set with the rival Rebels, Medicine Hat has yielded three of the four points available. Bob Ridley goes to his last commercial trying to put a positive spin on another in a long line of losses.

"You've got to be a fan to have been with them this long," Bob confides in me. "They have been awfully good to me. Provided me with a lot of great hockey over the years. How could you not be a fan of the Medicine Hat Tigers?"

More importantly, how could the club not be a fan of his? Ridley has given so much over the years. He's driven so many miles and made their story travel such an incredible distance. More than Lanny McDonald, Trevor Linden, Kelly Hrudey and all of the players who have come this way over thirty seasons, he embodies the spirit. He's the keeper of the Tigers history and the sage who foretells a return to prosperity.

All the fans are gone from the arena now. The ice is clean and Bob Ridley's day is almost done. Finished until 5 a.m. tomorrow when he'll turn up at CHAT radio and do the morning show as the sports director of the station. They're coming back from the commercial break and he'll put a final period on this game. Wrap it up. It's best not to watch during the signoff. Instead, I'll just listen to the voice of my new favourite team and imagine, through Rids, that better days are just around the corner.

"It was not to be for the Medicine Hat Tigers tonight, losing by a score of 5–2 against the Red Deer Rebels. That following a 3–3 tie against the same Rebel hockey club in Red Deer last night. The Tigers are going after the Kootenay Ice this coming weekend on Friday in Cranbrook and back home on Saturday. The Tigers will certainly be better in that series of games. That pretty well wraps it up from the arena. I'm Bob Ridley on New Country 1270 CHAT, bidding you all a very pleasant good night."

THE FAMILY

The Crawfords

Top: The Patriarch: Floyd's World Championship
(courtesy Floyd Crawford)

Bottom: Belleville's Hockey Clan
(courtesty Danielle Yohn)

✧ A TINY VOICE ANSWERS THE PHONE. "Pronto!" the child says. I'm calling a member of a famous hockey family who happens to be living in Italy, so I feel a little disoriented. "Is Susan Crawford there please?" I ask slowly and clearly.

"No . . . no," comes the hesitant response, followed by silence. Soon I hear a woman's lyrical tones as she makes inquiries of the child, the words drifting across the ocean. I imagine open shutters and a warm breeze wafting in from the piazza below, bicycles clattering over narrow cobblestone streets—not a hint of ice or snow or the Canadian game, and I worry I've gone down the wrong road.

"Hello, this is Susan Crawford," the woman's voice brings me back. I explain who I am and why I've called. Her younger brother Marc, the coach of the Vancouver Canucks, had suggested I call her. "Oh, she's the smartest of us all," he had bragged. "The smartest by far." Now, hearing my introduction, Susan laughs lightly and says that it was likely her other brother Louis, coach of the OHL Belleville Bulls, who gave me the number. "Both of their teams are doing quite well. I check them on the Internet every day," she says, and I can hear the excitement in her voice.

Susan Crawford is forty-five and moved to Rome with her physician husband a decade ago. Armed with a master's degree from the University of Ottawa and the ability to speak three languages fluently (French, English and Italian) she teaches English to Italian children and takes her seven-year-old son to soccer. Hockey is rarely played in Rome. "I miss it," she declares. "It's part of who I am."

Susan is the eldest of seven brothers and two sisters who grew up in Belleville, Ontario, an eastern Ontario city of 46,000. Her father, Floyd, played defence for the Canadian team that won the World Hockey championship in Prague in 1959. She remembers the parade, riding in the front seat of a convertible when her dad and the rest of the Belleville McFarlands returned in triumph.

Five of her seven brothers have played the game professionally, and all of them have made their mark on the ice, at least as juniors. Susan's sister, Danielle, won provincial championships as a member of the Belleville Legionettes back when women's hockey wasn't fashionable. Her mother, Pauline, met her father at a Chicoutimi rink where he was playing for the senior Sagueneens. Pauline Crawford is the ultimate fan; she still attends every single one of the junior games in Belleville.

The Crawford name is chiselled into most of the major team trophies, both professional and amateur, that hockey offers. Floyd and six of his sons are still chasing the puck across the far reaches of North America. Danielle is in the midst of a comeback at the age of thirty-four, following the birth of her second child. Although Susan is the only one who never played, hockey's in her blood. "Even though I can follow on the Internet, it's not the same thing. I miss being able to go to the games," she laments.

Something in her has been stirred by our brief transatlantic conversation. Ten years of absence from Canada wells up inside her and she sounds nostalgic—like an ardent follower waiting in line for standing-room-only seats. "I was just sort of there. I was a fan and a babysitter," Susan explains. "I really didn't contribute very much."

Susan was the first of the flock, born in Val d'Or, Quebec, the northernmost stop along Floyd's hockey trail. She was there in Montreal, holding her mother's hand and seeing her father off on his frequent travels. Later, with her brothers all playing hockey, dinnertime was organized chaos as the boys wolfed down meals on the way to games in Oshawa or Kingston or one of any number of places. "Hockey was always the major topic of conversation, if not the only topic of conversation," she remembers.

The outsider who cheered and followed their careers, Susan became a teacher in Belleville before moving to Italy. On visits home to Canada, she is confronted by her brothers' fame at every turn. When she returns to Rome, she finds herself longing for open spaces and winter's chill. It's during these times that she understands most clearly how, in her family, hockey is something bred in the bone. "First of all, my parents wouldn't have met had my father not been a hockey player," she reasons. "The fact that our family exists at all is because of hockey."

Before ringing off, Susan chats for a while about her middle brother, Marc, and her youngest sibling, Eric, who is eighteen years younger than she is. Both coaching for the same NHL team in Vancouver, they're involved in a late-season revival before the playoffs. "They're doing really well lately. They've come on in the last few games," she notes expertly. "When you called I was just going to check for last night's results." Across the ocean and through the years, big sister is apparently keeping score.

———

The patriarch won't reveal his age. The silver-haired, solidly built man with the bushy eyebrows claims he's twenty-two. "I don't go for this age bit," he huffs. "I think young, and my friends are young people. When I hit the rocking chair, I figure the game is over."

We are in the weight room of the Yardmen Arena in Belleville just before a late-season match between the junior Bulls and the visiting Kingston Frontenacs, longtime rivals in the Ontario Major Junior League. Floyd is the chief scout for the Bulls and although he is, by my conservative estimate, at least seventy years old, he still takes in upwards of two hundred games a year. Whether he's watching bantams, midgets or Tier II juniors, the eldest Crawford is constantly on the lookout for talent to stock his son Louis's team. Belleville is a perennial contender for supremacy in the league and much of it has to do with the quality of the players they have selected over the years.

Floyd's hockey career began in a section of Toronto very close to a park known as Christie Pits. His family lived on the north boundary of The Pits and his mother would let him trundle down the hill to skate on one of the seven outdoor hockey "cushions," as they were called back then. "I just fell in love with the game," he says, leaning against the back wall of the gymnasium. "I used to cry when my father came down and called me to come back home."

Crawford remembers interest in his playing ability when he was about fifteen. In the men's league at Ravina Gardens, games raged every Wednesday and Saturday night. The ex-NHLers who were in the army during World War II generally took to the ice on Saturdays, displacing most of the younger players like Floyd. He recalls jumping at the chance to compete with some of his idols when they were short of players.

Crawford was spotted by the Montreal Canadiens, an honour in itself, and went to the Habs training camp after signing what was called a "C" form. Floyd was, in effect, sold into servitude by one of the greatest outfits in professional hockey at a bargain basement price. "I signed a 'C' form for the grand total of $100," he tells me. "I carried the money around in my pocket for a few weeks' bragging rights."

But his path didn't lead to stardom and the National Hockey League. Instead, Floyd Crawford became an honest workman who made the game his life. His youngest son, Eric, had told me his dad's motto was "Have skates, will travel." Floyd hit the road, and after playing for the senior Montreal Royals, was traded unceremoniously north to the Chicoutimi Sagueneens.

In Chicoutimi, he met his future wife, Pauline Duval, a nurse originally from Buckingham, Quebec, who attended the games with her parents. It was a league comprised of some fine hockey players and developing talents in the late 1940s and early 1950s. Crawford skated against a young hotshot by the name of Jean Béliveau as well as future Canadiens stars Dickie Moore and Marcel Bonin. "It was an honour to play in that league with that calibre of hockey player," he says, eyes sparkling. "Hey, you've heard this before. At that time there were only six teams in the NHL."

Not quite good enough for the biggest rinks and the brightest lights, Floyd pursued the next best thing—the senior ranks, or the "journey downhill" as he refers to it. The newly married defenceman migrated to Rimouski and from there to Val d'Or.

Two children, Susan and Peter, were born to the Crawfords in Val d'Or, and work beyond the rink provided grocery money. Many of the players had jobs in the local copper mines while providing hard-hitting entertainment to isolated communities in the evenings and on weekends. But as with many mining economies, the boom times in northern Quebec didn't last. In the late 1950s they went bust. "Each little town was trying to outbid the other guys," he says. "That league folded because they ran out of money."

One Sunday night in Rimouski, Floyd Crawford got a call from a man named Drury Denes, who was to be the manager of a new team in Belleville. Wren Blair, later of Oshawa Generals and NHL fame, was forming an eastern Ontario Senior A league, which would involve teams from Toronto to Cornwall. The association aimed to rival the western part of the province, which had managed to capture the coveted Allan Cup on numerous occasions.

The wealthy Belleville businessman Harvey McFarland, who owned a construction firm that held lucrative highway paving contracts from the Ontario government, sponsored the team. The McFarlands were born, and Floyd Crawford was one of the left defencemen as well as the team's captain.

"I'm pretty proud of that," he says, a little misty-eyed. The McFarlands had a good season in 1958 and faced the Kelowna Packers from the B.C. interior in the Allan Cup final. Attached to the Canadian senior championship was the right to travel to Europe for the next World Championships, with the blessing of the Canadian Amateur Hockey Association. In the final series of the playoffs in Kelowna, the McFarlands trailed the Packers three games to one. Somehow they rallied to win and secured the opportunity to go overseas and represent their country. The one proviso was that the CAHA could recommend a few outside players to strengthen the lineup of the Allan Cup victors.

"As soon as the Allan Cup was won that's all anyone could think about," Crawford says, fire in his voice. "First and foremost, you wanted to be on that team. You didn't want some minor league pro coming in and taking your job. That's what I had on my mind: 'I've come this far, baby, and I'm going over there!' I was like a monk. I devoted my whole being to staying on that team."

That dogged determination was to become his trademark. "I loved the game tremendously and offered what I could," says the scout. "I wasn't a great player, but I worked hard every night."

It was just that simple for all of the McFarlands as they carried Canadian colours to Prague in 1959. The bunch of self-described "pluggers" had weeks of barnstorming across Europe before the tournament actually began. In the deciding game against the Russians, Floyd and the rest of the Canadians survived a strategic enemy breakaway from the opening faceoff, and goaltender Gordie Bell saved the day. Belleville claimed the title by a score of 3–1. As captain, Crawford was the first to stand on the podium in Czechoslovakia and accept the championship trophy.

"It was certainly the pinnacle of my hockey life," he says, showing me his lineup card. "The Russians were coming and we had tremendous respect for them. Going over there we had only one thing on our minds. We didn't want to come back with silver. We wanted gold. In the end, everything turned our way and it happened."

———

Floyd is anxious to get to the rink because the Bulls are honouring one of the club's favourite players from times gone by. Fifteen years after his retirement from the Bulls, Dunc MacIntyre remains the most prolific scorer in the history of Belleville's junior franchise. They'll hang his sweater in the rafters tonight and never let another player wear his number. MacIntyre played in the minors for awhile but at five feet eight inches and 165 pounds, he was too small in a big man's game. He switched to life as a policeman but Crawford and others in Belleville still refer to him as "the heart of the team."

Heart is what has kept Floyd Crawford at it for so long. The Belleville McFarlands folded a year after their world championship triumph when many of their best players left for better offers. Floyd joined an International Hockey League team in Omaha, Nebraska, for a season and then attempted to come home to Belleville. "I was going to raise my family, get a job and cut the grass," he says. "But the urge was still there. Four years later they talked me into going back to the IHL with Des Moines, Iowa."

Crawford returned to Belleville after a year in Des Moines and got involved in the game at its developmental stages. He coached midgets and minor midgets, soon taking command of the Junior B team in the area. They were called the Belleville Bobcats and in 1979, Floyd took them to a championship season complete with the Sutherland Cup.

A four-game sweep over the Windsor squad gave Belleville the crown, but Crawford wasn't satisfied. Chris Rutledge, who was the club's athletic trainer back then and is currently the Bulls' trainer, recalls Floyd's intensity. He describes how, after the final game, which the Bobcats won 4–0, Crawford refused to congratulate his players because he felt they had missed several opportunities to display their excellence. A bewildered Rutledge was forced to skip the celebrations as well and take the coach back to the hotel.

"He walked away from the arena that night," Rutledge confirms Crawford's absence from the victory party. "He never played for the Cup, he played for the game. He's an incredible man."

Floyd went on to coach in the Ontario Major Junior League, first with Cornwall and then with Guelph. It didn't last long and for the past fifteen seasons he's quenched his endless thirst for hockey as the head scout for Belleville. He has witnessed more games than he would have as a coach, and his schedule dwarfs the one he skated through as a player. Floyd has tickets to the rink six days a week for more than thirty weeks of the year. This is clearly more than a job, it's a calling. "I have never perceived it as a business," he emphasizes. "I just followed the game. A lot of people said I was a little weird doing that, but I chose my path and I provided for my family very well. They didn't suffer because of my hockey career."

In fact, they flourished and followed him into the trade. He insists that he never pushed his sons or daughters onto the ice, instead letting them find out for themselves what the sport offers. Floyd chuckles a little on the way to his excellent seat at the far end of the Yardmen Arena. "You going up to say hi to the general manager?" he shouts. I have no idea what he's getting at. Then I clue in that Floyd is talking about his wife, Pauline. He points to a section of the bleachers where the fans are already intently watching the first few moments of the game between the Bulls and the Frontenacs. "I'm not playing any violins here. I never made much money in hockey but I found a million-dollar woman!"

———

Her seat is just the other side of the Belleville Bulls Booster Club. She sits a few rows down and to the left so that she can keep an eye on the home team's goalie for two of the three periods of play. "Thank you, Hanna," says Pauline Crawford with a hint of a French accent. The third generation of Crawford women in attendance at the rink has just passed some potato chips to Grandma. Pauline's youngest girl, Danielle, is one row closer to the ice.

"Sometimes I can't come," Pauline admits. "If the game's on TV, I stay home. It's a lot quieter."

The thing is, very few of the Belleville Bulls games are telecast. It's the reality of junior hockey and so the loyal hockey mom is in her position at Yardmen Arena forty times or more a season, depending on the playoffs. For Pauline it must seem natural. After all, her son Louis is behind the bench, his wife and son in the seats next to her. The second oldest Crawford boy, Michael, is up in the press box scouting the Frontenacs should Belleville have occasion to encounter them in the post-season. Husband Floyd is brooding behind the glass in the office perched over the net. He's making a mountain of notes and grumbling, to be sure, at every inept move the Bulls make. For forty years and more, this has been Pauline Crawford's life.

"When I got married I knew he was going to be playing hockey," she tells me. "The first year we moved five times."

They started off the year in Chicoutimi, moved to Rimouski and then back to Chicoutimi, summering near Floyd's home in Toronto before heading to Windsor. After their sojourns in Abitibi and Val d'Or, Floyd took Pauline out of her native Quebec for good. It was on to Belleville and not long after that, he left for three months in Europe. With three young children and another on the way, Pauline stayed home and listened to the accounts of the McFarlands on radio and read about their exploits in the local newspaper, the Belleville *Intelligencer*.

"He went there to win," she says, smiling at the memory. "He was very serious about it." There is a calmness about her despite the frenetic atmosphere of the rink. She must be well into her sixties but at first glance she reminds me of a teenager. She's slender and her hair is pulled back from her freckled face in a youthful ponytail. Whenever she is forced to talk about her role in this hockey-crazed gaggle of men, her eyes crinkle with pleasure "They do what they want, that's the main thing," she admits. "They are doing it because they want to. The girls as well. They were all fairly athletic so I stood by that."

It has meant more than standing by for the mother of nine kids, eight of whom ended up playing hockey. You can bet that all of them took to the ice at or near the same time on Saturdays. I can just imagine her assuming the roles of short-order cook, chauffeur, confessor, seamstress, physiotherapist, cheerleader and schedule maker, as Floyd found his way in the world, which by necessity meant taking to the road. No wonder he calls her "General Manager."

"I guess I was organized," Pauline shrugs.

The most visibly accomplished of the boys is Marc, who coached the Stanley Cup–winning Colorado Avalanche. "My mother is a person who worries about very few things in life," the coach of the Vancouver Canucks explained. "That has served me well. This job comes with a lot of pressure and anxiety. Her philosophy has always been that things will work out. It's a big part of her personality, and it's a big part of mine too."

She seems so at home in the arena. Pauline's family surrounds her and the children play at her feet while the game flows by. She dispenses treats for the kids and blankets to cover the chilly bleacher seats. Her pace is unhurried; this game is just one of the many thousands she has watched. There have been days with practices at six, seven and eight o'clock in the morning, kids eating on different shifts and rolling on the highway to towns in opposite directions—not to mention her work as a nurse. Like the smoothest of skaters, she has taken it all in stride. "We had some days that weren't very good," she admits, when asked about having to keep tabs on young sons and daughters in so many places. "I guess that was why I had to get my driver's licence!"

She is a refreshing hockey mom. She cheers, but in her own quiet, reserved fashion. I know that the Crawford boys who played as professionals are reputed to be feisty. Louis stands calmly behind the Belleville bench for the moment, but as an American leaguer, he was a feared and rugged performer who accumulated more than his share of fighting penalties. I have seen Marc as the coach of Quebec, Colorado and Vancouver, witnessed him get red-faced as he exhorts his players with constant verbal cues. Pauline is not like her sons in that regard. When Kingston scores, she remains stoic and when Belleville finds the net, she allows just a little smile.

The same outlook has always dominated Pauline's approach to hockey. It was never her goal to marry a player or raise her boys to make it to the NHL. She is a fan of the game and became absorbed by the sport because Floyd loved it so dearly. It is clear, as I listen to her few well-chosen words, that her hopes for the children have always been consistent. "In fact the first one, Peter, was eight when he started. Most kids now start much earlier," she says, reflecting on how and why her kids became so enmeshed in the game. "It was because they wanted to. Some more than others, but they were never pushed to play hockey."

————

Peter, the oldest boy, feigns astonishment that I have located him in Springfield, Illinois, at the commodities firm where he has worked for the past decade. "How the hell did you find me?" are his initial words over the telephone.

He's forty-three years old and, along with his sister Susan, is the only one of the Crawford offspring not born in Belleville. Peter was born in Val d'Or while Floyd was still playing senior hockey in Quebec, but he remembers little of his father's on-ice exploits or the victory at the World Championships in 1959. "I never really thought about it until I was much older and it finally sunk in that it was a hell of an accomplishment," he recalls.

Being the first hockey-playing child of a dad who made his living by the game was not burdensome to Peter. He remembers a backyard rink, then starting organized league play when he was eight. By that time he was skating with other kids on the frozen

Bay of Quinte and battling in the road hockey wars in front of
their modest Belleville home. "We would make nets out of
chicken wire and shoot pucks at each other or at our wooden
garage," he says. "The garage eventually fell apart from taking millions of puck shots."

Typically Canadian, he matured in the game while playing
minor hockey near home. Although he didn't feel that his father
pushed him into being a player, Peter recognized the unspoken
cues. "He was always quite intense with off-ice strategy," Peter
remembers. "He was a big Lloyd Percival guru and always had his
Handbook of Hockey with him."

But it was Peter's mother who instilled in him the virtue of
competing at the highest level possible. According to Peter, his
mom was the most influential coach of all. "She probably knew the
game as well as any coach or general manager. She's seen so many
hockey games that she's an expert."

He got his break when he signed on with the Junior B
Collingwood Blues under the direction of former NHLer Eddie
Bush. Not drafted by an NHL team, Peter completed his junior
days and tried his luck at Union College in Schenectady, New
York. There he was coached by Ned Harkness, the one-time
Detroit Red Wings bench boss.

"I was an all-round player. I could do everything well," Peter
says, hastening to add that he doesn't want to sound as if he's
bragging. "I played every position on the ice except goal. They
could put me out at centre, left wing, right wing, defence, it
didn't matter."

Although he was not an exceptional player, he could make a living doing something that came naturally to him. He decided to
enter the hockey profession midway through the 1977–78 season as
a member of the Toledo Goaldiggers, an International Hockey
League squad from the American Midwest. In those days, the
Goaldiggers' name did not reflect the motives of the players on the

team. There wasn't a lot of cash but there was a chance to compete at a fairly high level.

Peter did win a pro championship, something to add to his father's world amateur title, by capturing the Turner Cup that first season with Toledo. The next campaign saw him move a touch further east to Michigan, with the Kalamazoo Wings. The team emerged with another Turner Cup triumph at the end of the playoff schedule, and Peter was sending home reports to his younger brothers that he was enjoying success as a pro hockey player. "Bobby, myself, Marc and Louis were all playing some type of professional hockey at the same time in the late seventies and early eighties," he confirms. "I don't know if they ever looked up to me or not. They just figured that here was their older brother, he's in the IHL, he's won a couple of cups and he's doing fine."

Whether they meant to emulate him or not, the record shows that four of his brothers followed Peter to the professional ranks, some at a much higher level and with varying degrees of success. For his part, the oldest son of Floyd and Pauline Crawford spent the final three seasons of his playing career with the Fort Wayne Komets of the IHL. His retirement brought him an opportunity to coach and manage in an obscure association known as the Continental Hockey League. Peter went to the Springfield franchise for a year and quickly discovered that an off-ice supervisory role wasn't something he enjoyed. He was persuaded by the owner to endure another season on the understanding that he would be assisted in learning the commodities trading business. For the last eighteen years, Peter has been working as a stockbroker.

Peter still coaches youth hockey in both Springfield and in St. Louis. The brand of play is nothing outrageously competitive, but it keeps his hand in the game. He also follows the progress of his many brothers who remain actively involved. In fact, he had just finished hosting a visit with Bob, the first of his siblings to make it to the NHL.

By trade, Peter Crawford is a stockbroker but deep down he
feels the tug of hockey like some sort of genetic programming.
"Just put me down as someone who enjoys playing the game—
period," he concludes. "Still do to this day, for fun and exercise.
That's it."

———

In the laundry room of the Yardmen Arena, the newly cleaned road
jerseys of the Belleville Bulls are hanging neatly, ready to be packed
for the impending playoffs. Leaning casually against one of the
giant washing machine doors, Michael Crawford jokes around with
the team's trainer, Chris Rutledge. He wears a black baseball cap,
slightly askew, a red Team Canada windbreaker and black jeans.
Completing the ensemble are grey woollen work socks and brown
sandals. It is a strange getup for the frigid weather that lingers into
March in eastern Ontario. This, however, is the look of a man
comfortable in his own skin. With a stack of statistics under his
arm, Michael, who now scouts for the Bulls, has the rare chance to
see a home game.

Only a year younger than Peter, Michael Crawford followed the
same unhurried route through minor hockey. His father, who continues to toil as the head scout with Belleville, is technically
Michael's boss. "He influenced us by introducing us to the game
and basically let us run free," Michael says of Floyd. "If you enjoyed
it, he enjoyed it along with you."

The other brothers acknowledge that Michael was talented,
some contend more purely skilful than they ever were. He played
senior hockey close to home with the Whitby Iroquois and later
with Woodstock when he was attending college in London,
Ontario. There were even a few pro games in the International
League when teams were short on players and he was called up
to fill a hole. Michael had a scholarship with Bridgewater State, a

college just outside Boston, but it didn't last long because they promised him the moon and delivered a lot less. He left hockey for some years and had a series of less-than-satisfactory "odd jobs," as he refers to them, before returning to the original path—something he believes is inevitable for every member of the Crawford clan.

Michael's eyes widen as he tips his cap back and describes how he became resigned to his fate. "In my case it took awhile because I didn't realize it. Everybody kept telling me that I was a skill player but I didn't understand until it was too late. Now I'm realizing that I have another gift, and that is that I can recognize players."

Michael makes Toronto his home base and travels in search of flourishing young players in order to feed his brother Louis's team. Sometimes he butts head with his father—they have, at times, divergent opinions on talent—but he generally enjoys the growing amount of time he spends in hockey rinks around the province. The first year as an associate scout, Michael took in about forty games and now he scrutinizes more than two hundred a season, despite the modest salary for what he does. "I'm enjoying myself immensely and my wife allows me to do this although the financial gain is not there," he says. "She also agrees that it's better for me because I seem to be much more at ease and much happier with myself and the family."

I sense that Michael was a restless soul when he was away from hockey. I remember how his father had talked about the intangible quality of the game that allowed people to define who they were. "A lot of guys found themselves," Floyd Crawford had said about his days in the mining towns of northern Quebec. It is becoming apparent that Michael is rediscovering himself as a junior talent scout.

It took a little convincing but Belleville's coach, his younger brother Lou, has come to rely on Michael's advice and is increasingly devoted to his intuition about young players. "At first I think he was a bit leery of my input, but after a few of the selections that

I recommended he realized that I know what I'm doing and now
he's looking forward to seeing what I have for him. Maybe I can
convince my other brother, Marc," he says, hoping to scout for
Vancouver and the NHL. "I think I have what it takes to get to the
next level."

————

Every household points to the first person who made it "big time,"
the individual who carried the family name forward. If the benchmark is the National Hockey League, then Bob is the standard
bearer of the Crawford clan.

The three oldest boys, Peter, Michael and Bob, are separated by
a total of three years. Bob was born a couple of days after his father
returned victorious from the World Championships in the spring of
1959. In the heart of Belleville, Bobby Crawford beat the pucks
against the old garage door with everyone else and developed a skill
that would take him to the pinnacle of the game.

Searching through some videotape from the early 1980s, I discover images of Bobby Crawford, dressed in the gaudy green
uniform of the Hartford Whalers. He steams down the right wing,
cocks his stick with an enormous back swing and launches a rocket
of a shot in the direction of the Buffalo Sabres goaltender, Tom
Barrasso. The pictures are from Crawford's breakthrough NHL
season of 1983–84, when he scored 36 goals and added 25 assists for
the Whalers.

"A lot of people think that I was raised to be a hockey player,"
he says. "It wasn't the case. We got as far as we did because we loved
what we did. In this sport if you don't love what you do, it doesn't
work. You can't force a kid to play. It's too tough. It's too tough
mentally, emotionally and organizationally."

Perhaps the reason Bob Crawford made it was his booming
shot. Whatever the reason, he was selected by the Cornwall Royals

to play major junior hockey when he was sixteen years old. "Bob was the first who went and got drafted," younger brother Louis recalls. "All of a sudden there was an extra potato on the table sort of thing."

Bob became a prolific scorer for the junior Royals. He played three seasons with them, one of which yielded a harvest of over sixty goals for the powerful right winger. Even more than the 246 games he played in the NHL, he points with pride to the first time his parents saw him as a junior in Montreal, at the fabled Forum. "I was a rookie and went in there and had a pretty good game. I came out of it with the Montreal press talking about Bob Crawford," he recalls.

The road ahead seemed clear: he was to be drafted into the National Hockey League at a time when the professionals were starting to reap the rewards of a burgeoning stockpile of talent. It was in the spring of 1979 and, for the first time, the top league was gobbling up underage players—the eighteen- and nineteen-year-olds who had previously remained off-limits as juniors. Many of the older, talented performers (like Ray Bourque) moved down in the order a few notches because of the increased competition for spots in the NHL.

Bob Crawford had expected to go in the second round of the entry draft. He remembers waiting by the telephone with his supportive father as the minutes turned into hours. "By six o'clock I started to question whether or not I was even drafted," he says. "I remember my father talking to me and telling me that I was going to make it. 'Whether you get a call or not, I've been around hockey my whole life and I'm not saying this because you're my son. You are going to make it into the National Hockey League,' he said. For a kid who was kind of in a state of shock, which most teenagers are on draft day, those were words of encouragement I'll never forget."

The first NHL Crawford was at long last claimed by the St. Louis Blues in the early fourth round of the draft. Bobby scored a goal in his first game playing for the Blues against the Vancouver Canucks. "My only claim to fame was for five minutes I was the leading scorer in the NHL," he says, jokingly. "It was the only game being played on opening night, and I scored the first goal to make it 1–0."

After eight games with the Blues in the first season, he was sent for apprenticeship training in St. Louis's Central Hockey League farm system with the Salt Lake Golden Eagles. Bobby spent the better part of the next three campaigns trying to impress the NHL club and in the process added two more championship victories to the Crawford trophy case. The Jack Adams Cup for CHL supremacy went to Salt Lake in both 1979–80 and 1980–81, and Bob helped lead the way.

His goal was to return to the NHL fold, however, and the family tenaciousness kicked into gear as he clawed his way back to St. Louis. "For me it was such a tough road getting there that by the time I finally made it I was more relieved than anything," he admits. "I remember near the end of my second year in Salt Lake City there was an article from St. Louis on all the prospects and I wasn't on it. I was looking at forty names and Bob Crawford wasn't one of them. I looked at that as a challenge. To some people it would have been devastating, but I didn't give up on myself."

Crawford's NHL career spanned more than two hundred games and included 71 goals and the same number of assists. Bob wore the sweaters of the St. Louis Blues, the Hartford Whalers, the New York Rangers and the Washington Capitals, before retiring in 1988 after a brief European tour of duty with clubs in Germany and Italy.

He founded and is co-owner of Champions, a business that owns and operates ice rinks and health facilities in the Hartford area. Bob also conducts hockey camps and is general manager of the Connecticut Clippers, a junior team that has recently captured the Metropolitan Atlantic Junior Hockey Championship. "You can add another trophy," he says when I list all the cups his family has won. "It was our first year in the league and they're proud of it around here, which is nice. Junior hockey is growing and it's always good to win a championship."

The former NHLer also informs me that he has just completed the purchase of a Tier II junior club in Port Hope, Ontario, close to the Belleville homestead. "I'm going to have Michael and Floyd help me with it," he says, confirming his absolute trust in his family where hockey is concerned. "Michael would like to get into it a little bit more. He's got a great mind and he's helping Floyd in Belleville. I know, between the two of them they'll do a great job."

The final story Bobby Crawford has for me illustrates the reverence he has for the family that shaped his outlook on life. Never a superstar, he recently found himself on the same podium in St. Louis with Hall of Famer Bobby Hull, who's also from the same hometown in eastern Ontario. Crawford told the audience that he grew up wanting to be just like Hull because the Golden Jet was his idol. He went on to explain that, although his own career had turned out very differently, it was at least as satisfying.

"There were probably only three years in my whole career that I actually went into the season knowing that I was on the team. And within the season I was always fighting to keep my job. We Crawfords were never the superstars. We were role players. We knew how to fit within a team and maybe that's why we made it."

Bobby Crawford's words apply equally well to his father, who fought to keep his job forty years earlier and because he persevered, came home from Czechoslovakia with the first championship trophy to be engraved with the Crawford name.

———

"My father was still playing when I was a kid," Marc Crawford says as he relaxes in the palatial surroundings of his Vancouver Canucks coaching office. On the giant television behind him, the Montreal

Canadiens are engaged in a battle with the Toronto Maple Leafs as the featured early game of the *Hockey Night in Canada* double-header. Andy Moog, the former Stanley Cup winner with the Edmonton Oilers and currently Crawford's goaltending consultant, is making notes on the game while the head coach chats.

"He played for the senior hockey team in Belleville and he was playing for Syracuse in the Eastern Pro League," Crawford continues. "We used to go down there every now and then. Just being able to go in the dressing room where there was lots of gum and all the pop we wanted to drink—you didn't need any money—it was great and I thought, now that's a pretty cool job!"

A year shy of his fortieth birthday, Marc has managed to claim one of the coolest jobs in the world, and there is an impish touch of mischief about him. He has grey hair at the temples but his short-cropped hair sticks up in the back, like the cartoon character Dennis the Menace but with dark hair. He is clearly at ease although his Canucks will face the red-hot New Jersey Devils in a couple of hours and Vancouver is still out of playoff contention— always cause for a coach to worry.

Marc Crawford doesn't fret about a lot of things. As a player, he won the Memorial Cup twice with the major junior Cornwall Royals, the first of his family to do so. It happened the year after Bobby left the club for the NHL at the outset of the 1979–80 season. The two were actually teammates Marc's rookie year in Cornwall. Bobby's departure brought another Crawford, Louis, for a brief stint with the Royals, but he soon moved to the Kitchener Rangers. In the 1981 Canadian junior finals, the Royals—led by Marc, who was by this time the captain of the team—defeated the Rangers.

For Floyd and Pauline it was the first time the Crawfords had competed on opposing sides. Floyd told me how they handled the situation: "Their mother and I told them we would be right between the two dressing rooms in the corridor after the game.

We would not be celebrating with the victor. We would practice neutrality."

Marc was a tournament all-star in the second championship year and turned into a grinding NHLer during portions of six seasons with the Vancouver Canucks. But his many goals and assists at the junior level did not translate into scoring success in the world's premier professional league. He seemed destined for a career on shuttle flights between Vancouver and the club's farm teams in Dallas of the Central Hockey League, Fredericton in the AHL and the IHL's Milwaukee Admirals. Marc's major pro experience amounted to 176 games and 50 points, as well as a supporting role in Vancouver's Cinderella appearance in the 1981–82 Stanley Cup final series against the dynasty-bound New York Islanders. The Canucks lost in four straight games but showed their grit and determination. It was familiar territory for the fourth boy in a family that puts a premium on hard work and perseverance.

"For the longest time I was convinced Harry Neale, our coach in Vancouver, thought I was Russian," Crawford jokes. "All I could hear whenever I was on the ice was Harry yelling, 'Crawfordov! Crawfordov!' I found out later that what Harry was actually saying was, 'Get Crawford off! Get Crawford off!'"

Harry Neale recognized something in Marc Crawford that he claims became more obvious with the passage of time and his own reflection on the elements of a hockey team's success. "Crawford is the great example of a player who had to exhaust every avenue to even get to the National Hockey League," says Neale, who coached and managed at the pro level for fourteen years and now works as the lead analyst on *Hockey Night in Canada*. "We would have been better off keeping him with the Canucks to make use of the dimension he gave us because we needed it to win games."

What Marc Crawford gave the Canucks was his ability to be the honest workman: to kill penalties and be tough on opposing stars. Checking the other team tirelessly is not always the most

glamorous aspect of the game, but it is essential for a team aspiring
to be a champion. It was this team approach that drew Neale to
Crawford's camp. "He was one of the only players I coached who
I thought had a bit of a feeling for the problems that the coach has
with reference to who dresses and who gets traded, who gets sent
down to the minors and who you are mad at."

To Harry Neale it came as no surprise that Marc turned to
coaching and found success after his playing days. "You can't tell by
how a player plays whether he's going to become a good coach or
not," Neale continues. "But you can tell whether or not he's got a
passion for the game and whether or not he loves the occupation as
well as the sport and I would have said that was the case even in the
middle of Crawford's playing career."

Marc turned to coaching near the end of his on-ice days. He
worked as the playing assistant coach with the Fredericton
Express of the American League in 1987–88, then moved the
next year to the Milwaukee Admirals. At twenty-nine he became
the general manager and coach of his old junior club in Cornwall
and before long had found his way closer to the NHL as the head
coach of the new AHL affiliate of the Toronto Maple Leafs in St.
John's, Newfoundland.

His first season directing the Baby Leafs was magic for Marc
Crawford. The dynamic young coach took his underdog team to
the Calder Cup final and a narrow seven-game loss to the Adirondack Red Wings. Newfoundland was an unlikely place to begin
full-time work in the professional coaching vocation. But Marc
came from a background of flexibility and open-mindedness when
it came to finding one's place in the game of hockey.

Following three seasons on The Rock, Crawford was lured
away by the NHL Quebec Nordiques and, at the remarkably young
age of thirty-three, became a head coach in one of hockey's most
demanding cities. Not only were the Nordiques under the micro-
scope because of years of ineptitude, they were also rumoured to

be leaving the province for richer business prospects south of the border. Into the vortex he stepped, his task to continue the club's quest for respectability. The Nordiques fans first referred to Crawford as the "plumber." His task was made more difficult by the simple fact that he was a unilingual coach in a French-speaking stronghold. His first move was to take French lessons.

"I didn't realize how big a factor that was for them to accept me as a coach," Marc says. "It was probably the wisest move I made while I was there. It opened up a whole new line of thinking. Being able to use the language to communicate with everybody made the experience so much more enjoyable."

The sometimes prickly Quebec media corps was immediately won over by Crawford's attempt to adapt. He became a darling, as did the Nordiques in their final year wearing the fleur-de-lis in Quebec City. Marc won the Jack Adams Trophy as the NHL's coach of the year and led his band of exciting young players to the Stanley Cup playoffs and a dramatic first-round series against the defending champions, the New York Rangers.

Crawford's sweat in the language classroom had partly been undertaken with his mother in mind. "I did make an effort for her," he admits. "And not only her. My aunts live close by and I knew it would mean a lot to them if I could pull off learning the language."

Pauline doesn't make a big thing of it. She speaks English most of the time these days and will only acknowledge that she was glad Marc tried his best. Floyd Crawford is much more openly impressed by his son's dedication. "When I heard about what he went through in order to be able to communicate with the French-Canadian journalists, it really did me proud," the patriarch declares. "He had the foresight and the desire to not just gloss over it. This is what he's all about. A pretty thorough guy."

Marc Crawford went south with the Nordiques to Colorado and led the newly dubbed Avalanche to the Stanley Cup in their first year of U.S. operation. The victory cemented Denver's once lukewarm allegiance to major league professional hockey and, at long last, engraved the Crawford moniker on hockey's Holy Grail. "Until I won the Stanley Cup we were the Sutters of the minor leagues," he says, referring to six famous NHL brothers from Alberta who, among them, have also won the top prize.

Marc's success with Colorado ensured his chance to coach Team Canada at the 1998 Olympic Games—an occasion that marked the return of the best NHL players to international competition. It was an undertaking doubly important to Marc because of his father's history with the World Champion Belleville McFarlands of 1959. Although the Canadians played well, they were stopped in their tracks by the Czech goaltender, Dominik Hasek, and relegated to a fourth-place finish. It was a huge disappointment for Marc, but he returned to coaching with the Avalanche and upon his dismissal in Colorado, delved into the broadcast side of hockey as an analyst before returning to Vancouver. With the Canucks today, he eagerly accepts a lion's share of the responsibility for restoring hope to the struggling franchise.

"I respect people who have to work hard for a living," he concludes. "They have to be in capacities that sometimes don't give them a lot of enjoyment or fulfillment outside of work. I really don't think that my brothers or my father have to look much past our work. We get a lot of fulfillment out of sports. We forge a lot of friendships. You get a lot of people with the same interests working in the same field. It's tailor-made for a fine and happy life."

————

The Belleville Bulls pack them in at the Yardmen Arena. Capacity is 3,500 when you count the three hundred or so regulars in the standing-room section. Known for their hard-hitting brand of hockey, the Bulls have turned a pugnacious attitude into a sparkling record over the past few seasons. Last year they claimed the Ontario Hockey League championship and challenged for the Memorial Cup under the direction of the fifth oldest Crawford son, Louis.

He stands almost motionless behind the bench as his players roar around just beyond his reach. There is an intense quality about Louis, which speaks of his burning desire and a latent need to impress a father who watches every turn, every shot, every pass, from behind the glass shield at the north end of the rink. Louis is completing his third year as the Bulls' boss. There can be no greater calling than to coach the team from home.

"It's a great hockey town," Louis told me following a loss to Oshawa a week or so earlier. "To be associated and working with your father and your brothers means that you had better do a good job or you won't be at it much longer."

There isn't much chance of his failing, although the defeat at the hands of the rival Generals at the Civic Auditorium was not welcome. Like all the Crawfords, Louis hates coming up short. "That's for darn sure! It's in our blood," he spat out. "We challenge each other and learn from Floyd, who's very competitive. I mean, he'll challenge anyone who looks at him in the wrong way. He's got a lot to offer and he's taught us a lot of great values."

Being somewhere in the middle of the pack forced Louis to scrap for attention. He was clearly in the shadow of the more gifted Bobby and the more charismatic Marc. But Louis was physically strong and in spite of an average skill level, progressed in the game to the point where he won a Memorial Cup as a left winger with the 1982 Kitchener Rangers. He cemented his place in the clan's history by becoming the first to claim the American Hockey League's Calder Cup, initially with the Rochester Americans and then with Adirondack. Louis was a tough customer who more often than not did his on-ice talking with his fists. In 650 AHL games played, he compiled an astounding 1,827 penalty minutes and stands fifth in that category on the all-time list. He claims everything he did was for the collective good, something his father would approve.

Louis claims his greatest personal achievement was following in the footsteps of Bobby and Marc. Struggling mightily, he finally made the lineup of an NHL club in the late 1980s. Mike Milbury, coach of the Boston Bruins, recognized in Louis the ability to work hard in the role of unsung contributor, and offered him an unlikely chance. Milbury himself had been that kind of player for many years in Boston. Louis suited up for a total of twenty-six NHL games with the Bruins, and scored a couple of precious goals for posterity.

"I think I'm still up there in the rafters of the Boston Gardens," Louis recalled the first of those two goals with obvious pride. "I'll remember that moment forever. It was nice to get rewarded for all the work."

Like his brothers, Louis remains in hockey because of his love of the game. Distinctly working class, he's proud of the fact that he punches a clock every day and finds a way to feed and clothe his family because of this sport. It's not a life of luxury but one of satisfaction and contentment.

Louis once swallowed his pride and played a few games for his brother Marc when Marc ran into injury problems as the rookie coach of the St. John's Maple Leafs. Louis had already given up his final year of an IHL contract in Milwaukee, wanting to get closer to home and his young family. He had played in Brantford and the lowly Colonial League as well as fought the battle with the bulge that plagues most old hockey players. Marc gave him a call anyway, knowing that when one is in need, the rule with the Crawfords is to reach out to someone you know best, like your brother.

"When I got out there, I didn't know how to approach it," Louis said. "I didn't know if I should just listen or get into a brawl with him like I used to when I was a kid. 'You're telling me to backcheck! What do you mean backcheck!'"

The arrangement lasted only a few games. Marc hoped that Louis would stay with the Leafs but his younger brother wanted to be done with the playing part of his hockey career. The most important part of the whole episode turned out to be the affirmation of their family connection. Marc and Louis had long been rivals in the junior and minor pro ranks. For a short time they were back on the same team and settled into a shared unspoken reverence for the game. "I respected the values of what he was doing and was grateful for the chance to play for him," Louis said fondly of his older brother Marc. "He's a very good coach, and I think I learned a lot just from the three games I was there."

The Belleville Bulls are coming back against the Kingston Frontenacs but Louis Crawford's expression does not change. He taps linemates on the shoulder pads and sends them over the boards. Inevitably they take no more than three strides and then collide with a rival player. It is the kind of hockey Louis wants them to play because it's the only way he knows—he has lived it firsthand. Louis is the coach. His father Floyd and his brother Michael are the scouts who have found him the talent he works with. His mission has been to fashion a team that reflects their common background.

"They appreciate a kid who will mix with my coaching philosophies and expectations," Louis says of the arrangement. "They understand what I need in order to get the job done at the junior level and give the kids the opportunity to go through what we as a family had the opportunity to go through. To make something of themselves in the game of hockey."

―――――

Not every member of the Crawford connection remains attached to the game on a day-to-day basis. Some have a purely ancillary role to play—to be a fan and to cheer the others on. Pauline leads the bleacher contingent. Louis's wife, Sherry, and their kids, Corbin and Logan, sit beside her. Danielle, the youngest Crawford daughter, is just a single row down, right next to her husband, Tim Yohn, who once played under Floyd as a member of the old Junior B Belleville Bobcats. Their kids, Hanna and Jacob, flick their eyes back and forth as the Bulls charge north and south on home ice. In the marketing office, over their left shoulders, is the son closest in age to Louis, Todd Crawford, who describes himself as the freak of the family.

"I had no scoring prowess whatsoever," sighs the slight, energetic thirty-six-year-old. He resembles Marc more than the others—the same tuft sticking up at the back of his full head of hair, a similar devilish quality to his demeanour. "I was moulded like my brother Louis. I was fast but didn't have the greatest hands in the world so I had to be a checking guy and I was not nearly as good a fighter as Louis, so that was probably why I never went anywhere."

Todd worked hard to play for the Tier II team in Belleville, which he did, becoming the sixth in his family to do so. Somewhat smaller in stature than the rest of the boys, Todd drifted towards track and field, a sport more suited to his physique. After competing as a triple jumper for the Canadian Junior Team in 1983, he won an athletic scholarship to Drake University in Iowa. There, Todd switched disciplines and became a long jumper with a personal best of 7.82 metres. "If I was a hockey player and I could do that I'd be making a million dollars a year," he croons.

While at Drake he even played a little intramural hockey, suiting up at every position and helping to teach his neophyte teammates about a game that was second nature to him. "I had a ball doing that because it got my blood going again," Todd says. "Track and field never gave me the same sensation."

Todd had always been impressed by his father's history with the McFarlands and the world supremacy they achieved long before he was born. Finding a way to be a member of a world championship

effort became somewhat of an obsession for the sixth of seven sons.
To that end, Todd won a place on the Canadian bobsled team.

"I was more of a fringe guy and was bumped on and off the
team, much like my brother Marc," Todd says. But he stuck with it
and in 1997 at the World Push Championships, he found a place in
the sled of future Olympic gold medallist Pierre Leuders. The
Canadian team prevailed to win the world title with a Crawford on
board. Todd had made his contribution to the burgeoning awards
treasure chest back in Belleville. "It was a real highlight for me
because I always wanted to aspire to a very high level, whether it
was hockey or any other sport," he says.

The quality Todd Crawford most exemplifies as a reflection of his
family is the sense of belonging. Even now as a teacher of grades six,
seven and eight special education students in Belleville, he is drawn
to this hockey rink like a magnet because he feels most comfortable
here. Our conversation is interrupted frequently by his sharp and
timely observations about the unfolding game. "Cheechoo's got
great wheels," Todd remarks on the Bulls' star right winger, now the
property of the NHL San Jose Sharks. Todd is the devout fan.

"The fact that you grew up in such a big family meant you
knew the pecking order. That helped us out a lot in hockey," Todd
says. "You knew you weren't a star so you played your role. If you
played that role you would get more ice time."

———

Danielle is the spitting image of her mother. She too is hockey
crazed and won Ontario championships as a member of the Belleville Legionettes in the early 1980s when her brothers Peter, Bobby,
Marc and Louis were playing pro. With her hair pulled back in a
familiar ponytail and sporting a military grey sweatshirt, Danielle
reclines on a chair next to the computer keyboard where birthday
announcements for the arena's scoreboard are typed in. She folds

her arms and intently follows the play, thankful for the break from her toddler, who remains down in Section 13 with Pauline.

"It came naturally. I wanted to play," she says, almost defiantly. "I remember getting a pair of boys' skates as hand-me-downs and you'd get teased by your classmates at school because you had boys' skates. I wouldn't put up with it. I'd show them who was faster and we would race."

Danielle never wanted to be a spectator. In a family of hockey-playing brothers she resolved to join the action and find her slot in the lineup. It wasn't always easy and there were many times when Danielle used every weapon at her disposal to remain on the roster. It was the same story that each and every one of the Crawfords came to know by heart.

"I remember being out in the backyard and being the only girl at home because my sister had gone away to university by then," she recounts. "Being the only girl, I recall being stuck in net a lot with my little brown snowsuit for padding and if I cried I didn't get to play much. So I'd make one good save and it felt OK. Good enough to make me stay in there."

Danielle's favourite player was not one of her brothers but Darryl Sittler of the Maple Leafs. She fondly remembers Bobby getting to the NHL and warning her that he would "grind" the Toronto captain into the boards. The kid sister lashed out at Bobby and exhorted him not to go anywhere near Sittler. "I looked up to my brothers," she explains. "But my childhood idol was Darryl Sittler."

Danielle attends every one of the Bulls games and still plays a little hockey herself. She's thirty-four and has lingering back pains related to the birth of Jacob eight months ago. Still, I sense a determination there, so similar in style to the male members of her family. She doesn't suffer fools and has clearly absorbed the same driven quality common to the Crawfords. Danielle was at the dinner table when Floyd came back from the hockey wars and she was obviously taking notes.

"I always knew when my dad's team had lost, I'll put it that way," she says. "He'd come home ranting and raving. But everyone said he managed to get the winners, the team that could win. He'd make the most out of whatever player he could get."

She predicts that she'll be back on the ice and in flying form soon. With a couple of painkillers, all her back discomfort will subside. If it doesn't then she'll go out there anyway and like a good Crawford, she'll struggle through it. "You've got to work with what you're given," Danielle declares. Maybe this is the Crawford mantra.

———

The baby of the family by a full seven years is Eric. On the cusp of his twenty-eighth birthday, the compact figure scoots around his tiny cubbyhole in the innards of Vancouver's General Motors Place while the other team practices. Eric's space is reserved for twenty-five VCRs and a dozen monitors labelled Master, Coach, Opponent, Penalty Killing and Powerplay. At his fingertips are two computer keypads and a laptop. Four telephones hang on the wall and black steel shelves of cassettes rise from floor to ceiling. Through the open door the Vancouver Canucks home jerseys hang pristine white, all pressed and ready for the game against the Devils in five hours. On the door is a nameplate: Eric Crawford—Video Coach. The room is a few footsteps away from the head coach's office. Just seconds from his big brother Marc's lair.

"Nepotism plays a role in why I'm here," admits Eric, tilting back in his swivel chair. "Marc and I have had some good experiences this year but there have been times when I've had to step back and remind myself that this is not only my brother, this is my boss and I have to get this thing done right now."

Marc hired Eric before his first full year behind the Canucks bench to become the team's video coordinator and "eye in the sky."

The younger Crawford's mandate is to break down each of the eighty-two games the team plays so that the coaches can work with the players to improve performance. It is a great opportunity for him to be involved with an NHL team at such a young age. It's true that Eric came by the job through his family connection, but he is also highly qualified to work in this area of the game.

As tradition dictated, the youngest of the Crawford troop played minor hockey in Belleville and then competed in Tier II junior leagues, in Wellington, Ontario and Springfield, Massachusetts. Eric graduated to the Canadian collegiate ranks with the St. Thomas University Tommies in Fredericton, New Brunswick, where he skated for five years under the direction of coach Alan MacAdam, a former NHL All-Star originally from Prince Edward Island.

Upon graduation from university, Eric pursued a teaching career back in the Belleville area and split his time between two schools instructing students in physical education, history and English. He was soon approached by the Tier II junior hockey team in Trenton, 19 kilometres west of Belleville, and asked to be the head coach of The Sting. His first year behind the bench Crawford took them to the provincial finals and then returned to the Maritimes and St. Thomas to work as the assistant to both the hockey coach and the athletic director. That experience complete, Marc brought him to Vancouver to help with the Canucks.

"It was kind of tough growing up and having to live up to your older brothers and your father, in terms of their play and their excellence," Eric says. "I learned pretty young that if I wasn't happy with myself and wasn't confident in who I was then I wasn't going to be very successful. Marc has given me an opportunity. I am incredibly thankful to him, and to my father for that matter, for getting me into this profession."

His boss, who just happens to be his brother, is in complete agreement. Marc Crawford has learned through the hockey wars that one of the principles of extended prosperity is the luxury of having faith in one's colleagues. In Eric he sees not only a qualified coach who brings the necessary expertise to the task at hand, but also a reliable worker who knows the value of team play. The resulting comfort zone will allow Marc to worry less about allegiances and more about the on-ice performance of the Canucks.

"His input is as good as anybody I've ever had in this position," Marc says in assessing Eric's contribution. "But that's not the only part of the job. You've got to have people that are loyal in this business. You have to let good people do their job but you have to have loyalty for sure. You can't always be worried about someone over your shoulder. It might make for an awfully long season."

Eric is not a very big person and he recognized early in his playing career that he would never have a chance at the NHL. He describes himself as "scrappy" and "in your face." With St. Thomas, one of the top-ranked university teams in the country at the time, he was the captain and the confidant of his accomplished coach. Eric is a student of the game, and somehow he has turned it into a personal credo.

"I think about the places that I've been with hockey," he says with refreshing amazement. "There was a time when I was in university and I was thinking about doing other things—maybe a master's degree. I was wondering and the whole time I had something in the back of mind and in my head that told me this game has got hold of me. It's a part of who I am and what I'm all about. It's definitely something that has shaped who I am."

———

The game in Belleville is drawing to a close and I think of all the Crawfords I have encountered. They are not the most famous Canadian hockey family. That distinction goes to the Sutters of Viking, Alberta, or the Richards of Montreal, maybe even the Hulls—Bobby, Dennis and later Brett who originated from the same town where I find myself this night. If fame and charisma were the defining characteristics, then some other clans might merit more consideration here.

Still, the sheer size of this family cannot be ignored. There are nine children, all but one of whom played at a high level. There are all those championships they've won, from the Stanley Cup to a world title. And staying power. Their playing days are over now, but each Crawford, like a moth seeking the irresistible warmth of a light bulb, clings to hockey's glow. The old man peers from behind the glass as his son coaches the home team, another boy keeps score and looks for talent, two more children cheer, the mother keeps a vigilant watch over her flock. And this is just one game in one place. In other towns, north and south of the border, four more brothers tightly orbit several other hockey rinks. And the oldest sister checks the standings from ancient Rome.

Just before leaving the Yardmen Arena, I tap Floyd Crawford on the shoulder to say thank you and good-bye. He is with his brood as they sit or stand beside him—in the bleachers—behind the bench. Like it or not, they have become convinced that the game is the family's living and more importantly its way of life. "It's the way we were brought up," Louis so precisely explained. "The game of hockey is like a breath that everyone has to take. The fresher, the better."

The old man who claims to be twenty-two shakes my hand as he turns his attention from the game for one brief but valuable moment. His words aren't so much boastful as they are insightful. "You could count on them every night. That was something that was within them," he says of the hockey family he has raised. "They have that tremendous competitiveness, and every one of them has a passion for this game. I'm very proud to be their father."

THE TOWN

Kamloops, B.C.

Top left: The '95 Champs
(courtesy Kamloops Blazers Hockey Club)

Middle right: Darcy Tucker: Town Favourite
(courtesy Kamloops Blazers Hockey Club)

Bottom left: The Blazers and the Billets: Kerry and Doris
(courtesy Doris Rubel)

✧ "WHAT ARE YOU DOING IN THE LOOPS?" Don Hay's first words on the phone from his office in Kennewick, Washington, cut right to the chase. He's currently the coach of the Tri-City Americans, a junior team in the Western Hockey League, but Hay remains a legendary figure in the B.C. interior—specifically in the city of Kamloops, the place he was born and where he engineered the greatest moment in the community's history.

"It's a really special town," Hay says. "I'm going to say there are 80,000 people there now and everyone's a Blazers fan. They might not all go to the games, but they sure know who the Kamloops Blazers are."

Hay worked as the hockey coach in Kamloops and many years before that skated as a player for the Rockets of the old B.C. junior league. Before moving closer to the coast and a spot on the roster of the New Westminster Bruins, Hay was touted as one of the brightest hockey prospects that ever emerged from this pulp and paper centre at the confluence of the North and South Thompson Rivers. From the top level of junior play in the country, he was drafted by the Minnesota North Stars, played semi-pro for three years and then returned to the town where he grew up to become a firefighter. For fifteen years he doused the flames and eventually came to lead the Blazers—the year they burned their way into the hearts of the people forever.

"It's a blue-collar town and it's always been a blue-collar hockey team," says Hay. "The people have always believed in the work ethic. It's just a part of that town. The pressure of the fans comes to bear on the players. When they put on the uniform it makes them play that much better."

Hay sought leaves of absence from the fire department from time to time when his coaching duties demanded, and he was granted them with few questions asked. Hay was an assistant under Ken Hitchcock when the Blazers first became community-owned after being purchased from the NHL Edmonton Oilers—saved from

a threatened move away from Kamloops to Swift Current, Saskatchewan. Five years of success followed and then another coach, Tom
Renney of Cranbrook, led the team to its first Memorial Cup victory in 1992. Don Hay was by his side, on the Blazers bench, for the
victory celebration in Seattle, Washington.

With that precious first title delivered, Renney left to go to the
Canadian Olympic program and the firefighter became the head
coach at the beginning of the 1992–93 season. Hay continued to
mould the Blazers based on a strong tradition established by Hitchcock and Renney, as well as excellent scouting and managing, and
returned Kamloops to the Memorial Cup tournament in 1994.
Again they were victorious, this time in Laval, Quebec, after
defeating the hometown Titans 5–3 in the climactic championship
game before a raucous and partisan crowd in the old arena. With
two Canadian junior crowns to their credit in the space of three
years, the team from Kamloops was building a reputation of dynas-
tic proportions. The folks at home were beginning to expect an
outfit that won all the time. They were the owners of the team and
it had become obvious that they reveled in the dividends their
investment had yielded.

"In the middle of summer if you went to the mall, people
would want to talk Blazers," Hay says, remembering the hothouse
environment. "If we were on a three-game losing streak and I went
to the supermarket, people would want to know why!"

Never was the air more searing in the arid foothills that surround the city than in the spring of 1995, when the Blazers hosted
the Memorial Cup at their brand-new Riverside Coliseum. There
were street parties, bands playing and 5,000 chanting fans dressed in
white every time Kamloops took to the ice against one of the
remaining three teams contesting the round-robin tournament: the
Detroit Junior Red Wings, the Brandon Wheat Kings and the Hull
Olympiques.

"Takin' Care of Business," an old Bachman Turner Overdrive

rock 'n' roll hit, had become the theme song of the Blazers and the public address announcer played it for the house every time the home side scored. The crowd was frantic and the visitors overwhelmed by the passion of the community. For the duration of the tournament, the rink on the river rocked to the beat of the hockey games, as did the entire town. Kamloops crushed Detroit 8–2 in the last exhilarating game. As the Kamloops captain, Darcy Tucker, raised the Memorial Cup above his head, the Detroit star defenceman Bryan Berard, who was to become the number-one NHL draft choice in less than a month, went to Colin Day, the president of the Blazers, and made a promise. "I hope we win the right to stage the Memorial Cup for the Ontario league next year," an overwhelmed Berard told Day. "Because if we do, we want the people of Kamloops to host it." Berard's wish was, of course, impossible to deliver, nevertheless it was his way of saying thanks to the people of Kamloops.

Don Hay finds himself in the hinterland of the game these days with some lingering homesickness. After the great Kamloops accomplishment, he went to the National Hockey League, first as an assistant coach in Calgary and then on to the Phoenix Coyotes in their first season—following the southern migration of the Winnipeg Jets. For some reason, Hay was let go by the Coyotes after he had directed them to a winning season and a thrilling seven-game opening playoff series setback at the hands of Paul Kariya and the Mighty Ducks of Anaheim. The next campaign saw him assisting again, this time with his former Flames boss, Pierre Page, in Anaheim. After another house cleaning, so endemic to the professional game, Hay decided to return to junior hockey where he would have much more control, not only as a coach but also as the team's manager with the Tri-City Americans.

It has also meant frequent returns with a visiting team to Kamloops for Don Hay—to the place he helped make famous. "For me it's really tough to go back there," he says with a sigh. "Even today, when I see video or pictures of the last game that we played there with all the fans wearing white and Darcy Tucker hoisting the Memorial Cup, it just sends shivers down my back. I have so many great memories, not only of the players but of the town."

Don Hay maintains a summer place in his native Kamloops, but goes away when the hockey season starts. The city belongs to those who currently wear the Blazer colours; former stars are welcomed but not deified. The attitude here when it comes to hockey is found in the motto, which succeeding generations of Kamloops Blazers have adopted and made law. In this hockey town, tucked into the very heart of B.C., they are "Takin' Care of Business," and say they always will.

―――――

The parking lot at the Stockmen's Hotel on the city's main drag is dusted by sand, which skitters around as the wind whistles by. It is early April and spring is just around the corner, the green grass soon to flourish in most parts of the country. In Kamloops, the warm air has already nestled in the Thompson River Valley and the water flows muddy and free past the downtown. Just beyond the shore, hills bordering on mountains rise in gentle curves—bald and brown in all directions. Scrubby bushes and a few short trees, but almost no sign of the lush vegetation I had expected from the rich interior of British Columbia. It looks more like Arizona, and I'm half expecting some tumbleweed to roll by as I make my way to the old Memorial Arena on Victoria Street.

For ten thousand years the aboriginal people of the Shuswap Nation have inhabited this bizarre extension of the Nevada Desert north of the border. Seventeen bands strong, the Shuswap presence is still noticeable in the city, which has evolved from a copper mining town to the production of pulp and paper, with cattle ranching still a going concern.

It has the feel of a frontier town, where cowboys roam the wide streets and where the largest hotel has a saloon complete with a casino in the lobby. This is the centre of the B.C. Lottery Corporation and Kamloops comes across as distinctly Wild West. Both historic railways, the CNR and the CPR, traverse the river and the highways converge at the city's threshold. The Trans-Canada and the Yellowhead make this the easiest way to get overland from the Pacific Ocean to points east. Everything, it strikes me, meets in Kamloops and like any junction, it's full of bustle and a well-deserved feeling of self-importance.

The hockey rink is a landmark building. It looks like a giant barn fronting onto the great thoroughfare running south. Memorial Arena is painted an odd pink and grey but its exterior is well maintained and the Canadian pennant flicks crisply from the peak of the five-sided roof, from the same pole that the Red Ensign flew when the building opened its doors in 1948.

An empty temple of hockey has a certain majesty about it; its grandeur is too often invisible when players crash the boards and crowds roar at billowing nets. Over fifty years old, Memorial Arena is well used but not rundown. The layers of gaudy yellow, blue, red and green paint glisten on the benches where a million people have sat over the years to watch the kids from this town compete. The meeting hall is the open balcony overlooking the bleachers. Underfoot, the hardwood floors are a rich oak. They are nearly flawless after all these years and retain a marvelous lustre. The very few creaks and groans tell me that the foundation is solid. The people care for this rink as if it was their common dwelling.

In the bowels of the arena and beyond the frozen extremities of the ice are the players' quarters. Thousands of them have come this way, from the tiniest of tykes to the Chiefs, the Rockets, Oilers and in more recent years, the Blazers. In the tunnels there are wooden walls between the minute dressing rooms and water drips incessantly from leaky faucets. "I grew up playing in the old barn," Don

Hay had told me. "When I coached the Blazers we'd have to bring in new recruits and there was never enough space in the dressing room to sit everybody. It ended up the young guys would have to sit on chairs outside the locker room and listen."

The capacity of the unassuming building is a modest 2,468. That's if you just count the folks who find a seat on one of the benches that ring the small ice surface. Another 1,500 or so could possibly find space on those pristine wooden floors. Standing room only, with the help of an understanding fire marshal who happened to work with the hockey coach, could get a tad more than 4,000 of the townspeople into this rink when Don Hay's Blazers were winning championships.

It's quieter now. The Blazers have moved and the "old barn" is devoted to the kids. A couple of lacrosse banners trumpeting the feats of the Okanagan Zone Champions dangle from the steel girders above. It's just a hockey rink now. The centre of attraction for the growing city has moved across town to the Riverside Coliseum.

———

Matt Recchi comes from the first family of hockey in Kamloops. His father, Mel, was a goalie with the local senior team and his older brother, Mark, the winner of a Stanley Cup with the Pittsburgh Penguins, has recently been named the Kamloops Male Athlete of the Twentieth Century. Mark Recchi Way is now the official name of a street that runs by the Riverside Coliseum— the major route to the new ice temple has been dedicated to the Philadelphia Flyers star who went a long way to putting this place on the map.

Matt is twenty-seven now and played briefly with the Blazers at the outset of the 1990s. He was a right winger who never quite caught on and has remained in Kamloops to work in the home heating business, all the while dabbling in his first love—the game

of hockey. Recchi is an assistant coach with the Blazers under former NHLer Dean Evason, himself a revered star with the Kamloops
Junior Oilers in the early 1980s. Together they extend the community's belief in tradition and lineage where the game is concerned.

"I think it starts early here," Matt declares while sitting beside
Evason before a game against their arch-rivals, the Prince George
Cougars. "When the kids are playing minor hockey here, they
learn to win. One day they may play for the Blazers but it starts
from the youth up. Everyone wants to play hockey, and everyone
wants to win."

Evason is dressed in a crisp white shirt and a silver necktie. The
ensemble complements his neatly combed hair. A native of Flin
Flon, Manitoba, Evason carved out a thirteen-year career in the
National Hockey League with stops in Washington, Hartford, San
Jose, Dallas and Calgary. With nearly 400 points scored and 1,002
penalty minutes to speak of his ultimate competitiveness, Evason
was a player of some distinction and won a gold medal with the
Canadian team at the World Championships in 1997.

Behind his desk, sweater number 20 of the Kamloops Junior
Oilers is encased in glass. He defines himself by his years playing in
the B.C. interior, especially his greatest triumph as the Western
Hockey League player of the year in the 1982–83 season. "It's like
a cult here," Evason tries to explain the hold that hockey has on the
people. "Everyone knows, lives and dies hockey, especially the
Blazers. There's a lot of pressure to perform—on both players and
coaches—but I think that's good. Everybody knows what's going
on all the time."

So great is the obsession with the game in Kamloops that it is
powering the city's hockey expansion on a daily basis. "They have
to turn kids away," Recchi says, shaking his head at the thought.
"There aren't enough rinks in the town. They just built another
last year."

"I have a ten-year-old boy and when I came back here I was

told he was on a waiting list to play," adds an incredulous Evason. Even the coach of the Blazers son is subject to the vagaries of a wildly booming hockey economy. "I told them they had to be kidding. How come all the kids couldn't play? He got on a team, but it was a very close call!"

————

On my next trip to the desert of the B.C. interior, the flight path into Kamloops brings the Central Mountain Airways Beechcraft off a steep left bank and down the approach. Zipping by the bottom of the airplane are the glistening waters of the Thompson River, interrupted by a series of sandbars reminding me of the Florida Keys. To the right of the plane is reality. The belching smokestack of the Weyerhaeuser Paper Products plant rises like a lighthouse guiding the little airship to its harbour. The sign beside the factory, the largest employer in Kamloops, is clearly visible: "Weyerhaeuser. The Future Is Growing."

Debbie Kirkpatrick works as a lab technician for Weyerhaeuser and is completing her first year as the president of the Kamloops Minor Hockey Association. She tells me that there are five arenas owned by the city and one private facility to provide the cherished ice time that 1,256 registered hockey players thrive on. The all-time high was 1,360 kids in the program, and that doesn't include all of the old-timers who play outside her organizational aegis.

She's spent six years on the executive and has assumed the presidency while juggling a full-time job and the needs of a bantam hockey player of her own—her son, Matt, is a goalie. Debbie also has control of an annual budget of more than half a million dollars. Most of the money is raised through registration fees but there are various fundraisers throughout the year, and each of the city-owned rinks has a canteen that turns over a large percentage of the profits to the association.

The town sponsors twenty-two tournaments each season, including the massive KIBIHT International Cup. The Kamloops International Bantam Ice Hockey Tournament has run smoothly for thirty-two years. From its modest beginnings in 1969, when only eight teams vied for supremacy, it has become a target for every thirteen- and fourteen-year-old player in North America. Its graduates include Mario Lemieux, Michael Peca and Kamloops' own Mark Recchi, not to mention hundreds of others who have gone on to distinguished careers in professional hockey, most notably the NHL.

More than 350 registered volunteers help with minor hockey in the city. "There are a great many more than that but those are the ones we know about for insurance purposes," Debbie adds. "This place has always supported hockey, and there is a large group of people involved."

They see the same rate of return on their ongoing investment that most communities do—no more, no less. The percentage of kids who graduate from Kamloops minor hockey to the professional ranks is only about 1 percent of the playing population. While there is great pride taken in the success of those like Recchi and Doug Lidster, who is a two-time Stanley Cup winner with New York and Dallas, the driving force is the town's team. The Kamloops Blazers are aspired to by most of the young players in local leagues. "If the Blazers haven't had a good year, we get a drop in registration," Debbie notes. It hasn't been the case very often since the team became locally financed. In fact, since the 1984–85 season, the Blazers have not had a losing record; a "down year" is considered to be one in which they fail to make the Memorial Cup finals. When they last won the Cup in 1995, at home in Kamloops, registration went through the roof.

"We had waiting lists and didn't know what to do with all the kids who wanted play," Debbie says. "All I know is this: the Kamloops Blazers are fantastic for our minor hockey association."

Given the prominent place on the waterfront that Riverside Coliseum now occupies and the aura of strength that the arena itself projects as well as the vitality of the team that plays there, it's hard to imagine that Kamloops almost lost its junior team. The building and the Blazers have become the anchors of the community, and many would contend they comprise its most valuable resource.

"It's almost motherhood now," Colin Day tells me, as we sit in the rapidly filling Coliseum. "You have to be very careful about saying anything bad about the Blazers. That's not to say we won't get people booing when we play bad, but don't knock the team away from the ice. We are a very big part of the community."

Day is a large and formidable man who wields the title of club president with a hefty measure of muscle in these parts. The son of a family who owned a popular soft drink distributorship in the city, Day became involved as a part owner of the team when they were still under the wing of the NHL Oilers in 1982. He bought a third of the franchise then and when crisis came, helped to move them out of the Oilers system in the spring of 1984. The team has become a profitable business venture under community ownership. "When we bought this franchise it was valued at about $350,000," Day says. "In today's market it's about a $5-million operation. We have seventeen employees and a payroll of about, $1.2 million a year. It's not a small potatoes operation."

It was the town, partly at Day's insistence, that recognized the value of the hockey team and saved it at its darkest hour. The junior Oilers won the first two rounds of the Western Hockey League playoffs in 1984 and eliminated the Seattle Breakers and Portland Winter Hawks before moving on to face the timeless Regina Pats in the final, with the right to play in the Memorial Cup tournament on the line. During that series the Edmonton Oilers management decided to sell the team when interest was at its peak. The Oilers announced that the club would be peddled to interests in

Swift Current, Saskatchewan, once the season was done. The news hit the people of Kamloops hard and drove them to take action.

"They had to fight to keep the team there," Bob Brown says. Brown was the general manager of the Kamloops team in the 1980s when the threatened exodus was averted; he remained with the franchise to guide it to Memorial Cup success in the 1990s. "All of a sudden the community got involved and bought it and saved it. So they had a piece of it. It was grassroots. They paid money and they worked their asses off to save the hockey club. There is a lot of pride in ownership, and it has continued to grow in the community."

Brown's own son Rob was a star with the Kamloops squad that emerged from the transition in the midst of a successful battle against Regina and advancement to the Memorial Cup, staged that year in Kitchener, Ontario. Dean Evason, the current coach of the Blazers, was a dynamic member of the lineup that eventually bowed to the Ottawa 67's, led by Brian Kilrea.

In retrospect, the greatest Kamloops victory occurred not on the ice but back home in British Columbia. It was evident that the group had cemented a loyalty between itself and the patrons that was based on the community's involvement and hard work. The legacy of that arrangement continues to be felt by the hockey team in this city. The players are constantly reminded of the fact that they are owned by the residents of Kamloops. The pressure to perform is immense.

"I don't know what would happen if we ever had a losing team." Colin Day almost cringes. "This situation forces us to be really attentive to what our fans want. We can't afford to give them a losing team. That's why we have all those banners up there."

The seats are filling up at the Coliseum as the squadron of elderly ushers bustles the folks to their places in the modern arena. Many of the hard plastic chair backs have metal plaques engraved with the names of season ticket holders and contributors to the rink fund. The building opened its doors in 1993 and cost the people of Kamloops about $21 million to complete. The massive fundraising campaign to modernize the franchise and house the Blazers has created a fanatical following for hockey based on the local attitude of "getting their money's worth."

"When I got there I found that the sports team was taking too much from the community." Bob Brown is remembering his introduction to the relationship between the city and the junior team. The thing that struck the ambitious general manager was the obvious lack of correlation between the success of the team and the number of people who would attend games. In the Memorial Arena, the Blazers were always winning but they would draw only 1,700 or 1,800 people, well below the capacity of the smaller-than-average rink. His first job was to get the players into the community and in the schools to talk to potential fans. It was an overnight success and the crowds improved. Then the building itself became a problem.

"I once saw a family of five come in and they had popcorn and it looked like they were really excited," Brown relates the example of one night when Memorial was full—3,800 tickets sold or about a thousand more than the fire regulations allowed. "Those people got down to where they were sitting and they had the worst seats in the facility. The thing that came to me was that these people wouldn't be back. The rink had become a liability in terms of selling tickets, except for the big games."

Colin Day and Bob Brown have had their differences over the years. Brown was let go in spite of the Memorial Cup successes and eventually found his way to the Tri-City Americans where he is trying to emulate the achievements of the Blazers in Washington. They do, however, agree on the value of a modern arena. "When the Coliseum was built we figured if we could average 3,000 or 3,500 fans a game then we would be doing great," he says. Day confirms the explosion in interest created by Riverside Coliseum's construction. The rink was fitting for a team that had won Canadian championships in 1992 and 1994. It was a reflection of the town's coming of age and the knowledge that not only was the team the best, the hockey environment was also "cutting edge."

"The building is an entertainment experience. It's not just the game," Day says. "People come here and they stand in corners and they visit and they talk and they might never watch the game. It has become a real family thing."

As I look beyond the ice surface from where we are perched, there are signs of gathering electricity. The sound system has begun to blare rock 'n' roll tunes and program sellers are hocking their wares. In the far corner of the wide-open concourse, a line has formed at the doorway to the "Takin' Care of Business" pro shop where the official merchandise of the Kamloops Blazers is being sold. I notice that the fans already in their seats sport the orange, blue and white colours of the local team to the virtual exclusion of popular NHL clubs like the Maple Leafs or the Mighty Ducks. Buying the home-grown product is what you do in The Loops.

The rink is beautifully constructed with a big league feel in spite of its junior residents. The wide sweeping roof flows to the uniformly blue seats. Both the upper deck and the symmetrical lower bowl boast individual chairs instead of benches, all with excellent sightlines. There isn't a bad vantage in the house and the scoreboard, while lacking a giant video screen to replay the action, has most of the bells and whistles. Along one side there is a marketplace of concessions where a hungry fan can purchase anything from pizza to nachos and even order a café au lait to top it off.

A well-appointed local sports Hall of Fame at the far end of the arena celebrates the accomplishments of Kamloops curlers, lacrosse players, football stars like Kevin Lapp of the B.C. Lions, and home-spun hockey stars such as Bert Marshall, once of the NHL Red Wings, Golden Seals, Rangers and Islanders. Harley Hook, the for-

mer Canadian Rodeo champion, has his place in the sun, his gloves
and cowboy hat there for all to see.

The banners Day referred to are bright red and line both sides
of the roof. WHL division and conference championships, dozens
of them, with the place of honour at the near end reserved for the
three Memorial Cup flags won by the Blazers. There are also
retired numbers—very few for a team that has been so prominent
and its graduating players so sought after. Mark Recchi's number 8
is there, as are a couple of others. Included is Dean Evason's number 20, indicating a reverence for the current coach of the Blazers
as well as an unspoken requirement for him to live up to his billing.

"Dean Evason is a saviour to these people. His number is retired,
and we don't retire jerseys lightly," Colin Day explains. "The fans
think he's a god, but I just hate the pressure they put on him."

The overall impression in Riverside, as the Blazers rush to the
ice and the Prince George Cougars glare towards their rivals, is of
an immense pot of water coming to the boil. The fans start chanting and clapping to the rhythmic pounding of the organ player.
The yelling bubbles over before the puck is dropped to signal the
beginning of the battle. Once the game gets underway the fans settle into a knowledgeable and reserved appreciation for what is happening. They cheer at the right times and demonstrate restraint
until the Blazers score. It is a crowd that has paid the freight to be
here and believes it deserves nothing less than the best.

"When this building opened, it created another 3,000 fans
instantly," Colin Day reckons. There are now 4,487 season ticket
holders for the Kamloops Blazers and another thousand people are
on a waiting list. Some of those who desperately seek full-time passage to the WHL team's regular schedule have to wait three or more
years to be satisfied. Already some of the faithful are providing for
the inheritance of their ducats in last wills and testaments. Admission to the hockey rink where the Blazers play has become a prized
position in this community.

"Quite frankly if you have tickets and you don't come to the game you had better have a good reason," Day says, all too seriously. "If you don't go then it's possible your neighbours will shun you. It's almost that bad."

———

In the foyer of the Flames' dressing room at the Saddledome in Calgary, Jarome Iginla, a native of Edmonton and a budding super-star, considers where he is and where he has come from. It doesn't take long to understand his appreciation for strong hockey roots that were nourished in the sandy soil of Kamloops. "They were three of the best years of my life and my hockey career," Iginla says of his time with the Blazers. "It's like the mini NHL. Coming from minor hockey you can't believe how serious the game is there."

Iginla is making the leap to the National Hockey League with fair success. Still only twenty-two, he is just completing his fourth full season with the Flames and has become the rock of the team—the trusty forward who combines hard-nosed play with a scoring touch. For the fourth time he has posted more than 50 points, and even though the Flames have missed the playoffs again, Iginla is establishing himself as a leader.

Coming out of the Edmonton development system, Iginla was highly touted, but the road to Kamloops and the Blazers required patience on the young forward's part. "Don Hay, the coach, told me and another rookie who was sixteen that we weren't going to get in all the games," Iginla remembers his initiation. "We would have to pay our dues. It was tough because we were used to playing a lot with our minor hockey teams and now we were watching. They gave us things to do up in the stands like stats or whatever."

Three fine seasons with the Blazers won Iginla the respect of the discerning people of Kamloops. He contributed to two Memorial Cup victories in 1994 and 1995 and at the triumphant

tournament held at Riverside Coliseum, he was named the Most
Sportsmanlike Player. Iginla is a charming young man still brim-
ming with an infectious happiness at playing the game even though
he is entering the prime years of his professional career.

He was chosen in the first round of the 1995 Entry Draft by the
Dallas Stars and proceeded to make the NHL's all rookie team in
1996–97 after being traded to Calgary so that the Stars could
acquire veteran and Stanley Cup winner Joe Nieuwendyk from the
Flames. The exchange was seen as high praise for Jarome's potential
in light of the fact that Nieuwendyk had fashioned legendary status
for himself in the Stampede City and his brilliant career was far
from being over.

Iginla is happy to reminisce about his days with the Blazers. He
talks about the year after the Memorial Cup when he scored 136
points in 63 games as a senior player on the club. Jarome hums out
the "Takin' Care of Business" theme song, savouring every note as
he throws himself back to a time and a town where he was the
centre of attention and where the hockey team meant everything.
"Fans would be dancing to it. You'd hope to blow out a team so
that you could hear it seven or eight times a night. Other players
can't stand that song. But me and my teammates in Kamloops just
love it."

Jarome Iginla's talent belongs to Calgary now but when he lets
his guard down, you can tell he still thinks of himself playing for
the Blazers—still analyzes the dynasty years when the citizens of
his adopted hometown made him feel important and drove him to
become the player that he is today. The Kamloops experience
ensured that Iginla would receive the undivided attention of 5,000
demanding hockey coaches every night he played. The payoff was
their delight in his brilliant performance.

"The town is so supportive, and they know whether you're on
a streak or in a drought," Iginla says. "They know what's going on

with you individually. They'd usually have some words of encouragement. Either that or they'd kick your butt!"

Down the hall from the Flames' dressing room, the expansion Atlanta Thrashers are shedding the sweaty gear of another morning skate which will ultimately lead to the next in a long line of opening season defeats. The Thrashers have become a collection of castoffs from the more established twenty-seven NHL teams, bolstered by a core group of young players who are far from realizing their ultimate capabilities.

Hnat Domenichelli was recently dispatched to Georgia from the Calgary Flames, where he was a teammate of Jarome Iginla's. The two had in fact been together for quite some time. They grew up as comrades in the Edmonton minor hockey system and both graduated to the Kamloops junior organization before being separated by the NHL draft—Domenichelli was selected by the Hartford Whalers while Iginla went to Dallas. They were reunited in Calgary a couple of years ago but things didn't blossom for Hnat as they had for his buddy Jarome.

"Every team in the league now has someone out there who was in Kamloops. Tonight I play against Jarome," Domenichelli says, a little wistfully. "You will never lose the friendships, and its good to see that everyone has done so well."

Domenichelli's pro career has failed to mirror what happened for him as a junior. Four years with the Blazers saw him rack up astounding scoring totals, including a season where he potted 59 goals and added 89 assists for 148 points. The tremendous outburst of offence took place over the course of sixty-two games when he skated on a line with his boyhood friend Jarome. There were two Memorial Cup championships, the same two that Iginla won, and Domenichelli rocketed to prominence as a Canadian Junior First Team All-Star and the country's Most Sportsmanlike Player in 1996. Since turning pro, the slight but speedy forward has experienced frequent trips to the American Hockey League to hone his skills and try to solve his lack of scoring prowess in the NHL. He appears to be finding the ice time he needs to improve with the developing squad in Atlanta.

"I think it definitely helped me as a professional hockey player," Domenichelli says, as he estimates the importance of his tour of duty with the Blazers. "Every person I come in contact with, I relate my time in Kamloops to them. We talk about the times we won in Kamloops and I guess that's why they pick me up. When I went to Atlanta they talked about how I'd won in Kamloops. You sometimes don't understand how important it is when you win but it always seems to follow you around."

Hnat Domenichelli was the "talk of the town" in his junior days, arguably the best player every time he leaped over the boards and onto the ice at Riverside Coliseum. There were occasions when he wove a near magic story line for the enraptured hockey following. The puck found his stick with uncanny frequency, then followed him to the net and the glory that only champions can know in the limelight of the season's last appearance at centre ice. The awareness came late to Domenichelli—the majority of his junior career was already done—that he was in a special place for hockey.

"I think it really sunk in when we hosted the Memorial Cup in my third year," he recalls. "We had about a five- or six-day period after the end of the regular season and the start of the Cup and the town really embraced us. It was blue and orange all over downtown and that's when I finally realized that this is really a hockey town and they really care for their players."

To be at the centre of attention was a startling revelation and Domenichelli admits to this day that he was unaware of the charismatic appeal that went along with being one of the better junior players in that setting. He had grown up to think of the Edmonton Oilers and dared to aspire to the life Wayne Gretzky and Mark

Messier lived. Now, with his ascension to the NHL complete, Hnat remembers his halcyon days in Kamloops and values their simplicity.

"You became a Blazer and I didn't realize it, but in Kamloops you were well known," he smiles. "It was a big thing to be a Blazer, people knew who you were and a lot of kids who played minor hockey in Kamloops wanted to be Blazers. After awhile you start to become a part of the community."

———

At Riverside Coliseum on a Sunday afternoon, the Blazers are involved in a seesaw battle with the tough Prince George Cougars. The teams are trading goals and that theme song hasn't been heard as much as the tentative fans would like. There is a disquieting nature about the crowd—its knowledge of the game's importance leads it to be reserved on the last day of the regular season. Every person knows that to get to the Memorial Cup this year, the local team must be able to handle the Cougars. Not only that, but the Prince George coach was the man behind the Blazers bench a couple of years back. Expatriate that he is in their eyes, Ed Dempsey and his new-found team from the north of the province are despised in this rink.

"The two best places to coach in this league are Prince George and Kamloops," the wiry little Dempsey barks out. "What makes those teams so great? People care!"

They cared so much in Kamloops that Dempsey was virtually run out of town after coaching the team to a mediocre season in his second year at the helm. He had been an assistant to Ken Hitchcock, Tom Renney and Don Hay—instrumental in the development of the Memorial Cup teams and a fixture of the franchise. Even so, the Blazers fans didn't accept the excuse that the cyclical nature of junior hockey made the less-than-fruitful years an expected thing when graduating players departed. They demanded a winner every year.

"No matter what you do it isn't good enough because they've seen so much that is good," the ex-Blazer coach says. "So many championships and so many good players. But even though the uniform stays the same the players in that uniform change. Number 12 now cannot be Jarome Iginla."

Brett Draney is trying to live up to the demands placed upon him as a leader of the Blazers and the only Kamloops boy on the current roster. It isn't easy but the nineteen-year-old left winger is giving it everything he's got. Draney has just scored his eighteenth goal of the season and when combined with 27 previous assists in the sixty-two games he has played, the total picture for the campaign has been a productive one. Now if the tall, sleepy-eyed young man can help get his team all the way through the playoff run intact, the throng of followers will be satisfied.

Up in the press box (which is astoundingly crowded for a junior game), a horde of analysts—both professional and amateur—record and discuss every significant move that Draney and his teammates make during the course of the afternoon. There is the usual contingent of professional scouts in attendance, getting in final evaluations of the prospects who will be eligible for the draft in June. Just less than a year ago, Brett Draney was named the 186th choice in the sixth round by Dallas. In all likelihood there is a bird dog at the Coliseum to watch him and make sure he's progressing to the point where he can be invited to the Stars training camp come September.

There is the local play-by-play caller on the radio. "The River" 97.5 FM, delivers every shift of every game to its listeners whether the Blazers are at home or on the road. Newspaper reporters from Kamloops and Prince George cover the game. The local television sports commentator has each successive goal committed to videotape with the aim of making the highlights his lead story on the broadcast that evening. Even the beauty queen, in full regalia, is in attendance, complete with a brilliant white sash covering her jet black pantsuit—a sparkling tiara adorning her regal locks. Miss Kamloops, Michelle Manus, has just engaged in a little colour commentary for the radio broadcast and gone so far as to express concern that the Blazers are struggling, just a touch, this afternoon.

"It means everything. It's a big part of the city. It makes it go," an exhausted Draney says, between periods. "The teams in the past did it and they handed the torch to us and now we've got to go out and prove that we are number one in Canada. Year by year we try to do that by setting goals and it usually works."

Draney is huge on his skates. Hulking far beyond the six-foot two-inch frame that's listed in the program, he tells me about what it means to be a Blazer, who he models himself after, and exactly what he believes is required to meet such inflated expectations.

"I've been watching this team since I was about six or seven and it's a privilege just to be on the team," Draney says. "Darcy Tucker was my favourite. He wasn't the biggest guy but he was gritty and he played hard every night. Darcy put up some pretty big numbers but he also led his team really well. He's a champion. I take my hat off to him because he was great to watch. The fans loved him and I loved him too."

———

Darcy Tucker loved playing in Kamloops and cherishes the connection he has to the people there, even though he has been separated by five years of professional hockey. Sitting in his underwear on a bench in the Toronto Maple Leafs locker room at the Air Canada Centre, the bruised and battered scrapper lets a broad smile wash over his countenance. With folded arms, Tucker leans back and regales me with stories of his time in the Canadian desert sun, when he became a hockey player and a better man.

"It seemed like every night when we went to the rink, we knew we weren't going to lose." Tucker shakes his long straggly

hair with lingering amazement. "A click went off in our heads as
soon as we stepped out onto the ice. We had a little chant before
every period that would trigger our minds as to what we expected
of each and every individual. It was 2–0 for us after the first five
minutes of the game. You ask players that played against us in Portland and Seattle and the rest of the teams in the Western League,
they hated coming to Kamloops, they hated it. They'd get off the
bus and there was always something in their pants. They were so
scared to come into our building. There was that kind of aura
when you came to Kamloops, you weren't going to get two points
in our building."

Tucker's words reflect the dominant club that he played for
from 1991 to 1995. In those four seasons, he toiled on three
Memorial Cup championship teams and is one of a small group of
players to have skated with the same franchise as it became a triple
Canadian junior champion. The other two, Tyson Nash and Ryan
Huska, were also Blazers and teammates of Tucker's.

A native of the farming community of Castor, Alberta, Darcy
combines skill with aggressiveness to pay his way in a much larger
man's game. At five foot ten and less than 180 pounds, he was not
high on the list of the NHL scouts despite his scoring ability and
propensity for inspired play as a junior. Tucker has been the celebrated captain of his team, a Canadian Major Junior League First
Team All-Star, as well as the Memorial Cup MVP in 1994. Still, he
was left until the 151st pick of the 1993 draft and scooped up by
the Montreal Canadiens' system. Never given much chance to
prove himself with the Habs, Tucker made the most of banishment to the AHL and was named the league's rookie of the year in
1996 with Fredericton. From there he was traded to a team in
Tampa Bay and proceeded to become one of the few bright lights
with the Lightning, scoring 20 goals in his first full season there.
This year, sensing a chance at the Stanley Cup, the Maple Leafs
added Tucker to their fold because of a belief in the intangible

"grit" factor which they believed to be the last missing element of their ultimate success. Their reasoning nearly paid off as the Leafs counted on Tucker's fiery nature and timely goals to oust a very good Ottawa team before falling to New Jersey, the eventual Stanley Cup champions.

"Playing there I've got my fondest memories of hockey," he says of Kamloops. "You only seem to remember the times that you win something or that you're on a winning type of hockey club. I'm already trying to forget those years I had in Tampa."

Tucker remembers more than the winning, however, and stresses that the chance to play for the Blazers had as much to do with the learning he did away from the ice as it did in the corners and faceoff circles at Memorial Arena and later Riverside Coliseum. "School was the hangout for us in our younger days," he says with a wry smile. "We'd walk around with our Blazers jackets on and we thought we were the cat's ass. We thought we were the next coming of God."

The trouble was, nobody in the community took much notice until the player demonstrated his worthiness. Tucker graduated from North Kamloops Senior Secondary School, but it wasn't a given. The hockey club made sure that there were no free rides and every Blazer would be held accountable for his actions. Colin Day, the team's president, has always stressed the notion that players had to become an asset to the city instead of a burden to it. "Our philosophy is going to be very strong, hard and fast," Day had said. "It's going to be family first, education second and hockey third. If you don't want to be a part of that system either as a player or a staff member, then go now so we won't have any problems. The Blazer 'B' is a worthy symbol and we had better do the best that we can so that the fans don't get on our backs."

Tucker chuckles as he reflects on his trials with the Kamloops credo not so long ago. A wealthy man now with a good life, he has the sense to understand what and who made his enviable position possible. In particular, he credits the Blazers management he played under for knowing what was right for young and impressionable players in the long run. "Bob Brown was the best executive I've ever played for," Darcy says, with conviction. "There was this tutoring program they put us through if we weren't doing well in school. I remember the last year I was in school with Ryan Huska and Tyson Nash. We were at the point where we knew we were leaving anyway. They caught us off guard and sent us to tutoring every Tuesday and Thursday night. Boy, were we pissed off. Bob Brown made us go anyway."

Darcy Tucker proved himself to the people of Kamloops and became a favourite son even though he was not born there. There was something about this tenacious little whirlwind that appealed to them, perhaps because he had become a reflection of the town itself. When he lived there, Tucker was a kid from a farm in a distant place learning to make his way. I went back to that picture of him holding the 1995 Memorial Cup high above his head for the crowd to see and wonder if it was an unspoken message to the people of Kamloops that he had made it happen because of all they had meant to him.

"They have a great system there with the billets," Darcy tells me. "Everybody was put into a family situation. It was like you were going to your own home. They have a lady who runs the billets there named Doris Rubel and she just seems to have a grasp of the whole situation."

Her base of operations is a small duplex on the north shore of the Thompson River at 645 Sydney Avenue. Outside Doris Rubel's home the relentless sand skitters by and she waves at me through the front window with the dainty lace curtains half drawn. I am to let myself in. Reaching for the silver knob on the screen door, I notice a little handwritten sign: No Salesmen, No Religion, No Hockey Players. Upon turning the handle and crossing the threshold, I can hear the giggling of two women who have secured safe passage for generations of junior hockey players in this part of the world.

"I didn't have time to bake today but would you take one of these store-bought muffins?" Doris asks, while ensuring that her daughter Kerry presents the mid-morning snack promptly. "We'll have two coffees, dear, and I don't think I'll take any sweetener in mine this early in the day." She is diabetic and doesn't see as well as she once did, but at sixty-four Doris Rubel still has a network to run. It all happens from this tiny kitchen where minuscule vases of flowers decorate her table and where the refrigerator is covered head to toe with snapshots of her favourites: Hitchcock, Sydor, Brown—all faces I immediately recognize. They are the boys she has looked after, the members of the team she has nurtured, the mouths she's helped feed and most significantly, her legacy to the townsfolk who love the game.

For thirty seasons Doris has been the billet coordinator for top-level hockey in Kamloops. The Chiefs, the Rockets, the Junior Oilers and now the Blazers have her to thank for good homes in which to live. She has to find twenty-five households a season, beginning in late August with training camp and continuing to the end of May, depending on how far the local team can extend itself during the inevitable playoff battle. Each family willing to house a player receives $330 dollars a month to cover expenses (read food, as junior hockey players are ravenous creatures and completely capable of emptying most well-stocked cupboards.) Doris tries to ensure that each player has a partner or "buddy" living in the same home so as to avoid loneliness. There are a few things to keep in mind when it comes to choosing the pairings. "Some veterans can live alone. The others can share a room, but its better if they have their own space," she says. "And definitely don't put two goaltenders in one house. I have never done that!"

She chuckles constantly and refers to the pictures on her refrigerator frequently. "They change all the time," Kerry chips in.

"Most people take them because they love hockey and they like having teenaged kids around."

"I tell them it's not a money-making thing," Doris adds. "You don't do it for any gains in the end but I do get a lot of Christmas cards. Daryl Reaugh, the colour analyst for the Dallas Stars, he comes back every summer and he brings flowers, big bouquets of flowers. That was very nice. It's the relationships though, the friendships, and for them to know there's a bed or a meal for them whenever."

Doris and Kerry don't take players into their own home anymore because Doris is recovering from a stroke and had been recently diagnosed with diabetes. Kerry has enough on her hands looking after her mother, and the two of them maintain and oversee the network of families who take care of the players.

"You don't want to come across as being too tough, but the players have got to understand that there are rules to be followed," Doris explains. "If you look around at the pennants it's because they've been good kids and we've had good billets. They are very good people."

It strikes me that this is like my favourite aunt's home, much like that special place where conversation is conducted over a good meal, and where almost anything can be said without fear of its reaching the wrong people. Doris Rubel's home is safe ground, and I imagine most hockey players who have encountered her would agree. "What is said in this house, stays in this house," Doris makes her point emphatically. "They have to trust me and I think that I've been fortunate that way. I don't think there's a boy that's gone out of this town that hasn't trusted me. That means a lot to me."

The belief that Doris was central to each player's happiness and the team's success was confirmed unanimously. "She was the mother hen for everybody," Mark Recchi, the Philadelphia Flyers star, had told me. He lived at home during his time with the Blazers but always knew there was someplace to go and someone to listen. "She took care of everybody."

Darcy Tucker likened her to a confidante and most of all, his friend. "Guys used to go over there and have perogies at her house." Tucker smiled. "They could go there and discuss problems they had—the problems with their billets or if they loved their billets. They could bring people for dinner or whatever. Your family could come and stay."

While Doris and Kerry have cared for the players over the years, they also remain loyal to the team first and foremost. Tucker remembered that Doris in particular had a feel for what was happening away from the ice. "We couldn't do anything there without her finding out and if she found out then she was giving us the wink," Tucker said, wide-eyed. "She was like the mother figure for all of us guys."

Bob Brown managed the Blazers to tremendous success for many years but contended that he could never have done it without a proper billeting program and with Doris and Kerry Rubel at the heart of it all. Brown was responsible for the product that went on the ice, whether it won or lost or had the talent to succeed. He relied on Doris to make sure the players were good citizens of the town and represented the Blazers well with the people of Kamloops.

"She never laid any of the billet problems on me or the coach. She handled them," Brown recalled. "She wasn't looking for a crown or anything else. The problems that she handled are so numerous that we probably couldn't count them. She's had a big impact on that franchise and is a rare breed."

The boys have kept in touch. In the living room there is a big television set that was purchased for Doris by Bob Brown's son, Rob, and a few of the other former Blazers who return for a summer reunion at the end of the NHL season. It's not much considering all that Doris has meant to them but she doesn't need anything more. There are special pictures on the bookshelf behind her favourite easy chair. "To Doris and Kerry—All My Love Forever," one is signed by Pittsburgh Penguins star, Rob Brown. Canadian Olympian Corey Hirsch, a goaltender, writes, "To Doris and Kerry, You can run but you can't hide! Thanks for everything." Just to the left is an image of Kamloops native Doug Lidster and former Blazer Darryl Sydor hugging the Stanley Cup won last spring by the Dallas Stars. Beside the precious mug is a beaming Doris Rubel. They have brought her there.

Doris and Kerry reminisce for awhile about the players they have seen come and go. They show me the gold pendants the club has made for them as commemorative gifts to remind them of each Memorial Cup victory. They refuse to wear them until the second round of the playoffs "when things get really serious," according to Doris.

Schooling is important and Doris and Kerry monitor attendance. The players are expected to help out by offering to cut their billets lawns in the early Kamloops spring, wash a few dishes, put their formidable loads of laundry in the right pile so that it can be handled in an orderly fashion. The tangible rewards beyond the $330 dollars a month are relatively few. They are invited to team banquets and they get seasons tickets to watch their favourite boys compete. To Doris it has become the central force in her life. It boils down to the fact that she loves hockey and the atmosphere surrounding the games. Until a year ago her sons operated the lights at Riverside Coliseum and in some way her whole family is involved.

The family, it turns out, is an extended one and this miniature kitchen table is always welcoming. "It's the friendships," Doris says. "Someday someone will phone and ask, what's for lunch? Last year in the playoffs there were anywhere from five to seven guys and they had to have something for the game meal. They don't even live with me. There have been so many guys. We watch them start here and then grow up."

Doris finishes by reading a few lines from the notes she's

prepared concerning the subject of food and how the billets should feed the boys. "I tell the billets no chili. Spaghetti is good but it's a different kind of sauce. No fish—that won't carry them through the game. No sausages, they're too greasy. They have to have something that's going to get them right through three periods so they're not full in the first and hungry in the third." The list is particular and exhaustive.

"Would you like another little cup of coffee, dear?" Doris is asking me. It's like Darcy Tucker said. Like being in my own home. The great players and coaches stuck to the refrigerator door became demystified to me. Recchi and Brown and Evason have suddenly become like family. I allow my gaze to fix on the coach of the Stanley Cup champion Dallas Stars, Ken Hitchcock, who had been the distinguished mentor in Kamloops through the mid-1980s. He has always been special to Doris Rubel.

"I used to make Hitch's lunches when they were on the road," she says, with great satisfaction. "I'd do chicken for him and salads and maybe a few carrot sticks. He loved peanut butter and honey for his treat."

———

"So you spent some time in my hometown," Ken Hitchcock is saying in the blasting heat of Dallas, Texas. "I should say my adopted hometown."

His team, the NHL Stars, commenced the defence of its Stanley Cup title against an outfit from the city where Hitchcock was actually born. The Edmonton Oilers had proven problematic for the Stars in playoff tournaments of the recent past. In 1997 the Oilers knocked off the heavily favoured squad from Dallas in seven games thanks to a dramatic overtime goal by Todd Marchant at steamy Reunion Arena. The next year it took five games for the Stars to get rid of Edmonton in round two and just last season the Oilers were tenacious again, every game was close and Dallas escaped with a four-game opening-set sweep. It turned out to be character building for the Stars—they went on to handle every adversity and claim their first Cup in franchise history. This season, the pattern repeated itself and Dallas almost won again. The Stars' aging and injury-riddled lineup lost to New Jersey in a thrilling six-game Stanley Cup final.

Hitchcock loves hockey beyond the salary and prestige it affords him. Somewhat of a history buff, the amiable forty-eight-year-old has an appreciation for the lessons of lineage as they apply to success in the game and life in general. Ken coached in Kamloops from 1984 to 1990, and was directly affected when the franchise was saved by the residents of the town and remained in the B.C. interior. "The city, the families and the community had to step up and pay for it," he explains. "It was theirs and they felt a real attachment to everything—you were treated with the utmost respect and adored."

During his time at the controls in Kamloops, Hitchcock amassed a record-breaking .693 winning percentage. He was named the Western Hockey League's coach of the year twice and in his last sparkling season with the Blazers, 1989–90, he was honoured as the Canadian Junior Coach of the Year. There were also a couple of appearances in the Memorial Cup tournament, in 1986 and 1990, but never the win that the coach had planned and prepared for. "To be right there . . . I could have handled it if we had been outplayed but the two times that I went to the Memorial Cup we lost both times in overtime and it was really heartbreaking," he says. "The other thing that bothered me was that I knew when I left in 1990 that we had built the depth of quality players in the organization to be terrific for about four or five years."

Hitchcock turned out to be prophetic as the Blazers won three Memorial Cup championships in the succeeding five years. In the meantime, he had gone to the professional ranks first as an assistant in Philadelphia, then to the International League to take over the Kalamazoo Wings before assuming command in Dallas when Bob Gainey decided to concentrate on managing the Stars midway through the 1995–96 season. As the NHL has unfolded for him in Texas, Hitchcock is constantly reminded of the hothouse environment in Kamloops, which shaped his understanding of the winning process.

"It was very, very intense," he says, trying to describe the passionate following for the Blazers. "It couldn't have been better experience for me because it made a lot of things that happen at this level seem like you'd done it before."

Although the NHL counts only a half dozen of its teams as being based in Canada, there is still an overwhelming influence exerted by natives of this country on the franchises, which operate in the American Midwest, eastern seaboard and sunbelt. It's as if the people who occupy the top hockey positions in the administrations of those teams try to transport the characteristics of Canadian communities south of the border and recreate a familiar environment for the game. The evidence of this is clearly obvious in Dallas.

"We have three fabrics here. There is the Montreal Canadiens and obviously the involvement with Bob Gainey. There are the Peterborough Petes, the involvement of Doug Jarvis and Bob Gainey. And there is the Kamloops connection, which is my contribution," Hitchcock notes. "All three organizations have the same type of philosophy. It's a family-first type of philosophy where we like to keep everything inside the bubble. We like to bring in as many people as we can that we are familiar with and surround ourselves with those types of people, both players and management style."

In effect, Hitchcock has tried to at least partially move Kamloops to North Texas and make Dallas a hockey town where winning is expected and depth of character is essential. So it is that the

Stars have traded for players such as Dean Evason, a Blazers legend. They drafted Jarome Iginla, another distinguished talent refined in Kamloops, only to be forced to move him to Calgary in order to get proven star Joe Nieuwendyk on side. Defencemen Brad Lukowich and Darryl Sydor are key to the Dallas blue line; both have won Memorial Cups with the Blazers. Chris Murray, a rugged forward and native of Port Hardy, B.C., has been added to the Stars lineup to toughen the team up for a second consecutive run at the Stanley Cup. Murray is a proven winner having been key to two Blazers Memorial Cups in 1992 and 1994. General Manager Bob Gainey advised his son, Steven, to hone his skills in the demanding Kamloops environment and then drafted him in 1997. The younger Gainey now plays in the Stars farm system with the Michigan K-Wings.

There are other, more subtle connections. The strength and conditioning coach of the Dallas team is J.J. McQueen. He has been invaluable to the Stars as he has maintained and improved the physical readiness of one of the oldest rosters in the National Hockey League. Players like forty-year-old forward Guy Carbonneau and thirty-five-year-old goaltender Ed Belfour, swear by him. McQueen was working at the air force base in Kamloops when Ken Hitchcock hired him to help the Blazers in the late 1980s. He has since travelled south at the urging of his loyal friend the former junior coach.

Daryl Reaugh from Prince George, B.C., is now the dynamic colour analyst on the Dallas Stars television broadcasts. He played in goal for the Blazers the first year Ken Hitchcock was coaching there and went on to a career in professional hockey mostly in the AHL but enjoyed a brief stint of twenty-seven games with the Edmonton Oilers. Reaugh, in his current position, comes across as young, energetic and entertaining. He has a devoted following of viewers in Dallas and he espouses the same principles which dominated his time with the Blazers. "They didn't want to be associated with a loser," Reaugh says, of the fans in Kamloops. "There was accountability. That city owned us. You had to answer to them."

The Stars are remarkably approachable professional athletes and it seems to come from the top down. They compete in a very demanding situation where hockey is not endemic to the community and they live in the shadow of the tremendously popular Dallas Cowboys of the National Football League and vie for attention with strong franchises in both the NBA and Major League Baseball. Still, the Stars are bonding with the people of this city and creating a love for hockey that may endure. The formative years in Kamloops are paying dividends.

"I feel a connection and a loyalty to that town," says twenty-seven-year-old Darryl Sydor, a key member of the Dallas defence. Sydor once scored 105 points in a single season for the Blazers and was a member of that first Kamloops team to win a Canadian Junior Championship in 1992. He is originally from Edmonton but married a local girl and I can remember seeing a picture of Darryl and his twin sons, Parker and Braden, on Doris Rubel's refrigerator door. He had called her a few nights before I was there to talk about a slip he had made which allowed another team to score. He was still connected to his beginnings.

"I'm from Edmonton but a lot of my growing up has been done in Kamloops," says the all-star defenceman. "I moved there when I was sixteen and I feel like a lot of people that you met for the rest of your life—your friends—are there. They taught you about life, the way you could win and your attitude about playing. It seems like if Dallas makes a deal it's a guy from Kamloops or a guy that's been in Kamloops. There's a connection there."

Daryl Reaugh agrees with Sydor and claims the background he gained while playing with the Blazers and living in the home of a Kamloops couple reflects a worthwhile trait unique to professional hockey players. He still calls his former billets Wally and Shirlaine Reutlinger, twice a week. Reaugh also maintains regular contact with Doris Rubel as do Hitchcock, Sydor and so many who have been influenced by her. The embracing arms of the hockey town reach them all—even in the Lone Star State.

"God bless everyone of them that would take hockey players in," Reaugh exclaims. "They are the friends. They have been the constant. There you had to learn to respect people that you didn't grow up with. It was like being part of an extended family and you end up with a game that's like it is. God, I hope it never changes!"

Ken Hitchcock has battled so many things to be where he is. Not the least of which was a weight problem, which threatened to seriously affect his health. There was a time when the articulate, master coach couldn't bend over to tie his skates. "Morbidly Obese" was the medical term for his condition and it became the subject of ridicule and immense frustration for Hitchcock, a devoted hockey mind. Through will power and the help of the people in his adopted home town of Kamloops, "Hitch" prevailed and as I watch him skate around the ice today, I think of Doris Rubel and the "treats" she used to pack in his lunch box in the junior days.

"My lunches changed. She used to pack me a lunch that you needed a caddy to carry," the Stars coach chuckles. "Then when I went on a diet it was this little brown bag that everybody used to laugh about. She's the greatest cook in the world."

It strikes me as a little silly that I am talking to the coach of the Stanley Cup Champions about his appreciation of good cooking on the morning of a playoff game. Then I understand that Ken Hitchcock finds our conversation to be of great significance. He has been reminded of another time and more importantly, another place where someone made a difference to his hockey career. He will not forget the lessons of Kamloops and its people.

"She is the one that really helped me to stay with the diet to be honest. That's why I treasure her so much." Hitchcock gives the billet lady her due. "I don't think I could have gotten that first year done without Doris Rubel. When I started to lose weight I ate a lot of meals with her and she kept me disciplined and determined. If I didn't eat the right thing she would stick a fork right through my hand. She was very hard with that stuff and it worked out great for me."

———

Kamloops, its residents will tell you, means a meeting place, in the language of the aboriginal people who live in the area. On a Sunday evening, where the arms of the Thompson River converge and create a calm pool of water, the grand and spacious hockey rink on the shore is full of neighbours and friends.

In section T at the northwest corner, Doris Rubel sits in her seat draped by a dark brown cape and donning a sparkling gold tennis visor. With her daughter Kerry at her side, Doris resembles a riverboat gambler and when the play is on she is not to be interrupted—she's concentrating on the hand she and the Blazers have been dealt.

"If they don't win tonight I'm in deep trouble," Mary Lane says, as she taps Doris on the shoulder when the whistle halts the action. "Why is that, dear?" responds the inquisitive billet lady. "I changed something for the pre-game meal. No garlic bread with the spaghetti!" A hushed and nervous reply has the patrons in the immediate vicinity captivated.

Doris waves her hand and comforts Mary who has three of the Blazers living at her house. Shaone Morrison, Mike Munro and Davis Parley are three of the older players who will soon become eligible for the NHL draft. Every detail of their junior hockey existence has been attended to with care and with pride. Mary's been billeting players for fifteen years and she nervously jiggles a cowbell waiting for Doris to solve another potential problem.

"Don't worry, Mary, it'll be just fine," Doris offers. "At least their breath will be better in the dressing room!" Everyone laughs with relief, and the fans settle back in their seats to watch the game recommence.

The small problems as well as the large ones seem to disappear in this place. Doris and the others take care of them—find a way for the hockey players to excel. Sometimes it's as simple as listening to them when they have a need. "We had one boy who was living by himself because his buddy had got sent to another team, so he was lonely," Doris says. "Sometimes you know that they are hurting when no-one is supposed to know that."

Craig Bonner, the assistant coach of the Blazers, is referred to by Doris and the rest of the locals as "Bones." He's only twenty-seven and has seen a bright future interrupted by a series of knee surgeries. A stalwart of the Kamloops defence in the late 1980s and early '90s, Bonner captained the team before Darryl Sydor assumed the reins and helped win the first Memorial Cup in 1992. Not drafted, he was signed by the Dallas organization as a free agent and went to Kalamazoo to play for his old coach Ken Hitchcock who had faith and took him in. There has been a divorce, which Doris helped him through, and now Craig has found his place back in "the Loops" at the end of his injury riddled playing career. He's an assistant coach to Dean Evason and has been in the same capacity with other coaches for the past four seasons.

Bonner is a native of Edmonton, but made his way in the world right here. In this hockey centre, the rite of passage which takes young men from the status of prospect to professional, is assisted by those who welcome young players and rarely consider them as out-siders. "I just think it's all about leaving home," Craig Bonner says. "The players leave home at such a young age and come from places that are fifteen to twenty hours away. The biggest thing here is the comfort. When you are seventeen or eighteen the transition involved in leaving home is a difficult one. If you are comfortable where you are, then the transition is easier."

These players, I have come to understand, will always belong to them. No matter where they are originally from or where they end up, each kid who pulls on the Kamloops Blazers sweater, even for a single game, will be bragged about and revered in this rink and its satellite community. The home team is winning again as time clicks away at Riverside Coliseum. The Prince George Cougars are soon to be vanquished and the folks of Kamloops, I imagine, will sleep easy tonight.

There is a little man shuffling around just outside the dressing room, arranging things for the victorious team's arrival from the ice. Greg "Spike" Wallace is the equipment manager for the Blazers and has been with the organization since day one. He was born in Kamloops forty-two years ago with a hole in his heart and could never play hockey. So he volunteered to help the high-school football trainer, went to college in Ontario to become accredited as an athletic therapist and, by way of Victoria, where he worked with the Junior Cougars in the early 1980s, returned to Kamloops and has been with the Blazers to this day.

"Obviously I'm not the guy that's scoring the goals and all that kind of stuff. I've accepted that in my life," says the jovial Wallace as he hurries to distribute towels and water bottles in the stalls. "It's just helping these guys make their careers. I've made my career successful and I want to see these guys be successful."

The dressing room is immense, better than some of the clubhouses I have seen in the grandiose and ultramodern arenas of the National Hockey League. Two attendants or "stick boys," Craig Kerwandy and Richard Minaker, sixteen and twelve years old respectively, hop to the marching orders of Spike and his assistant, Pete Friedel. The position of "stick boy" is a prestigious one in Kamloops and has been handed down to these fellows by older brothers—helped along by the fact that Spike knows one of the guy's fathers.

While they hurry, I look at the vast list of players' names

engraved on the wall, clearly visible to every locker in the room. It serves as a reminder to the current players that they will, in a tangible way, always be a part of the team. There are 260 names in all—Scott Niedermayer, Greg Hawgood, Ken Daneyko, all great players who have fashioned lasting NHL careers.

Slogans are stencilled neatly on plastic boards and screwed firmly into the glossy concrete blocks. The most telling, Spike figures, has been left by Ken Hitchcock, the Stanley Cup champion coach who has been recently inducted into the local Hall of Fame here, a man born in Edmonton who thinks of this team as his home. "The crest on the front is more important than the name on the back." It is by the door on the way to the ice—a reminder to honour the people they play for.

"The slogan has been a way of life," Greg Wallace says. "In the wintertime you walk down the street and everyone talks the Blazers. Even if they don't come to the games physically they are still a part of it. You can't get away from it."

The players are starting to return and I can hear the roar from the crowd, the "Takin' Care of Business" song in the background. I know that Doris Rubel and the rest of the billets are cheering from out there and will be soon rushing home along Mark Recchi Way to prepare post-game nourishment for the boys. Darryl Sydor or Darcy Tucker might call to find out the score and to relay the news of the latest goal they've delivered for Dallas or Toronto. Colin Day is sure to be a satisfied club president, as the last of the tickets for the upcoming playoffs against Seattle will be gobbled up in the wink of an eye. Registration for spots in the Kamloops Minor Hockey Association is about to go up, and come Monday morning, down at the Weyerhaeuser pulp and paper plant, Debbie Kirkpatrick will be fielding dozens of calls from prospective hockey parents.

Spike puts away the last of the sticks on the rack by the workbench where his tools are all neatly arranged. He folds his arms and looks at the replica Memorial Cup banners as well as the names of the players who made great things happen. Wallace considers the current youngsters and stresses they've been given everything they could possibly want or need in order to be great. As only someone from here could undertake, he considers the furthering of hockey in The Loops to be his duty.

"There are nights I lie awake and wonder what I'm going to be doing in ten years," he concedes. "I may not be doing this but I would have a very difficult time leaving Kamloops. People leave but it always seems like they come back here. The community is very strong. People are always there to give support or to volunteer. There's no question, it is a very proud hockey town."

It's like so many Canadian places. Kamloops is so demanding of those who play the game while wearing its colours. So honoured when its heroes still call it their home.

THE HERO

Ron Ellis

Everything I Wanted Him to Be

✧ "BE CAREFUL WHAT YOU WISH FOR," Ron Ellis is saying as he stands beside hockey's Holy Grail. "All I ever wished for was to win the Stanley Cup just once and it came true."

We are in the Great Hall of the Hockey Hall of Fame in downtown Toronto. Ron Ellis, who now works at the Hall of Fame in the public affairs department, is older and a little rounder than I remember him. The sideburns and the brush cut are gone and his beautiful blue-and-white sweater has been replaced by a black sports jacket with the Hall of Fame's crest embroidered on the left front pocket. He wears grey flannels and a necktie. My hero is into his fifties now but I still recognize the young player I worshipped more than three decades ago when the Leafs were kings.

He chuckles every now and then at the smallest things as we move through the rooms, looking at the exhibits together. "Are you sure you've got time for this?" he asks. I have all the time in the world for Ron Ellis. Meeting my hero is something I've waited what seems an eternity for.

———

We had crossed paths in recent years at Maple Leaf Gardens when I had the rare opportunity to broadcast a game from the grand old building on *Hockey Night in Canada*. Ellis was active in the Maple Leaf Alumni, so we had brief encounters in the halls near the dressing room or in the press section, which was suspended from the ancient roof.

At the All-Star festivities in the new Air Canada Centre, I had been installed by my producer at the players' bench as the former Leafs took on the Heroes of Hockey in an old-timers' game. It preceded the much-anticipated gala, which featured the young superstars—Pavel Bure, Mats Sundin, Paul Kariya and all the rest.

I was transfixed as Ellis took his place in the warm-up alongside Frank Mahovlich, Darryl Sittler, Lanny McDonald and Rick Vaive, a more recent favourite of mine and like my hero a legendary Toronto right winger. Wearing his familiar number 6, Ronny Ellis adjusted his elbow pads with great frequency, just as he had done many years before. He tapped his shoulders to make sure his equipment was in place and hopped around the corners, his skates constantly moving and digging ferociously into the ice. All the same mannerisms—the ones that I had copied religiously throughout my unremarkable playing career.

While circling the ice and fielding passes from Norm Ullman and Errol Thompson, a couple of his former teammates, Ellis happened to breeze by the penalty box; he lifted the blade of his stick like a scoop and flicked it, sending a sprinkling of snow into my face. Accelerating for the next rush on net, he looked back and winked—the same wink I had seen in the picture commemorating his first goal at Maple Leaf Gardens.

———

In the Hall of Fame, we end up talking like old friends. I had fretted about the whole encounter, hoping that my connection to this personal icon could withstand the harshness of reality. Ron Ellis was, after all, just a retired professional hockey player and subject to the same frailties as any man.

"Could you take me to your favourite place in here?" I ask him. "Show me what means the most to you."

Ellis smiles and motions me on. Without a moment's hesitation he leads me to the "Forever Rivals" display featuring the teams that moulded his passion as a player, the Toronto Maple Leafs and the Montreal Canadiens.

"That's me in the middle there, surrounded by some pretty good players," Ron says, pointing to a colour portrait that shows him attacking the Habs' net to the chagrin of Larry Robinson, Serge Savard and goalie Ken Dryden. Darryl Sittler, his Maple

Leafs teammate, is providing support. All of these legendary figures, with the exception of Ellis, have already been inducted into the Hall of Fame.

More than anything else, Ellis loves the connection he has to the famous rivalry and to the original six teams that formed the National Hockey League in his day. Born in the small town of Lindsay, Ontario, he was an air force brat who moved around quite a bit during his childhood years as the family followed his dad's postings. Ron was first scouted by the Leafs in Ottawa; "Punch" Imlach and "King" Clancy had spotted him as a young centreman. "I remember them coming to my house to talk to my parents," he says. "They came up the driveway and I was peeking out my bedroom window. I can see it as plain as if it were yesterday."

They passed him on to the Weston Dukes, where Ellis starred at the Junior B level, then graduated to the Marlboros, the team his father once played for. He followed in his father's footsteps and beyond, helping his team to capture the Memorial Cup in 1964. His contemporaries included Pete Stemkowski, Mike Walton and Wayne Carleton, all of whom prospered alongside Ellis in the Toronto Maple Leafs system and went on to enjoy substantial careers in the NHL.

Ellis wasn't sure he was cut out for big league hockey. In fact, he had considered education to be his primary goal and had almost committed to one of two scholarship offers from American schools when "Punch" Imlach urged him to turn pro halfway through his final year with the Marlies. But Ron remained skeptical because the Leafs were a talented team at centre ice, his natural position, and he saw little opportunity to make an immediate impact with the storied franchise. His coach with the Marlboros, Jim Gregory, convinced Ellis to move to the right wing because he knew Toronto would be trading some of its older stars in that slot.

"I was very fortunate. I think to be successful in professional hockey you've got to work hard, you've got to be committed, you have to pay the price and sacrifice, but at the same time you have to get the breaks along the way," Ellis says. "I'm very thankful for the breaks. I liked playing centre and I didn't want to move, but it was the biggest break of my life and I've told Jim Gregory that many times."

Gregory went on to become the general manager of the Maple Leafs and presided over much of Ellis's professional career in Toronto. He has since been instrumental in the development of the NHL's Central Scouting Bureau as its former director and is currently the vice-president of Hockey Operations with the NHL. Ellis remembers Gregory as a mentor, the man who made it possible for him to play professionally at the Gardens. "My dream was to play with the Leafs and to finish with the Leafs," he declares. "That ended up being my goal and fortunately it worked out for me."

Ellis indicates his old Northland helmet, which is on display in the "Forever Rivals" exhibit. Bowl-shaped and scuffed from the nicks of a thousand stick blades, it has a white number 6 stencilled on the back and is a similar model to the one former Hart and Art Ross Trophy–winner Stan Mikita of the Blackhawks wore. Ellis himself was one of the first Maple Leafs to wear a helmet and in a sense helped to pioneer the practice in the NHL, not completely by personal choice.

In the mid-1960s the National Hockey League featured contests on all of the major holidays and there were very few breaks during the course of the regular season. On Christmas Eve 1964, very early in Ron's rookie year, he got the puck caught in his skates during a game against the Blackhawks. Making the mistake of looking down to find the disc, he was popped in the jaw by a Chicago defenceman's shoulder—both players were in full flight. "I was out cold on the ice for about ten minutes. Red Kelly was leaning over me and thought I was dead," Ellis relates the story, which was told to him after he came to. "Things have changed a lot. They finally carried me off the ice on a stretcher. Not knowing as much as they do now about concussions and so on, I was back out playing the next period!"

Ellis survived the accident to play well in the next game against Montreal, which was a fast end-to-end affair devoid of much physical contact. In Boston the following night, however, things were a little different. The Bruins home rink was smaller than the norm and there was bound to be less room for a speedy player like Ellis to operate. The result was a broadside from the rock-solid defender Leo Boivin after Ellis passed the puck. "I took the check, but that collision sent my brain against my skull and down I went. I was out for the next ten games."

The helmet was donned a few years later after Toronto had won the Stanley Cup in 1967 by beating Montreal in six games, the clincher coming at Maple Leaf Gardens. Ellis scored the first goal of the final game just over six minutes into the second period. He gobbled up the rebound of a Red Kelly shot and lifted the puck past Lorne "Gump" Worsley, the Canadiens goaltender. "It was special to score the goal because it was in the Gardens," Ellis says, understating the importance of his accomplishment. "Just to play in the National Hockey League was tremendous," he explains. "But once you're there, your next goal is to win the Cup. The Stanley Cup is a dream come true for any Canadian kid."

Still, as he reminisces about the glory of it all, I am struck by the fact that Ron Ellis and I are not currently beside the Stanley Cup. He had shown me his name etched into the precious mug's side when I first arrived. Now we are staring at red, white and blue sweaters—at the "Flying Frenchmen" and the staunch defenders of the Maple Leafs, such as the late Tim Horton, his jaw jutting forward like chiselled granite. For Ellis, it's not the winning that matters so much as the struggle and, beyond that, the challenge the two teams represented to each other as well as in the eyes of the fans.

"The Montreal-Toronto game was the one where all of Canada would tune in. It was very special whenever we played them," Ellis says. "I liked their style. It was more of a wide-open skating style, and that was what I really loved. I enjoyed those games when you could try to fly up and down with them. I always enjoyed playing Montreal."

As we move through this arcade of hockey history, we gravitate to the growing collection of material in the international section of the museum. There, Ellis's Team Canada jacket from the "Summit Series" is on display alongside the famous picture of the Paul Henderson goal, which ensured victory over the Soviets at the eleventh hour. Ellis had teamed with Henderson and Bobby Clarke to form one of the most effective threesomes for the Canadian side throughout the historic tournament. He was originally an unheralded choice for the roster as selected by coach Harry Sinden, a squad made up of superstars and a few key role players of which Ellis was the most important.

"I think that series touched the core of our Canadian character," Ellis comments. "It was the way it evolved. If we had won all eight games like everybody said we would, then it might not have had the same appeal. We had to make a comeback and win the last three games with the deciding goal coming with 34 seconds left in Game 8. When you add all that together, it makes for the series of a lifetime, and it's definitely the highlight of my career."

In a way, the Summit Series and his supporting role in the great drama are representative of Ron Ellis as a hockey player. It was a tenaciously fought battle where nothing came easily and the foot soldiers led the way to a narrow victory, one that has been savoured by Canadian hockey fans ever since. "To play against the Russians you had to be a two-way player," Ellis insists, nearly thirty years after the fact. "We had to be a well-balanced team. I contributed by helping to shut down Valery Kharlamov."

The record shows that the Paul Henderson–Bobby Clarke–Ron Ellis line was the only triumvirate employed unchanged by the Canadian side in all eight contests. As the series wore on, they neutralized the big Soviet scorers and Henderson miraculously produced game-winning goals. Ellis did not score in any of the titanic struggles and maintains that it is a personal disappointment to him, but one that has been overshadowed by the part he played in the overall team success. "I was injured in Game 1, hyperextended my neck. I couldn't shoot the puck and I thought it was over, maybe the end of my career," he reveals. "I had to go to Harry Sinden and tell him that I couldn't shoot the puck."

In the end, Ellis persevered and played his role at coach Sinden's urgings. "I just liked doing my job," Canada's number 6 admits. "One of the things that I'm most proud of is the fact that people appreciated the way I played. So even if I wasn't scoring, I could still do a job for the team."

Ron Ellis lingers by the showcase where Team Canada 1972 is forever celebrated and considers the road that took him to the pinnacle of the game. He was painfully shy in his early days with the Leafs, and I hear the trace of a stutter as he recounts the struggle to overcome his initiation to the life of a national celebrity. Ellis, it turns out, loved playing professional hockey, but found it difficult to deal with fame once he found himself removed from the ice surface.

"I used to walk down to the rink on Church Street and the fans would be all along the way saying hello and good luck," he recalls. "I appreciated it but I was a pretty quiet guy. I sometimes found it hard to accept."

Ellis partly overcame his aversion to public appearances with the help of the man who made the ice at Maple Leaf Gardens. The late Doug Moore enjoyed playing the guitar and singing folk songs to pass the hours while sitting in the boiler room of the ancient building. A few others joined him, including Ellis, who had helped his father run a tourist resort north of Huntsville, Ontario, in the off-season. There, Randy and son Ron had staged a sing-along once a week to entertain the guests. The star right winger found that music was a way to become more extroverted and agreed to travel with Moore to retirement homes in the Toronto area to provide elderly hockey fans with a little fun as well as a glimpse of one of their favourite Leafs players. It was the same logic, I learn now, that brought Ron Ellis to my Parkwoods Civitan hockey banquet and afforded me the rare chance to be close to my hero when I was a child.

"I didn't completely understand the impact that the game or the Leafs or my career had on people until I retired," Ellis says, shaking his head. "It humbles me. It really does. After I retired I did a little appearance on the East Coast and I had a father come up to me with his son. He wanted me to meet the boy. Ron Ellis Smith was the kid's name."

There are other stories of the people who have followed his career. At one meeting in the Maritimes a man presented Ron with a complete register of every one of the 640 regular season points he scored with Toronto, listing the game, the team the Leafs were playing against and the time of the goal. "He told me that he admired the way I played," the retired star explains, still incredulous. "He told me that I had meant a lot to him."

Ron Ellis played 1,034 games in the National Hockey League and all of them were with the Maple Leafs. He dreaded the thought of being traded to another club and desperately wanted, not to be a star, but to be a useful and consistent hockey player. He strove for all-around effectiveness, killed penalties and was a threat to score on any power play. "Some people called me robotic," he says of his detractors. "But that was a conscious decision. Those days you weren't allowed to come off your wing. I developed a style, and I'm proud of that style. The coaches knew they could count on me, and I'm honoured to be able to say that."

Ellis was, however, demanding of himself to the point of obsession where his on-ice responsibilities were concerned. He turned every small mistake into a disaster and played each game over and over again in his mind until the joy of playing hockey at its highest level became a huge burden. "Playing in Toronto was a grind," he winces. "I was worn out emotionally because I took the game home with me. I was so critical of myself. The game was with me twenty-four hours a day. I think I might have been able to play another two or three years if I'd been able to relax a little more."

As it was, after Ellis played eleven full seasons, he decided to take a leave of absence. He had just signed his best contract and was coming off his most productive campaign, having scored 32 goals and 61 points during the regular schedule of 1974–75. "For the sake of my family I thought I should take a break," he says. "It was a good training camp and a good exhibition season, but I knew in my heart that I had to take a break."

During the time away from the NHL, Ron ran a golf club just north of Toronto in Aurora and was involved in a home development firm. Both ventures met with only average success. All the while, he was playing with the NHL Oldtimers, which gave him the chance to tour with former teammates and adversaries as well as enjoy what he missed the most, the camaraderie and friendship of the team atmosphere. In 1977, Alan Eagleson, the player agent and head of the NHL Players Association, requested that Ellis interrupt his retirement to play for Canada at the World Hockey Championships in Vienna, Austria. Ellis rose to the challenge by working out religiously for four months in order to get back into shape. He played well for coach Johnny Wilson and alongside other stars like Phil Esposito. The next season Ron found his way back to the NHL with the Leafs (they still owned his playing rights) and provided Toronto with an additional 56 goals over parts of four seasons before retiring for good in January, 1981.

Once their hockey careers are over, many players find it difficult to find their place in the world. Ron Ellis is no different, even though he had prepared himself for life beyond Maple Leaf Gardens. "We all knew that one day we would have to find another job," Ellis says. "I was always thinking of that and preparing for that. I never took the summers off. We didn't make enough money in the NHL back then. We made good money but it wasn't like it is today."

He spent time as a physical education teacher, working in an insurance firm and owning a sporting goods store in Brampton, Ontario. Nothing seemed to fit, and Ron embarked on a period of intense depression because of the enormous pressure he felt to be as successful off the ice as he had been on it. "Those things are all part of what happened to me," he says, reflecting back on that difficult period. "It all came to a crashing halt for awhile. Fortunately for my family, we were able to move through that with the help of my doctors, and I think I'm a better person for it. I'm more content now."

Ellis has returned to hockey's fold and admits he has found salvation in the simple things that first fired his ambition. He's not a member of the Hockey Hall of Fame, but he serves the game by his work there and feels he has found his niche. It is not, he says, about the money because he never found much of it in spite of striving heartily for the riches that a career in professional hockey might provide. His first contract with the Leafs was $8,000 a season. His last was lucrative in its day at $150,000, but a far cry from the millionaire salaries doled out in the NHL today.

"Things have changed. I think that money sometimes infects the soul," Ellis says. "We knew back then where we wanted to play. I hoped that I could be a professional hockey player and I wanted to be a Maple Leaf."

A little boy and his father approach us. The boy steps forward with a simple request: "Can I have your autograph, Mr. Ellis?"

This is something I never had the chance to do; I never got close enough to my hero to utter those words.

"Why of course you can," Ellis says. "But tell me, young man, did you ever see me play?"

The father is quick to respond and I can tell he is about the same age as I am. "No sir, but I did," he says, shaking Ellis's hand. "You wore number 11 first, then number 8, but you were my favourite when you had that big number 6 on your back."

Ellis smiles and musses the little boy's hair after handing back the Hall of Fame program and the black magic marker. The father and his son have a souvenir of their time here—a brush with a former star that played a game they love.

Ron Ellis is third in Toronto Maple Leafs history with sixteen seasons spent wearing their colours. He is one of only five players to wear that blue-and-white jersey for more than a thousand games. Ellis is third on the Leafs' all-time goal scoring list and leads the way in that department when it comes to right wingers. He is one of the most accomplished Toronto Maple Leafs in the history of the team and yet, on this day, a little boy asking for his signature gives him more pleasure than all the celebrity he ever had. "It's the major part of my life," Ellis says, as we walk on. "Hockey is the work of my life."

We make one final stop in the Hall of Fame. Near the exit, an exhibit commemorates the role of the family in the game of hockey, displaying artifacts with a connection to the Richard, Hull and Mahovlich families, to name a few of the more famous NHL clans. Ellis slows and points to a stack of three uniforms. At the bottom is the white wool sweater of his father, Randy, who played for the Marlboros. Next is the Team Canada top that Ron wore at the World Championships in 1977. On top is a white jersey with the initials R.M.C. emblazoned on its chest. This is what Ellis's son, R.J., donned when playing for the Royal Military College as part of the 112-year hockey rivalry with West Point Academy in the United States.

It was decreed before the annual match a few years ago that the

Most Valuable Player from the RMC team would have his sweater donated to the Hall of Fame and put on permanent exhibition. Ron Ellis Junior was voted MVP and the result has been that the lineage of one particular hockey family will not go unnoticed. It's a very small thing, but to Ron Ellis it is a great honour.

"I'm so proud of him. He had a good career there," Ellis says of his son, who now flies Hercules aircraft out of the Canadian Armed Forces base in Trenton, Ontario. "They didn't have a great team but he had a wonderful four years there and he set some records. He can be thankful to the game."

———

Now it's time to say so long to Ron Ellis of the Maple Leafs. It seems to me that he is the product of something good, and I don't hesitate to tell him so. It's comforting to know that he remembers the town he came from, is thankful to the coaches who taught him, reveres the only professional team he skated for, and values his family connection to the game above all. Ellis, I am relieved to discover, is everything I had hoped my hero would be.

There is, near the entrance to the Hockey Hall of Fame, a mural-sized picture of the current Stanley Cup champions. In this case, the jubilant Dallas Stars are depicted and Ron Ellis makes an admiring remark about one of the better players on the team. "I really like that young fellow, Mike Modano, because of the way he plays," my hero says. "I love it when guys like him dance." It is this sense of wonder and magic that creates devotion on the part of hockey fans.

In meeting a childhood idol for the first time, there is always the danger of grand illusions being destroyed. But in my experience today, the trip has been worth the taking. I am reminded of the caution Ron Ellis offered very early in our discussion. "Be careful what you wish for," he had warned. I leave his company wishing my hero and I could talk about this game forever.